Biblical Foundations
of Freedom

Robert Robinson

Biblical Foundations of Freedom

Destroying Satan's Lies
with God's Truth

Art Mathias

Wellspring Publishing
ANCHORAGE, ALASKA

Wellspring Ministries of Alaska
2511 Sentry Drive
Anchorage, Alaska 99507-4469
907-563-9033
e-mail: akwellspr@aol.com
Website: akwellspring.com

ISBN 0-972-0656-0-1

Printed in the United States of America

Contents

Preface

Ecclesiastes 1:9 says, "The thing that hath been, it is that which shall be; and that which is done is that which shall be done: and there is no new thing under the sun." God continues to teach His people through His Holy Spirit, and His truth is coming forth in many places throughout the earth. In light of this Scriptural truth, I submit that no thought of man is truly "original," especially mine.

This book is about anger, hatred, jealousy, rejection, fear, pride, bitterness and other sins, and how they separate believers from God, creating "disease" in our souls and physical bodies. These concepts are not new. They have been taught by countless others.

Let me explain why this book was written. In January 1999, I was healed of a disease called Environmental Illness. I had become allergic to most foods and clothing fibers. I was prayed for and had hands laid on me by two different pastors and their elders in an effort to receive healing, but I was not healed. Why not?

Sometimes God cannot heal us of our diseases. This may seem like a shocking statement, but it is not. I firmly believed that God could heal me, but He didn't. I have come to understand that God could not heal me without violating His holy nature, because of my unrepentant sin. Does this statement shock you?

Why should God choose to bless us if we choose to disobey Him? Deuteronomy 28 and many other passages graphically lay out the blessings of obedience and the curses, or consequences, of disobedience. In these curses are listed all the diseases of mankind. Disease is the result of sin, either Adam's or our own. We live in a fallen world, and Scripture says there will be infirmities because of the fall. An example of this is the blind man in John 9.

Before sin entered into the world there were no diseases. Praise God, there will be no diseases after the Great White Throne Judgment when Satan has been bound and thrown into the abyss forever.

As Christians, we have an active part to play in this temporal life. Our part is to obey the Lord. When we choose to live the way God commands, He delights in blessing us. He teaches us that we are to draw nigh to Him, and He will draw nigh to us (James 4:8). We are to seek first the kingdom of God, and His righteousness, and then all other things will be added (Matthew 6:33). These verses show that there is a level of responsibility and obedience required to receive His blessings, and to enjoy a very close and personal relationship with Him. We can walk in the "cool of the evening" with God, as did Adam and Eve, if we have dealt with the sin in our lives.

When I went before God and dealt with my sins of unforgiveness and resentment, and cast out the spirit of fear, God was faithful: He healed me. He produced a radical change in my health that was obvious to many people. People started asking what had happened. I had changed physically, and they saw the difference in my appearance.

As I shared my story, I encouraged others to study and to apply Biblical principles to their own lives. They were healed of allergies, chronic fatigue syndrome, fibromyalgia and many other diseases.

As the months passed I became inundated with requests from people wanting help. I did not know how to respond because I was new to the concept of a healing ministry. However, I knew that I could not turn these people away. I founded Wellspring Ministries because of the need to help others learn how to apply these powerful, healing Biblical principles to their own lives, just as I had done.

I started setting up appointments, and Linda Follett became my first ministry partner. We shared these truths from the Bible with our ministry clients.

As we tried to be more effective helping others, we developed our own unique methods and materials. I began teaching a twelve-week series at my church that required the development of handouts, and this book is the result.

We pray that God will use this book to change lives by restoring a right relationship with Him through His Son, Jesus Christ.

Most of us do not understand what sin is. We have become immune to sin so that we do not understand that sin in our lives separates us from God. God called each of us to be holy and set apart. We are to be in this world, but not of it. Sadly, many of us are "leavened" by the things of this world. Then we wonder why God's power is not evident in our lives or our churches.

Jesus did three things while He was on the earth: He taught repentance, He cast out demons by His word, and He laid hands on the sick and healed them. And then He laid down His life to forever free us from the bondage of sin. In Mark 16, and other passages, Jesus told us (and continues to tell us) that after His ascension and the coming of the Holy Spirit we should do these same things.

The events of Matthew, Mark, Luke and John relating to freedom from sin and ministering to others should be happening in our lives today. God never changes. "For I am the LORD, I change not..." (Malachi 3:6a).

If we apply the principles of sanctification taught in the New Testament, then the power of God will be evident in our lives and churches.

At Wellspring Ministries, we have seen God heal many people.

One woman had been allergic to literally every food. She stands five-feet, five-inches, but only weighed seventy-nine pounds. Following just ten days of understanding and applying scriptural truths to her life, she could eat more than fifty foods and had gained back eight pounds. Now her weight is normal. Her sickness and decline had lasted more than twenty years.

Another woman was healed of multiple sclerosis. Others have been healed of allergies and fibromyalgia.

We have seen fears and phobias conquered, and people set free from fear-driven lives. Others no longer have migraine headaches, reflux, heart disease or ovarian cancer. Many have been set free from multiple personalities. Others no longer carry shame from their past because God has set them free through His forgiveness.

Jesus healed all these people. He alone will heal you because He is not a respector of persons. What He has done for one, He will do for another, if we meet His conditions. What is the status of your relationship with Him? Are you separated from Him in any way?

How do you feel about God the Father? Is He a loving, caring God or does He carry a big stick, ready to punish you? Do you really believe that He is the giver of every good and perfect gift? Do you believe that if it is not good and perfect it cannot be from God? (James 1:17).

How do you relate to others? Are your relationships with members of your family or others fractured?

How do you feel about yourself? Do you love yourself? God teaches that you need to love yourself before you can reach out to love others (Matthew 22:37-40).

It is in broken relationships that most of our problems in life and many of our diseases take root. Spending time studying this book and applying its life-transforming truths will help free you from these diseases. I guarantee that you will walk closer with God, heal relationships with others, and find how to "walk worthy" of the high calling of Jesus Christ (Colossians 1:10, I Thessalonians 2:12). Herein is shared knowledge and understanding to change your life by bringing you closer to God and providing you the tools to change your life, heal your diseases and restore wounded relationships.

Art Mathias, Ph.D.

Acknowledgements

First, to my wife, for allowing me to spend fifteen hours per day during the fifteen months of study and teaching I invested in writing this book, and for her priceless help reviewing my work.

To Linda Follett, my "right hand," who was always there to proof, edit and help with this book.

To Pastor Henry Wright. The first nine chapters of this book are adapted from his teachings.

The chapters on the Kinsman Redeemer and the Armor of God are adapted from the teachings of Kay Arthur, Precept Ministries.

All Scripture is quoted from the 1611 Version of the King James Bible, unless otherwise designated.

Introduction

Ephesians 6:12 teaches, "We wrestle not against flesh and blood, but against principalities, against powers, against the rulers of the darkness of this world, against spiritual wickedness in high places."

Our true enemies are not other people, but Satan and his demons.

There are two totally opposed kingdoms at war, and we are the prize. Ephesians names this a spiritual war, and we have no choice about participating. Let us accept this fact and become educated how to win instead of living in defeat. He that is within us is greater than he that is in the world (I John 4:4). We will always win when we do things God's way; we will always lose if we do things our own way.

To win a war, a military commander first needs a clear idea of the character, tendencies and strategies of his enemy. He masters knowledge of his enemy's strengths and weaknesses. Hosea 4:6, says, "My people are destroyed for lack of knowledge: because thou hast rejected knowledge, I will also reject thee, that thou shalt be no priest to me: seeing thou hast forgotten the law of thy God, I will also forget thy children." God has given us His knowledge, and sent His Holy Spirit to teach us (John 14:26). In the Bible, we have everything we need to understand and combat the wiles of the devil. God has given us everything that we need to have victory in this war. Let's choose not to reject His knowledge. The first section of this book teaches the major methods Satan uses to attack us.

God's kingdom consists of God the Father, God the Son — Who is Jesus Christ — and God the Holy Spirit. Satan's kingdom consists of Satan and his powers, principalities and demons. Satan's principalities have a pecking order. There are stronger ruling demons and lesser demons that answer to, serve, and protect each principality. These demons form the front rank of the army of Satan.

God's nature is love, joy, peace, longsuffering, gentleness, and the other fruit of the Holy Spirit. Satan's nature is hatred, envy, jealousy, unforgiveness, resentment, anger, murder, violence, rejection, fear, self-hatred, self-murder, bitterness, fornication, adultery and the like.

In this war between these two kingdoms, God gave us a free will. We have the ability to choose whom we will serve (Deuteronomy 30:19, Joshua 24:15). The evidence of whom we are serving is heard in our words (Matthew 15:11). It is what comes out of the mouth of man that defiles him. If we are submitting to the Holy Spirit, our speech will be proclaiming His nature of love, joy, peace, longsuffering, etc. He lives in and through us. We are a vessel in service to Him.

If our mouths spew hatred, unforgiveness, resentment, fear, bitterness, violence, rejection, self-hatred, etc., then we are showing that we are controlled by one or more of Satan's demons. These demons can live through us. We are, all too often, their vessels of self-expression.

There is only one Holy Spirit, so all of God's nature and fruit comes from Him and is expressed through us. But Satan has innumerable demons. Thousands can be in the same person at the same time. Jesus cast out legions of demons from one man, and sent them into a herd of pigs (Luke 8:30-31).

In this book, we have called each nature, or fruit, of Satan by the name that indicates how that nature expresses itself. Thus, each demon has its own name, i.e., "the spirit of fear" (II Timothy 1:7).

The Holy Spirit manifests His nature through people. Satan and his demons are the counterfeit of the Holy Spirit and they also manifest their nature the same way — through people.

Just as God is truth, so Satan is a liar.

God is love, joy, peace, longsuffering, gentleness, goodness, faith, meekness, and temperance (Galatians 5:22-23) — perfection personified.

Satan is hatred, murder, violence, unforgiveness, resentment, rejection, fear, jealousy and envy, lies (Galatians 5:19-21) — imperfection and degradation personified.

Which area of our everyday life gives us the most trouble? Is it not fear, doubt, unbelief, rejection, jealousy, envy, bitterness, sexual sin, lust, greed, etc.? These words describe the very nature of Satan. Could these be the names of the principalities and powers of Ephesians 6:12? It would seem that this host of evil principalities and powers would show evidence of the major battles with Satan in our lives. This study will show how each of these areas is nothing but the lies of Satan he uses to try and defeat us.

We are in the process of being changed into the image and likeness of God through the renewing of our minds (Romans 12:2). We must understand the condition of our mind in its present state. What lies of Satan have we believed? We must identify them and allow God to replace them with His truth.

Why is it that one minute we can joyfully be driving down the road singing praise songs and praying, yet when someone cuts us off, we fly into rage with angry and coarse words spewing out of our mouths? How can we praise God one minute, and the next minute be cursing (James 3:11)?

Let's go back to the beginning of time, and learn about the origin of sin and its nature.

The Spiritual Battle

MANKIND HAS FREE WILL

God created mankind with a free will. We are sovereign in our choices. We are told to choose each day whom we will serve. Whomever we choose to serve, we become a servant to him. The evidence of whom we have chosen to serve is seen in our speech, because it is what comes out of the heart of man that defiles him. Our fruits are either of God, our Creator, or of the enemy, Satan.

God's Kingdom

GOD THE FATHER
GOD THE SON
GOD THE HOLY SPIRIT

The Nature of God

Love
Joy
Peace
Longsuffering
Gentleness
Goodness
Faith
Virtue
Purity
Wisdom
Justice
Honesty
Fairness
Sincerity
Knowledge
Understanding
Grace
Mercy
Excellence
Forgiveness
Compassion
Devotion
Truth

But those things which proceed out of the mouth come forth from the heart and they defile the man.

MATTHEW 15:18

⇦ CONVICTION ... OR TEMPTATION ⇨

A double-minded man is unstable in all his ways.

JAMES 1:8

Satan's Kingdom

SATAN • POWERS
PRINCIPALITIES
DEMONS

Satan's Nature

Rejection
Hatred
Violence
Jealousy & Envy
Condemnation
Shame
Pride
Guilt
Lying
Lust
Greed
Covetousness
Revenge
Retaliation
Slander
Critical Spirit
Fear
Terror
Unforgiveness
Unmerciful
Self-Pity
Gossip
Self-Centered

In this life, our testing comes through the decisions we make. If we choose to obey God and to make quality decisions that honor (agree with) Him, we receive His blessings. If we choose to serve God, we also choose to allow the Holy Spirit to manifest through us, and we exhibit the fruits of the Spirit. As a result, we have the peace that passes all understanding.

If we choose to serve Satan, the consequence is that his evil spirits, which represent his nature, will manifest through us. God never causes evil; it is our choice. If we choose to disobey God, and follow Satan, we receive Satan's blessings. In our disobedience, God turns us over to our own devices, and allows us to go our own way. This is always of Satan, the devil, whom God calls "the enemy." As a result, we lose our peace and joy.

CHAPTER ONE

What is Sin?

As I study the Bible, I find its teachings sometimes differ from my personal
theology. I don't try to adjust the Bible's teachings to match my theology. I adjust my
theology to match the teachings of the Bible. Have you ever done that? There is hardly
a day that goes by that the Bible doesn't instruct me to make an adjustment in my life.

This study will require you to search the Bible, and you need to be willing to
examine some of your long-held personal beliefs. God reveals Himself to us progressively, as we are able to understand more and more. As we learn more we gain a deeper
understanding of His Word.

Please do not "throw out the baby with the bath water," if you don't agree with any
part of what I present. As humans, we all see things through a dark glass (I Corinthians
13:12). There is much that we don't yet understand. Satan loves to sow seeds of doubt
and unbelief, to steal God's Word from us. So before you agree or disagree with my
teachings, be fully convinced yourself from the Word of God (I Thessalonians 5:21).

Our intent is to openly expose the devil so that his ways will be perfectly visible.
With the eyes of the Spirit, we need to see so clearly that we will be changed forever.
In some cultures the devil is out in the open and easily discerned. But in other cultures,
like ours, he is more hidden. This means we need to dig deeper to discern how he has
deceived us.

If you become uncomfortable with some of these teachings, it may be that the Holy
Spirit is convicting you. We pray that everything that is hidden will come to light. Then
we can deal with it, restore a right relationship with God, and gain freedom in Christ.
The very sin that we will not deal with today is the very sin that will destroy us
tomorrow. "The wages of sin is death" (Romans 6:23).

DEFINING TERMS

Before we begin, we need to define some spiritual concepts about who we really
are. Do you realize that you are a spirit? And that you have a soul? Do you know
that your soul and spirit are two different entities? They are. And we also have a body.
We are body, soul and spirit.

Our body is the visible flesh and all its parts. We need to understand that the
word "flesh" is used two different ways in Scripture. Many people think, "Well, that's
just my old flesh. I've got to get my flesh under control. I'm going to crucify my flesh."
Do they mean they're going to kill themselves? Are they going to kill their body?
Of course not.

To crucify the flesh has nothing to do with the physical body. It has to do with the "body of sin" (Romans 6:6). When I use the word "flesh" from now on, I mean the concept of the body of sin, our old man, the old nature, or the Adamic nature. A study of the nature of Satan, our old man, the old nature, the flesh, or the Adamic nature reveals that they all share the same characteristics. In reality they are synonyms. When I mean the physical body, I'm going to call it the "body."

I Thessalonians 5:23 says that we are to be sanctified wholly in our spirit, soul, and body. The Bible doesn't call the body the "flesh"; it calls it the "body." The word "flesh" almost always has a spiritual meaning.

Romans 6:6 says, "Knowing this, that our old man is crucified with Him, that the body of sin might be destroyed, that henceforth we should not serve sin." We are to crucify our old man, the old nature, the flesh or the Adamic nature; thereby destroying the "body of sin," that "we should not serve sin (Satan)," so that we will not serve sin, but God. This verse equates the old man, the body of sin, and sin. It teaches that we are to crucify or destroy the body of sin, so that we will not serve sin. In His death, Jesus enabled us, through the power of the new nature, to crucify and destroy the works of the devil in our lives.

The body of sin (Romans 6:6) is Satan and his demons, which manifest in our lives through the old nature, the flesh, or the Adamic nature, which we are to destroy. The body of Christ is the Church, and is made up of all believers.

Scripture tells us to be "in this world, but not of it" (John 15:19, 17:14-16, 18:36). Here, "world" is not the planet Earth. Strong's Greek Dictionary defines *kosmos* as an "orderly arrangement...by implication the world (in a wide or narrow sense, including its inhabitants, literal or figurative...)." The Greek work *kosmos* translated as "world" refers to humans, to all of mankind. Scripture calls the physical earth as "earth." People are called "the world." Thus it makes sense to say that we are to be "in this world but not of it."

John 15:19 says, "If ye were of the world, the world would love his own: but because ye are not of the world, but I have chosen you out of the world, therefore the world hateth you." The physical earth or the planet Earth cannot hate. Only people can hate.

If I said, "I'm in this planet, but not of it," it would be illogical and nonsensical. If we're alive, we're on this earth whether we like it or not, so we can't say we're not part of it. Speaking spiritually, however, we can live in the world of mankind but we don't have to participate in its nature. This is the meaning of the Scripture that says we are "in this world but not of it."

We are in a world that is ruled by Satan. II Corinthians 4:4 names Satan as the god of this world, meaning he is the god of mankind. Out of this world that is subject to Satan's rulership, God has chosen for Himself a people that He calls the body of Christ

(I Corinthians 12:27). By default, we are either a member of the body of Christ or a member of the body of Satan (Matthew 6:24, 12:30, Romans 6:16).

The body of Christ is each and every believer. We became members of the body of Christ when be became born again (John 3:3) and received the new nature or the nature of Christ. In the born-again experience we became the Temple of God.

I Corinthians 3:16

"Know ye not that ye are the temple of God, and that the Spirit of God dwelleth in you?"

Under the New Covenant the Holy Spirit dwells in each believer giving us the power and authority to crucify the flesh and thus have victory over Satan and sin in this life. We no longer have to be slaves to sin, but we can be holy as He is holy. God has commanded us to be holy as He is in many verses (Leviticus 11:44). He has also commanded us to go on to perfection (Hebrews 6:1). Would He command us to do something that was not possible? Has He laid a trap for us? Of course not!

The New Covenant is better than the Old Covenant because the Holy Spirit lives in us and we then can have power over sin and Satan in this life. Both the Old and New Covenants are conditional. Obedience has always been required.

James 2:17

"Even so faith, if it hath not works, is dead, being alone."

James 2:20

"But wilt thou know, O vain man, that faith without works is dead?"

James 2:26

"For as the body without the spirit is dead, so faith without works is dead also."

True faith is never alone. There will always be a change in heart and behavior if there is salvation. Obedience is always required. We cannot just be hearers of the Word.

Romans 2:13

"For not the hearers of the law are just before God, but the doers of the law shall be justified."

Understanding the concept that we have a spirit, soul and a body is vital. I pray that you will pay close attention, and accept the Holy Spirit's teaching to achieve a clear understanding of God's truth in this matter.

I Thessalonians 5:23 says, "And the very God of peace sanctify you wholly; and I pray God your whole spirit and soul and body be preserved blameless unto the coming of our Lord Jesus Christ." Paul is teaching that we are to be sanctified in our whole spirit, soul and body. As we have discussed, the body is our physical being. It is the home for our spirit and soul. It is appointed once to die. At the resurrection we will receive a new, glorified body (I Corinthians 15:35-58).

By definition, we have a body, a soul and a spirit. Our physical body is home to our soul and spirit while we live in the physical world. Our soul consists of our intellect, mind, emotions, memory and will. Our spirit consists of our conscience and intuition — intuition facilitates tapping into spiritual things. Our conscience tells us whether things are from God: good; or not from God: evil.

When God created Adam he did not have an "old nature" or the "flesh." God called, and therefore created mankind from before time began (II Timothy 1:9). The Greek word translated "world" in II Timothy 1:9 is aionios which means "eternal, forever, perpetual, or before time began." In our original creation we did not have a sin nature. The sin nature entered into this world (kosmos), or mankind, when Adam sinned.

This is why Paul said in Romans 7:17 and 20, "it is no more I that do it, but sin that dwelleth in me."

In Romans 7:18 Paul says, "For I know that in me (that is, in my flesh,) dwelleth no good thing...." Paul is separating himself from his sin. We may do evil, but we are not evil. The "sin that dwelleth in me" is the flesh or the old nature. It was not part of our original creation. We are created in the image of God and God does not have a sin nature.

When Adam sinned, the spirit of man died to God. This is why we must be born again to be saved or justified. In the born-again experience our spirit is re-born to God. The law of God was given to show us our sins. It was never intended as a means of justification. We could never be justified by the law even if it were kept perfectly. It was intended as a means to sanctification.

When we became born again we received the new nature, the new man or "inward man," which is the nature of God (Romans 7:22). It is His Holy Spirit that lives in each and every believer. Therefore, the spirit of every believer is owned by God. He has declared us righteous (justification) and set us apart (Rom. 4:25). But at this point a war began in each of us: a war between the old nature, or flesh, and the new nature.

This begins the second part of justification we call sanctification. Leviticus 11:44 says, "For I am the Lord your God: ye shall therefore sanctify yourselves, and ye shall be holy; for I am holy...." As believers we are required to set ourselves apart to God. We are to crucify the flesh. We are to purge ourselves of all iniquity. II Timothy 2:21 says, "If a man therefore purge himself from these [iniquities], he shall be a vessel unto honour, sanctified, and meet for the master's use, and prepared unto every good work."

Romans 9:8 says, "They, which are the children of the flesh, these are not the children of God: but the children of the promise are counted for the seed." The "children of the flesh" are the children of Satan. Galations 3:29 says, "And if ye be Christ's, then are ye Abraham's seed, and heirs according to the promise."

This war is fought in our soul. Our soul consists of our intellect, mind, emotions, memory, thoughts and will. It is in this area of our existence that we fight against Satan. It is in this part of us that Satan tempts, entices and sometimes controls believers. As we cleanse ourselves of all sin and iniquity, we gain victory, and destroy the works of the devil. We accomplish this one sin and one iniquity at a time. This is why II Corinthians 10:5 teaches us to cast "down imaginations, and every high thing that exalteth itself against the knowledge of God, and bringing into captivity every thought to the obedience of Christ."

I Timothy 4:1-2 says, "Now the Spirit speaketh expressly, that in the latter times some shall depart from the faith, giving heed to seducing spirits, [lying] and doctrines of devils; Speaking lies in hypocrisy; having their conscience seared with a hot iron."

Many people have consciences that are seared, rendering them ineffective, leaving them unable to discern between good and evil.

What does it mean to have a seared conscience? It means that the spirit — for conscience is a part of the spirit — has been tarnished or perverted. It is being led by the flesh, or Adamic nature, instead of being God-led through the Holy Spirit. A person with a seared conscience cannot tell the difference between right and wrong from God's perspective. If a person's conscience is seared, their spirit is dead to God. Understanding the seared conscience concept allows us to see more clearly the meaning of Proverbs 16:25: "There is a way that seemeth right unto a man, but the end thereof are the ways of death."

Hebrews 4:12

"For the word of God is quick, and powerful, and sharper than any two-edged sword, piercing even to the dividing asunder of soul and spirit, and of the joints and marrow, and is a discerner of the thoughts and intents of the heart."

God's Word is a discerner of the thoughts and intents of the heart. The heart is often used as a synonym for the soul or inner most part of us. I am grateful that the Word of God is able to separate the soul from the spirit (Prov. 4:23, Matt. 15:17-20). He knows our hearts and gives us time to repent. To be complete persons, we need to have head knowledge, but this knowledge must become part of our heart so that we might experience the truth. Once we move head knowledge to our heart we will be set free from Satan's power and achieve total victory over him (John 8:31-32).

The spirit and soul will live forever. The body will return to dust at death, but all believers will receive a new, glorified body like the one that Jesus had after His resurrection. In His new body, He ate, walked through walls, and traveled instantly from one place to another.

THE SECOND HEAVEN

Scripture doesn't speak specifically to the existence of a second heaven, but Paul said he was caught up into the third heaven (II Corinthians 12:2), the realm where God resides. Jesus referred to it in Luke 10:18: "I beheld Satan as lightning fall from heaven." If there is a third heaven, it follows that there must be a first and a second.

The physical world, planet Earth, is the first heaven.

Ephesians 2:2-3

"Wherein in time past ye walked according to the course of this world, according to the prince of the power of the air, the spirit that now worketh in the children of disobedience: Among whom also we all had our conversation in times past in the lusts of our flesh, fulfilling the desires of the flesh and of the mind; and were by nature the children of wrath, even as others."

Satan is called the "prince and the power of the air." He is a fallen archangel that seeks to do evil in the hearts of the "sons of disobedience." Satan rules this world and the earth from an invisible plane called the second heaven — not located in the physical world.

I have never seen Satan. I have never seen a demon either, but I sure have dealt with them. I have cast demons out of people and heard them talk to me through people. I have told them to be quiet by the authority of Jesus Christ, and they have obeyed. Scripture clearly shows that there is a physical and a spiritual world. The spiritual world is invisible, and home to the fallen angels (demons).

Using New Age psychic techniques, modern man has found ways to tap into the second heaven. People who practice such techniques allow demons to overtake them and rule them through psychic power, divination, fortune telling, and lying signs and wonders (II Thessalonians 2:9). The devil uses humans to do his deeds on this earth.

Satan and his demons usurped the God-given rights of man when Adam sinned. Satan become the holder of the title deed to the earth and became the god of the world or mankind. He began to rule in the earth through the men he manipulated or influenced through his demons. If these demons don't already control someone, they seek to influence or tempt them through spiritual attacks.

Referring to Lucifer, Ezekiel 28:13 says, "Thou hast been in Eden the garden of God; every precious stone was thy covering, the sardius, topaz, and the diamond, the beryl, the onyx, and the jasper, the sapphire, the emerald, and the carbuncle, and gold: the workmanship of thy tabrets and of thy pipes was prepared in thee in the day that thou wast created."

There are several important points in this verse. First, we see that Lucifer is a created being, an angel of God, and had both a spiritual and physical body. Lucifer wore on his body all the jewels and precious stones that provided his "covering." It is my opinion he lost his physical body when he sinned and become known as Satan.

Every example of demons in scripture is one where the demon or demons were manifesting through a person or animal. They searched out human or animal bodies to inhabit, control or manifest their nature through. Therefore I do not believe that the fallen angels or demons have a physical body of any kind. This is not true of angels that still serve God. There are at least 104 examples of angels appearing to men in Scripture (Hebrews 13:2).

Ezekiel 28:13 says that Lucifer was a created being. Colossians 1:16 says, "For by Him were all things created, that are in heaven, and that are in earth, visible and invisible, whether they be thrones, or dominions, or principalities, or powers: all things were created by Him, and for Him." John 1:3 also refers to Jesus as the Creator of all things.

Jesus Christ created the heavens and the earth including all things visible and invisible. God the Father created all things through the Word, Who is Jesus. Jesus is the spoken Word and He is also God.

Ezekiel 28:14, referencing Lucifer, says you are the anointed cherub. Whenever you encounter the word "anointing," know that it refers to the work of the Holy Spirit in and through a created being, whether angels or humans.

Ezekiel 28:15 says, "Thou wast perfect in thy ways from the day that thou wast created, till iniquity was found in thee." Where was iniquity found? It was within Lucifer. Verse 17 locates iniquity in his heart, which is his spirit.

Revelation 12 describes the battle in heaven when one-third of the angels followed Lucifer, declared war on God, and were cast out of heaven. In Luke 10:18 Jesus said, "I saw Satan...." He didn't say Lucifer, but rather, "I saw Satan fall like lightening from heaven." This verse is in the past tense. Satan has fallen from heaven; it is no longer his home. Lucifer is now called Satan, and the angels that were cast out with him are called demons.

Satan wanted to be like God and one-third of the angels joined him in his rebellion. It is the same lie that is at the root of all false beliefs and false religions.

Why can't we see Satan? We can not see Satan because he is a spirit. Jesus dealt with many invisible principalities and powers — demons that would speak out loud in synagogues or through people — and He ordered them to be quiet. Demons actually used the lips and vocal chords of people. They had no bodies of their own. They were using the person's body to manifest their nature (Mark 1:23-24). So, when Jesus said He saw Satan fall like lightening into the earth, it must have been in a dimension that we cannot see, yet it was very real...and still is.

As spirit-beings, demons spoke through people or animals. They did not have a physical body. Demons seek to control or influence a person to show their nature through them; they have no other means of doing so.

We have learned that Satan is a created being; that Jesus is the creator; that Satan and his demons exist in an invisible realm called the second heaven; that sin first existed in heaven in the person of Lucifer; and that Lucifer's name was changed to Satan when he rebelled and was cast out of heaven to the earth. The third heaven is no longer Satan's home but he still has access to the third heaven and God to accuse us (Revelation 12:10).

The King James Version of the Bible calls demons "devils." The Greek word translated "devils" or "a devil" is *daimonion*, and means "a demonic being." In this study we are making the assumption that these demonic beings are the angels that fell with Satan.

How did sin enter into this world?

Romans 5:12 says that by one man sin entered into this world. The one man is Adam. Since sin entered into this world, it had to have come from somewhere. Jesus said that He saw Satan fall like lightening to the earth, and in Genesis 3 Satan takes the form of a serpent when he tempted Eve.

The story begins in Genesis 2:16-17 where "the LORD God commanded the man, saying, Of every tree of the garden thou mayest freely eat: But of the tree of the knowledge of good and evil, thou shalt not eat of it: for in the day that thou eatest thereof thou shalt surely die."

But in Genesis 3:3, Eve says to Satan, "But of the fruit of the tree which is in the midst of the garden, God hath said, Ye shall not eat of it, neither shall ye touch it, lest ye die."

Eve added the words, "neither shall you touch it." It is possible for us to be around evil and yet not sin. Jesus was tempted in the Wilderness by Satan and He did not sin. Temptation is not sin. But many times, Satan tricks us into believing that we have already sinned when we haven't, so that he can provoke us to go ahead and actually do so.

In Genesis 3:4-5 Satan continues, "And the serpent said unto the woman, Ye shall not surely die: For God doth know that in the day ye eat thereof, then your eyes shall be opened, and ye shall be as gods, knowing good and evil."

Satan asserts that God is a liar and that He is withholding something good from us. If we can access that which was withheld, we can be like God. Here the father of lies is calling the Father of Truth a liar. Satan always attempts to blame God for what he (Satan) has done.

Verse 6 says that Eve yielded to temptation, ate the fruit and gave some to Adam. He also ate. That act of disobedience to God was the event that allowed Satan and sin to enter into this world. Through Adam, sin entered into the world. Adam, as the spiritual head of the home, had the responsibility before God to set aside or correct Eve's sin (Numbers 30:6-8). He did not fulfill his duty, and additionally, he partook of the fruit (sin) himself.

What is sin?

We can explore what changed in Adam and Eve's lives for clues.

When Adam and Eve sinned, they became double-minded, developing a sort of split personality (James 1:8). They were still drawn to God, but something was wrong; something separated them from Him that had not been present before eating the fruit.

What entered into Adam and Eve that had not been there before they sinned? What entered into their lives that God did not create in them?

They showed doubt, doubting God's Word; unbelief, not believing God's Word; and rebellion, disobeying or rebelling against God's Word. Satan lied to Eve telling her that she would not die, but rather she would be a god like her Father, able to discern both good and evil. This new mindset created double-mindedness, sometimes believing God and other times believing Satan.

What was the first thing Adam and Eve did after they sinned? They discovered their nakedness and became ashamed, so they took leaves and covered themselves. Then they hid from God. Before they sinned, God would walk and talk with Adam in the cool of the evening just like we talk to each other (Genesis 3:8). After sinning, Adam was afraid of God. Satan wins a victory when we become afraid of God so that we hide from Him.

Adam and Eve experienced condemnation for the first time. How many of us have had to fight off condemnation after we have sinned? Romans 8:1 says that if we are following after the spirit of God, there is no condemnation. Condemnation comes from believing the devil instead of Jesus Christ.

Adam and Eve felt shame. They had been created naked, but now felt unclean and had to put on clothes.

What did Adam do when God asked, "Why did you do this?" Adam said, "the woman whom thou gavest to be with me, she gave me of the tree, and I did eat" (Genesis 3:12). Adam refused to take personal responsibility, adding to his sin. The first man quickly learned to blame others and his wife. We had a good teacher who taught us the same behavior. We often blame others, even when we know that we're at fault. To become the spiritual leaders of our homes means taking responsibility for our actions.

The garden is also the first incidence where man blamed God for what went wrong. Adam implied that his sin was God's fault. God gave the woman to him. He reasoned that if God had not given him the woman, the sin would not have happened.

When we blame God, we are trying to rid ourselves from all responsibility and accountability. The truth was that Adam used his free will to choose to disobey God. Each of us does the same thing when we sin. We should not blame others; we should accept the responsibility and be accountable for our actions.

Some of the most powerful principalities and powers of the devil show up in the behavior of Adam and Eve after they sinned. We see lying, shame, condemnation, doubt, false accusations, and unbelief. For the first time, lust of the flesh, lust of the eyes, and the pride of life are evident (Genesis 3:6, I John 2:15-17). These are the same root problems that Christians still fight today.

This was just the start of what Adam's sin allowed Satan to bring into this world.

Eve gave birth to Cain and Abel. Years later, Cain killed Abel: the first murder. Why? God regarded Abel's sacrifice as more excellent than Cain's. Cain's soul filled with bitterness and jealousy, driving him to commit murder (Hebrews 11:4, Genesis 4:8).

God did not reject Cain, He rejected his sacrifice. God required a blood sacrifice as a sin offering and the best animal was to be sacrificed. Cain chose instead to bring crops from his fields. God demonstrated this act of sacrifice Himself when He killed an animal to provide clothing for Adam and Eve.

Cain perceived God's reaction to his sacrifice as a personal rejection. It was a lie from Satan, and he meditated on it. Satan's evil nature started to bubble inside him, and Cain might have said, "I hate Abel. I wish I could just get even with him." Jealousy, resentment, unforgiveness, hatred, violence, and murder rose up within Cain — all elements of bitterness. Overwhelmed by them, he killed his brother.

God saw Cain and said, "Cain! Where's your brother?" (Genesis 4).

Cain lied, saying, "I don't know, am I my brother's keeper?" Cain lied, and he was now afraid of God.

God said, "How come I hear your brother's blood screaming in My ears from the dirt?" (Genesis 4:10).

God's perfect creation began fragmenting and degenerating as a result of Adam's sin. Why did this happen? How could this be?

We see that through Adam's sin, Satan and his demons "entered into this world" (Romans 5:12). Satan and his demons gained the title deed to this earth and became the god of this world or mankind. They brought their natures of unbelief, rebellion, lying, fear of man, unforgiveness, resentment, anger, hatred, violence, murder, and bitterness with them. Satan uses these to influence us to become afraid of God. Fear is Satan's number one tool to destroy our relationship with God. Fear is the opposite of faith. If we are in fear, we are not trusting God.

In this study, we name each demon with the attribute its nature represents, i.e. fear, anger, hatred, etc. Each demon falls under a ruling demon, or principality, that forms a part of Satan's hierarchy (Ephesians 6:12, Luke 11:26).

Taking this one step further, I want to suggest a radical but essential idea. I suggest that sin is more than just an action, or a thought, or falling short, or missing the mark. As sovereigns of our own free will, when we choose to sin we open the door for Satan's demons to manifest their nature through us. Wow! That is a scary thought! Consider this carefully.

Ephesians 6:12 says that we wrestle against powers and principalities, and spiritual wickedness in high places. The sins that entered this world with Satan form his powers and principalities. With what do we wrestle? Unbelief, doubt, rebellion, unforgiveness, resentment, anger, hatred, violence, murder, bitterness, rejection, jealousy, envy and the like. These are the sins that entered into this world with Satan through Adam, and we continue to wrestle with them today.

I have chosen to call these sins "spirits," "entities," or "beings," because the Bible uses these words to describe them. These sins are the character and manifestation of Satan and his spirits. Let me explain.

Numbers 5:14 says, "And the spirit of jealousy come upon him, and he be jealous of his wife." The Hebrew word used for "spirit" is *ruwach* (Strong's 6307). It is the same word that is used for the Spirit of God.

A lying spirit is seen in I Kings 22:23: "Now therefore, behold, the LORD hath put a lying spirit in the mouth of all these thy prophets, and the LORD hath spoken evil concerning thee."

A spirit of whoredoms or idolatry is found in Hosea 4:12: "My people ask counsel at their stocks, and their staff declareth unto them: for the spirit of whoredoms hath caused them to err, and they have gone a whoring from under their God."

Isaiah 61:3 speaks of a spirit of heaviness or depression. "To appoint unto them that mourn in Zion, to give unto them beauty for ashes, the oil of joy for mourning, the garment of praise for the spirit of heaviness; that they might be called trees of righteousness, the planting of the LORD, that He might be glorified."

Acts 16:16 speaks of a spirit of divination. "And it came to pass, as we went to prayer, a certain damsel possessed with a spirit of divination met us, which brought her masters much gain by soothsaying."

The Greek word used in the New Testament for "spirit" is *pneuma* (Strong's 4151). It is used both in conjunction with defining evil spirits and the Holy Spirit, just as the Old Testament used the same word for both.

In Mark 5:8, Jesus commanded an unclean spirit to come out of a man, "For He said unto him, Come out of the man, thou unclean spirit." Jesus asked this spirit its name, and the spirit's audible answer is recorded in verse 9. It claims the name, "legion, for we are many." The word "legion" was used for a Roman legion of six thousand men. This man had thousands of demons in him that drove him to insanity. This shows graphically how demons can affect mental health.

Mark 9:25 shows Jesus casting out a deaf and dumb spirit. "When Jesus saw that the people came running together, he rebuked the foul spirit, saying unto him, Thou dumb and deaf spirit, I charge thee, come out of him, and enter no more into him." The boy received the ability to speak and hear. This shows how demons can affect physical health.

In Luke 13:11-13, Jesus casts out a spirit of infirmity and heals a crooked back. "And, behold, there was a woman which had a spirit of infirmity eighteen years, and was bowed together, and could in no wise lift up herself. And when Jesus saw her, He called her to Him, and said unto her, Woman, thou art loosed from thine infirmity. And He laid His hands on her: and immediately she was made straight, and glorified God." This oppressive spirit actually affected the woman's posture and appearance.

II Timothy 1:7 says, "For God hath not given us the spirit of fear; but of power, and of love, and of a sound mind." Fear forms the basis for many mental health problems. Fear is a sin. We will deal with this in greater detail in a later chapter. Fear is another spirit that God did not give us.

There are many other Scriptural references to evil spirits negatively influencing our lives. These few examples I have provided should help you understand that Scripture repeatedly refers to various sins, diseases and infirmities as "a spirit." These evil spirits are real beings, just as is the Holy Spirit (though they are not equal in power since they are created beings and the Holy Spirit is God's Spirit). These evil spirits brought sin into this world, but they also brought mental and physical illness and death with them. If we allow them dominion in our souls, then they will manifest their natures in our character and in our bodies.

Revelation 21:4

"And God shall wipe away all tears from their eyes; and there shall be no more death, neither sorrow, nor crying, neither shall there be any more pain: for the former things are passed away."

The "former things" consist of the evil that entered this world through sin. At the end, when God binds Satan and casts him into hell forever, his curse on this world and on us is broken. Sorrow, pain, and crying will be banished as will be disease, illness and death in God's new heaven and earth. These negative circumstances will all perish forever with Satan, showing once again that he is the author of evil.

PERFECT HATRED

Given how much damage sin has done to God's creation, I hope you will develop a perfect hatred for sin and Satan's lies. Genesis 3:15 says, "I will put enmity between thee and the woman, and between thy seed and her seed; it shall bruise thy head, and thou shalt bruise his heel." Enmity is the strongest word in Hebrew for hatred. God created this kind of hatred, not Satan. Satan has twisted this so that we hate one another, ourselves or God. But God put hatred between Satan and us. We need to learn to direct this God-given hatred at Satan, where it belongs. We need to hate what God hates: evil and sin.

What follows next is one of the most important life concepts that I have ever heard. When we choose to sin we are allowing a demon to manifest his nature through us. As people understand this truth, they are set free from the evil influence of Satan. Realizing this truth is so repulsive to a believer that it generates a powerful God-given hatred for sin and Satan. It creates a very strong determination to stop sinning. Hatred is redirected to its proper target: the devil.

Revelation 12:11 says, "And they overcame him by the blood of the Lamb, and by the word of their testimony. . . ." I want to tell you about Joan (not her real name). I met Joan at a seminar Pastor Henry Wright taught in Anchorage, Alaska. He taught about the spiritual roots of disease, and during the seminar he asked people to write what he calls a "yucky pucky" list of sins and situations they need to deal with in their lives. During the last night of the seminar, ministry teams helped people deal with their "yucky pucky" lists.

On that night almost every one in the church lined up needing ministry. More than 150 people wanted help. We started ministering to them at 9:00 P.M., and continued until 4:00 A.M. It was wonderful seeing the Holy Spirit work in the lives of these people.

Around 2:00 A.M. there were four people working with Joan and they asked me to help. She sat on the steps leading up to the platform, and I sat down beside her. Her "yuck pucky" list was several pages long. Though I was tired and didn't have my glasses with me and could not read her list, I easily spotted three large letters: SRA. I thought, "No, this can't be." I asked her, "Is this Satanic Ritual Abuse?"

"Yes," she said.

My heart flip-flopped a couple of times. I had never dealt with anything like this before and I asked the Holy Spirit to help us.

"It was not your fault; you were a victim. In the name of Jesus, I release you from all guilt and shame," I said.

She started to sob and all of us held her. Her body started to go rigid and her fingers and hands contorted. I didn't know what to do. I looked at Pastor Wright and he said, "Cast out the spirit of insanity." I had only done something like this once before when I cast the spirit of fear out of myself. "This can't be any different," I thought, so I said, "In the name of Jesus, I command the spirit of insanity to leave."

Immediately she fell limp. We had to hold her tightly, or she would have fallen off the steps.

In what seemed like several minutes, but was only a few seconds, Joan revived and her hands returned to the rigid and contorted positions they'd been in before. "Well, there must be more to do," I thought.

She refused to look me in the eye, so I gently took her chin and turned her head toward me. Then I commanded all the unclean, foul spirits to leave. Nothing happened.

Then I demanded in Jesus' name that the spirit tell me its name. The most guttural voice I have ever heard said, "hatred."

I was on uncharted ground, but with a Holy boldness I commanded "hatred" to leave in the name of Jesus. The voice retorted, "No, I don't have to, I'm justified."

Wow! What a statement! What did it mean? "No, you are not justified; leave her now in the name of Jesus," I demanded.

"She hates everybody," the demon growled.

I ordered the demon to be quiet, and we carefully led Joan through forgiveness of everybody that had ever abused her. It took more than an hour. We commanded the principality of bitterness and all its supporting demons of unforgiveness, resentment, retaliation, anger, hatred, violence, and murder to leave in the name of Jesus. They did.

My wife helped during this session with Joan. As we discussed it later, we felt certain that Joan could not have been a born-again believer. How could a true Christian have resident in her all those demons? I had pondered this after casting the spirit of fear out of myself a few months earlier.

We wondered if we would ever see Joan again, and had no way of contacting her since we only knew her first name.

Joan walked into my office about three weeks later. "Do you remember me?" she asked.

"Are you kidding? Of course I remember you. How could I forget?"

We talked for an hour, and set a follow-up time for continued ministry. I learned to my great surprise that she was definitely a born-again, spirit-filled Christian. I checked that out carefully.

I spent about six hours in ministry with Joan during two different sessions. She had been ritually abused for several years and developed several personalities along with other problems. God delivered her from them all. Now she has only one God-given personality. Praise God!

My experience with Joan was very important in several ways. I had to examine and adjust my theology several times. She was a born-again Christian occupied by demons that spoke to me through her. Four other people had also heard them. One demon called itself "hatred." The demons obeyed me, just like Jesus said they would. I learned that sometimes demons will not leave if they are, indeed, justified in staying.

Ephesians 4:27 says, "give not the devil a place." The word "place" in Greek means a right or a room. If they have a right to indwell someone, they will refuse to leave. Sin justifies their right to refuse to leave.

This incredible lesson has helped me to help others many, many times. Since meeting Joan, I have had several similar experiences with other people.

I have learned through God's Word and my own experience that despite being born again and filled with the Holy Spirit, we all still struggle against the two spiritual kingdoms that simultaneously exist upon the earth. As we get deeper into this teaching, I will prove this as truth from the Word.

The Apostle Paul had much to say about his walk with the Lord and he spoke boldly. I'm glad he taught as he did so that I can quote him. I'm going to open the Bible, and let God speak to us through it. When we have finished our study, we can each judge its truth for ourselves.

I want to review a few facts before moving ahead. In Ezekiel 28, we saw a picture of Lucifer as an archangel of God. And Lucifer rebelled because iniquity was found in his heart (Ezekiel 18:15). The heart refers to the spirit. Vine's Dictionary refers to the heart as "the sphere of Divine influence; the center of man's inward life; hidden springs of personal life; the seat of spiritual life."

We are created as triune beings; we have a spirit, and a soul, and we live in a body. We are created in God's image. This is an important distinction. Some teach that the soul and spirit are the same, and this is not so.

If you died today, your body would return to dust and your soul and spirit would go in one of two different directions.

If you have accepted Jesus Christ as your personal Savior and are spiritually re-born as taught in the Bible, your spirit and your soul would return unto the Lord to await the redemption of your body at the "first resurrection." The Bible says the dead in Christ shall rise first, and then we who are alive and remain shall be caught up together to meet the Lord in the air (I Thessalonians 4:16).

If you have not accepted Christ, a different eternity awaits you. There is life after death for the sinner. Some think that when a sinner dies, they drift off into an eternal oblivion. The Bible teaches that sinners are sent to a place called "the lake of fire." It is a place totally and permanently separated from God. "And whosoever was not found written in the book of life was cast into the lake of fire" (Revelation 20:15).

The Bible teaches that there is a resurrection of those who died without accepting Christ, called the damned. It says that their body, soul and spirit will be reunited and they will stand before God the Father at the great white throne judgment (Revelation 20:11).

If you're a believer, Scripture says the dead in Christ shall rise first. They will receive a glorified body. If you are still alive on the earth when Christ returns, you will be caught up to be with Christ. All believers will stand before Jesus in heaven at the judgment seat of Christ to answer for every idle word (II Corinthians 5:10).

We are a spirit, we have a soul, and we live in a body. Lucifer is a spirit and he had a body when he was in heaven. The Bible says that within him were the tabrets of music and the ability to make music, and that every precious stone was his covering. He was the "anointed cherub" (Ezekiel 28:13-14). In Colossians 1:16, we read that Jesus Christ created all things, visible and invisible. All things include Lucifer.

As a created being, the Holy Spirit anointed Lucifer to fulfill the will of God. The Bible says that iniquity was found in his heart and he rebelled. Sin existed in his spirit, in his very nature (Isaiah 14:12-15).

The sin of Adam and Eve allowed Satan into this world and he brought spiritual and physical death with him. Sin has its origin in our heart, in our spirit, and in our very essence as humans. Lucifer's sin and rebellion resulted in his being thrown out of heaven, and he died to God spiritually.

When Adam and Eve sinned, they died to God spiritually and were thrown out of the Garden. To be spiritually alive again we must first be born again which makes our spirit alive to God again. Then, with our new natures, we gain the power and authority to destroy or crucify the flesh, which is the works of the devil in our lives.

I reject a doctrine of eternal security that implies that if we are born again we can "live like the devil" and still go to heaven. Scripture requires obedience to be His disciples. We have a responsibility to live Godly and Holy lives. We have the responsibility to conquer or crucify the flesh and become holy, as He is holy. We can accomplish this under the New Covenant because the Holy Spirit now lives in us, giving us His power and authority. We can accomplish this, both logically and experientially. Have you ever had victory over one sin? If so, why not two, or three, or all of them?

We are holy, as He is holy when His nature of love, joy, peace, longsuffering, gentleness, etc. is manifesting through us.

Adam's and Eve's sin brought spiritual fragmentation. They became double-minded and unstable in all their ways (James 1:8). We see this same behavior in many Christians who act Godly one minute and devilish the next. We have done this ourselves. How can this be? It is because we are not whole before God. Some part of our nature is not of God. It has not been sanctified. This study is designed to identify this destructive part of our nature and destroy the lies supporting it.

Jesus said in Luke 10:18, "...I beheld Satan as lightning fall from heaven." Where is Satan? We do not see him but we know that he is here. He tempted Jesus and he's present in the world today, though he is invisible. He's not in heaven, but he has access to heaven (Revelation 12:10); he's not in the physical world. Where is he? He exists in the second heaven.

Paul wrote that he was caught up into the third heaven where God exists (II Corinthians 12:2). The Bible implies that the first heaven includes the atmosphere around us: our air, the planets and the physical creation. The second heaven is a spiritual realm not in the physical world, and it's not in the third heaven where God exists. We live in the first heaven, on the planet Earth.

We can access the second heaven through Jesus Christ, by the Word and the power of the Holy Spirit. We also have spiritual access to the third heaven, but not physically as yet. Our access to the third heaven comes through prayer and walking in the Spirit.

How do we know that we have access to the second heaven? The second heaven has access to us. This is proven by the fact that Satan and his demons can possess, influence, tempt or control a human. To do so, they obviously have access to us.

Where is Satan's kingdom? It's all around us. Satan is called "the prince of the power of the air," but he also has access to us. Ephesians 2:2 says, "Wherein in time past ye walked according to the course of this world, according to the prince of the power of the air, the spirit that now worketh in the children of disobedience."

Romans 5:12 says, "Wherefore, as by one man sin entered into the world, and death by sin; and so death passed upon all men, for that all have sinned." The "world" means mankind: you and me. If sin entered the world, it had to come from somewhere else. Sin came from Satan's realm: the second heaven.

While Adam and Eve lived in the Garden of Eden, Satan existed in the second heaven, invisible to them. Satan inhabited a serpent in order to speak to Eve.

This is an essential point and it is imperative that you grasp it. "The body of sin" in Romans 6:6 consists of Satan's kingdom as it exists in the second heaven today, and it counterfeits the kingdom of God, working its evil purpose through and upon mankind.

The Bible provides numerous examples of people who turned away from God to serve the devil. That's why the Bible says emphatically that if your Father is not God, then Satan is your father. "Ye are of your father the devil, and the lusts of your father ye will do. He was a murderer from the beginning, and abode not in the truth, because there is no truth in him. When he speaketh a lie, he speaketh of his own: for he is a liar, and the father of it" (John 8:44).

How could Satan be my father? It depends on which kingdom I choose to serve. We cannot live in-between these two kingdoms. The Bible says we are in this world — Satan's dominion — but we are not of it. Satan's kingdom exists in this world (in mankind) and so does God's kingdom. Jesus said in Matthew 12:28, "But if I cast out devils by the Spirit of God, then the kingdom of God is come unto you."

God intended that mankind would serve His kingdom on this planet, not Satan's kingdom. But sin and disobedience entered the world through Adam.

By Jesus Christ's obedience on the cross, sin was defeated. And it is through His shed blood and His Word, that we have the power to overcome the devil and his kingdom, including principalities and powers, demons and spiritual wickedness. God sent Jesus to die, to overcome sin and death, to rise again and to once and for all time defeat Satan. In so doing, He defeated Satan's power over us.

Why do you think God gave us so much information that exposes the devil and the kingdom of darkness? So that we would not be ignorant!

If my enemy were a wolf, but I had no idea what a wolf looked like, how could I know if he was good or bad? I'd approach the wolf and say, "Oh, kitty, kitty, kitty," and I'd quickly lose a hand! God told us about wolves in sheep's clothing. "Beware of false prophets, which come to you in sheep's clothing, but inwardly they are ravening wolves" (Matthew 7:15). God warned us about the consequences of sin and disobedience. The question we must answer is, and it has both temporal and eternal implications: will we put forth the effort to learn, or will we remain ignorant?

Often we fall into Satan's trap because we don't know enough to even identify him. Isaiah 5:13 says, "My people are gone into captivity because they have no knowledge." It's time for the church to wake up and understand that we are in an all out war of epic dimensions! The war for our souls rages in the heavenlies, and Satan fights aggressively to destroy our spirit, so that he will be glorified in God's place.

There is a spiritual phenomenon I don't understand: how an evil spirit and the Holy Spirit can be in the same place at the same time. I don't understand how good and evil can co-exist in me. But it is true because I know that what sometimes comes out of my mouth is evil, and I am ashamed of it. I also know without a doubt that the Holy Spirit lives in me and that I'm a child of God, but sometimes I act like the devil.

How can the Holy Spirit and demons co-exist in the heavens? Revelation 12:10 says that Satan stands before God day and night "accusing the brethren." It's a mystery to me, but I know it's true because they have access to me. In this life, we all see truth through a dark glass. There is much that we can't understand but we know to be true to our observation and experience.

WHY DOES SIN EXIST IN THE WORLD?

The Bible shows clearly in John 1:29, that Jesus came to earth to take away the sin of the world. Since Jesus came to take away the sin of the world, why is sin still here?

Some Christians are snared by a theological trap that claims, "I'm born again, I'm spirit filled, Jesus paid the price, it is finished, and I'm immune to the devil." "All my past, present and future sins are automatically forgiven." If so, why are they oppressed, depressed, filled with diseases and have all types of evil operating in their lives? Why do they constantly repeat the same old lies, even when they know the truth?

Let's wake up, acknowledge and learn about our enemy, and then defeat him. We have the power and ability to do this because the provision has been made, and the debt has been paid. Under the New Covenant we have the Holy Spirit living in us. But the work of Jesus on the cross and His resurrection must be appropriated in our lives each day. We must forgive others or God does not forgive us (Matthew 6:14-15). If we confess our sins He will cleanse us (I John 1:9). What happens if we do not forgive others or do not confess our sins? We must become doers of His word and not hearers only (Romans 2:13, James 1:23-25).

Being born again doesn't make us immune to evil. It means we have the power to overcome evil. Jesus died for sin as the ultimate sacrifice and rose again to give us the power to defeat Satan (I John 2:14, 4:4).

The blood of Jesus is the ultimate atonement for the forgiveness of sins. The Old Testament animal sacrifices provided a covering for sins, but not forgiveness. Jesus' blood provides total forgiveness of sins, if we forgive others and ask God to forgive us. His resurrected life gives us access to the victorious power of the Holy Spirit.

While the cross brought forgiveness, the power of Christian faith comes from the indwelling of the Holy Spirit. In this way we have all three members of the Godhead — Father, Son and Holy Spirit — living in and through us.

Jesus said if you have seen Me, you have seen the Father (John 14:9). This should be true in our lives. We should be manifesting the nature of God, as Jesus did, so that people see God's nature in our actions, hear Him in our speech, and understand Him in our attitudes. This can happen only through the power of the Holy Spirit acting in and through us. The Holy Spirit has been sent to convict us of our sins and then help to defeat Satan's lies in our lives.

Sometimes we think that if others around us would only get their act together, we could live more holy and peaceful lives. But holiness doesn't depend on somebody else's life; it starts in our own life. We are told not to judge others. We're told to look first into our own spirit. Matthew 7:5 teaches us not to worry about the little speck in somebody else's eye, but to get the beam (log) out of our own.

Jesus came to take away the sin of the world, and He came that we might have life and freedom, and have it more abundantly. His gift of life means that we can triumph over Satan's warfare against us as he tries to steal our peace and health. Satan can only steal our peace if we choose to let him.

I John 3:8 says, "He that committeth sin is of the devil; for the devil sinneth from the beginning. For this purpose the Son of God was manifested, that He might destroy the works of the devil."

For this purpose the Son of God came, to destroy the works of the devil. This is an awesome truth! And because He lives in us we can do the same thing in our lives. We do not have to commit sin! Some teach that we will never be able to accomplish this until we are in heaven. Where is your faith? Is it in the delivering power of Jesus or in the grave?

John 8:34 says that we're not to be "the servant of sin." The nature of Satan represents sin, and he uses his evil power to sway us toward him. When we yield to him and his evil nature so that it shows in our actions, it becomes our sin. Then we become sinful beings who need to repent and be cleansed by God.

The Bible says if we ask God to forgive us, "He is faithful and just to forgive us our sins and to cleanse us from all unrighteousness" (I John 1:9). Matthew 6:14-15 says that if we don't forgive others, God will not forgive us, thus emphasizing our responsibility to be part of the process. God does His work through us.

God wants us to confess when we have yielded to Satan and his kingdom. True repentance is a Godly sorrow for our sins against God and the evidence is a complete turning away from the sin. Then we will receive God's cleansing and blessings. It is also our responsibility to resist the devil. Once we have repented, the devil will come and tempt us to return to the sin. We must learn to say "no" to the devil (James 4:7). Before, and after the act of repentance, is a time of spiritual warfare within us that is addressed in Romans 7:22-23: "For I delight in the law of God after the inward man: But I see another law in my members, warring against the law of my mind, and bringing me into captivity to the law of sin which is in my members."

Some people serve sin in many ways; they serve many unclean spirits. The Bible says that if you continually commit sin, you become its slave (John 8:34). The Greek word for "servant" is *doó-los*; and it means a voluntary or involuntary slave, and is frequently used for someone in subjection, i.e. a servant.

A person who is bound by alcohol or drug addiction has become a slave to sin. This positions them as a slave to one or more evil spirits who control their actions and attitudes. If it were not so, they would have the freedom to resist the sin in their lives that such addiction inevitably creates.

Many people struggle with pornography and obscenity, obsessive or compulsive behavior and other unclean and destructive habits.

Some struggle with more common problems such as hatred, anger or bitterness. If a person can't stop hating, they have become a slave to the demon of hate, and hate has become their master. A person who is filled with criticism has become a slave to a spirit of criticism. It becomes natural for them to criticize because a critical spirit has become their master.

Loss of self-control over any aspect of our life indicates that sin has made us unable to exercise our free will under God's control. Sin becomes our master and we are enslaved. The sooner we recognize this truth and deal honestly with ourselves and with God, the quicker we'll be set free.

Romans 7:15-16 says, "For that which I do I allow not: for what I would, that do I not; but what I hate, that do I. If then I do that which I would not, I consent unto the law that it is good."

Paul is being very honest with us that even he struggled with sin. He was struggling with why he did that which he hated — and did not want to do — and why he did not do what he wanted or allowed. He admitted that when he sinned he was calling the law of sin good, and the law of God evil.

Paul wrote in Romans 7:17 and 20, "Now then it is no more I that do it, but sin that dwelleth in me." Paul was painfully honest about his own struggles with sin, but he had learned how to separate himself from it. He loved himself, but hated his sin. He recognized that his old nature or his flesh was not him. It was not part of Paul that was created before the foundations of the world in God's image. It was added by Satan, at the fall of man, when Adam sinned. He also recognized that because of the New Covenant, we can crucify the flesh and have victory over the sin that dwells in us.

Romans 7:23-25 says, "But I see another law in my members, warring against the law of my mind, and bringing me into captivity to the law of sin which is in my members. O wretched man that I am! who shall deliver me from the body of this death? I thank God through Jesus Christ our Lord. So then with the mind I myself serve the law of God; but with the flesh the law of sin."

Jesus is our deliverer from the body of death. He is our deliverer from sin and disease. He came to heal the broken hearted and to set the captives free (Isaiah 61:1-3, Luke 4:18-19).

Much of our "captivity" to sin begins while we are little children resulting from misunderstanding of events or because of "lies" told to us by adults. Satan often uses adults to place within children doubt, fear, lack of self-confidence, self-hatred and any number of negative influences. Working thusly, it makes his warfare less difficult than trying to attack adults who have well-grounded faith systems.

Adults commonly tell children that their predicament happened to them because "you are shameful," "you are dirty," "it was your fault." They say, "you are nothing but a liar," "you're selfish," "I can never trust you." These lies result in children who believe "I am not loved," "I can never be safe," or "I've gotta stick up for myself."

These lies establish a life pattern that becomes our master. We self-destruct by constantly repeating the lies, each time reinforcing them. Long after the original event, the resulting shame and self-condemnation destroy our peace. Though the original event may have required correction, or the original abuse was terrible, it is not the most serious problem. It is the constant repeating and reapplying of the negative lessons learned from the event that is the most serious issue. How we interpret and react to the original event deeply affects our lives.

Only the truth of God will destroy the works of Satan. Victory comes not from changing our environment to avoid negative events, but from interpreting events through the prism of God's truth. This requires discernment.

Satan's first line of attack is in our thought life. Can you tell the difference between the truth and a lie? When your emotions well up within you, do they flow from truth or are they based on a lie? The next chapter will guide us in learning to examine our thoughts and emotions, testing them to see if they are God's truth or Satan's lies.

CHAPTER TWO

Discernment

DEFINITION

What is discernment? It is a common enough word, but I wonder if we have ever really stopped to understand its meaning?

The dictionary defines "discernment" as "the ability to see clearly, to perceive, to distinguish, or to recognize." In Hebrews 5:14, the Greek word *diakrino* is translated as "discern." It means, "to separate thoroughly good and evil."

In contrast, Romans 14:21 uses the word *astheneo* translated as "weak." It means "weak; strengthless; without power to distinguish sufficiently between right and wrong, good and evil, or lawful and unlawful." It speaks to the ability to distinguish between the truth and a lie.

Hebrews 5:14 says, "But strong meat belongeth to them that are of full age, even those who by reason of use have their senses exercised to discern both good and evil." A mature Christian prays for and practices discernment in the conduct of their life. In so doing, they have learned to tell the difference between good and evil, and then choose to do what is good.

Hebrews 5:11 says, "Of whom we have many things to say, and hard to be uttered, seeing ye are dull of hearing." Paul desires to teach us in depth about Christ, but we are unable to hear his teaching. He is not speaking to our ability to distinguish sounds, nor speak the words written on a page. Our difficulty in learning is not because the concepts are too complicated. Paul's frustration with us is that our attitudes are wrong and these wrong attitudes block the imparting of the kind of teaching we really need.

He continues this thought in Hebrews 5:12-14: "...when for the time ye ought to be teachers, ye have need that one teach you again which be the first principles of the oracles of God; and are become such as have need of milk, and not of strong meat. For every one that useth milk is unskilful in the word of righteousness: for he is a babe. But strong meat belongeth to them that are of full age, even those who by reason of use have their senses exercised to discern both good and evil."

Many of us have been Christians a long time. We should be teaching others, but because we have not aggressively pursued truth we have become insensitive to it — dulled. So, we start at the beginning, once again having to be taught the most basic Christian doctrines. Our growth has been stifled and we are like unweaned babes (I Corinthians 3:2, I Peter 2:2). Milk-feeding was a common metaphor among early writers to express the idea of imparting elementary principles of religion and science. They compared sucking to learning; infants to beginners; and meat to those who had mastered basic principles and now sought a deeper level of understanding.

In Hebrews 6:1-2, Paul describes the first principles of Christ. "Therefore leaving the principles of the doctrine of Christ, let us go on unto perfection; not laying again the foundation of repentance from dead works, and of faith toward God, Of the doctrine of baptisms, and of laying on of hands, and of resurrection of the dead, and of eternal judgment."

As believers, what do we practice in our diverse denominations, and even within denominations? We argue if repentance is necessary for salvation. We argue about how to baptize, and whether or not God still heals people or performs miracles. We dispute over the issue of a literal hell. Yet God created one Church and one Scripture. The Church consists of too many unweaned babes unwilling to move beyond basic principles to the real issues of faith that unite us all in Christ.

Paul implores us to go beyond first principles, to grow out of childhood. He points us toward perfection. Would Paul tell us to go on to perfection if it were not possible? We are never to rest until we achieve adulthood as believers, mature in Christ. We need to be capable of consuming the strong meat of God's Word, capable of teaching God's Word, and capable of applying our Biblically-informed senses to discern between good and evil, lies and the truth. This requires a lot of hard work and effort on our part.

John 12:40 says, "He [Satan] hath blinded their eyes, and hardened their heart; that they should not see with their eyes, nor understand with their heart, and be converted, and I should heal them." As we yield to Satan, he blinds our eyes and hardens our hearts — our attitudes — so that we don't understand Godliness (II Cor. 4:4, I John 2:11). Satan's first goal is to prevent us from receiving new birth (conversion). Failing that, he strives to keep us from maturing so that we can enjoy a deeper walk with God. Satan desires to prevent us from receiving spiritual healing that could result in physical healing.

Jeremiah 17:9-10 says, "The heart is deceitful above all things, and desperately wicked: who can know it? I the LORD search the heart, I try the reins, even to give every man according to his ways, and according to the fruit of his doings."

We cannot trust our feelings. Rather, we must rely only on the Word of God taken by faith. God's rewards for us are directly related to obeying His Word, not to how we feel or think about it. Disobedience reaps the "fruit of our own doings." We must study to show ourselves approved, rightly dividing the Word of truth (II Timothy 2:15). And we must apply the truths to our life that we learn from our study.

In Psalms 139:23-24 David said, "Search me, O God, and know my heart: try me, and know my thoughts: And see if there be any wicked way in me, and lead me in the way everlasting." David passionately asked God to examine him, to know his heart, to renew his spirit, to test him, to examine his thoughts, to root out any wicked way in him, to direct him to walk in God's way. Are we willing to make the same request?

We need to seek His face for healing. II Chronicles 7:14 says, "If My people, which are called by My name, shall humble themselves, and pray, and seek My face, and turn from their wicked ways; then will I hear from heaven, and will forgive their sin, and will heal their land."

We need to draw nigh to God to be cleansed. James 4:8 says, "Draw nigh to God, and He will draw nigh to you. Cleanse your hands, ye sinners; and purify your hearts, ye double minded."

Cleansing our hands requires repentance, a turning away from sin with a determination not to repeat it. Cleansing our hearts requires us to confess our sins, forgive others and ourselves, and ask God for forgiveness. Then we are not only declared righteous and blameless, but we become righteous in our experience, putting us in a position to receive healing of both spirit and body.

Our first life priority should be to seek God and His righteousness. If we do this, He promises to bless us. The blessing results from our choice of putting Him first in our heart, mind and actions. Matthew 6:33 says, "But seek ye first the kingdom of God, and his righteousness; and all these things shall be added unto you."

God's ways are orderly. He plays the dominant role in all creation, but in His order of things, we must take personal responsibility for our actions. He gave us a free will and we choose, situation by situation, whether or not to obey Him. God never changes nor moves away, and is always faithful to do His part. But He will not bless us when we have chosen sin that separates us from Him. God longs to bless us as we obediently surrender our lives to Him (I Samuel 15:22).

James 4:7 says, "Submit yourselves therefore to God. Resist the devil, and he will flee from you." We are to submit to God and put Him first in our lives. By resisting the devil, he will flee and God will step in to provide His blessing.

Romans 16:20 says, "... and the God of peace shall bruise Satan under your feet shortly. The grace of our Lord Jesus Christ be with you. Amen." This verse needs to be a constant reminder that we have victory over Satan through the Lord Jesus Christ.

SPIRITUAL WARFARE

Two spiritual kingdoms are at war here on earth, and we're caught in the middle (Revelation 2:16). Many of us are aware of this spiritual warfare and the ongoing battle for our souls, but others are blind. II Corinthians 2:11 says, "Lest Satan should get an advantage of us: for we are not ignorant of his devices."

We must know Satan's devices so well that we can recognize and discern his lies. God warns us not to be ignorant in Hosea 4:6: "My people are destroyed for lack of knowledge." God wants us to comprehend truth about Him and Satan so that we can be victorious over evil.

Satan attacks us in three dimensions: 1) spiritually, 2) mentally (in our thoughts), and 3) physically.

Satan attacks us spiritually by trying to weaken and destroy our faith in God. He attempts to counterfeit everything that is of God. He presents God as mean-spirited, selfish, jealous and vindictive. He wants us to believe that God is withholding good things from us. He tries to trick us into blaming God for our hardships and diseases, when in truth, Satan is the author of everything negative. He wants to replace faith in God with fear and superstition.

How many times have we heard someone say, "I don't understand why God would allow my wife to die?" God is the author of life, not death. Satan authored sin and death and published it first on the hearts of Adam and Eve. It then found a ready home in the hearts of all humans. God the Father is the giver of every good and perfect gift (James 1:17). Therefore if it is not good and perfect, it is not from God. As I have learned to accept this simple truth at deeper levels in my life, I have gained greater and greater levels of peace and joy.

Satan attacks us physically by bringing disease and death to our bodies. Disease and death entered this world by Satan's instigation through one man's sin (Romans 5:12). Disease and death will be banished forever in the New Heavens, while Satan is bound forever and condemned to the abyss. Deuteronomy 27-28 graphically illustrate the contrasts between obedience and disobedience to God-righteousness and sin. Every manner of disease is listed in the consequences of disobedience.

During each miracle of healing that Jesus performed, He cast out demons or forgave sins, or both. All diseases are from Satan. Disease found its root in Adam's original sin, but takes root in our own sin as well. Every disease is rooted in separation from God, which is the ultimate effect of sin.

Not every disease is the result of our personal sin. In John 9 is the story of the man that was blind from birth. The disciples asked Jesus whose fault it was: was it the sin of the parents, or the sin of the man? Jesus answered, "neither." In a fallen and cursed world, calamities happen that are not the fault or sin of an individual, but the result of Adam's sin. Sin and Satan are still the cause. The point of this story is that the "works of God should be made manifest" in the healing of the man. The whole point of this story is that Jesus healed and thus destroyed the works of the devil.

As we consider discernment, understand that it is the primary weapon we will use to win this spiritual war. The key is to understand that the battles are fought in our minds. We need to learn to take captive every thought. Recognize that not every thought we have is our own, so when thoughts enter our mind, we need to examine them to see who sent them.

Satan attacks us mentally and emotionally through our thoughts. Satan uses three types of thoughts in his attack. Expect them; know they are coming.

Satan accuses God to us. He'll say, "God doesn't love you. After all, He allowed and did not stop September 11." He employs a wide range of tactics, bold and subtle, to try to get you to believe the lie that God either won't or couldn't possibly love you.

Satan accuses others to us. Satan will accuse me, this ministry, our church, our husband or wife, our kids, or anyone else. He'll plant doubts and suspicions in our minds about others. "This ministry doesn't really help anyone," or "If my husband would only understand, then we could get along," or "My dad is right. I really am no good."

Satan accuses you to yourself. Have you ever struggled with feelings of guilt, self-accusation, unloveliness, self-rejection, or self-hatred? You say to yourself, "I'm no good; nobody loves me," or "There I go again, I'll never get it right," or "I'm just a failure." At some time in our lives, we have all faced this type of self-rejection. How could we, who are supposed to love ourselves, say such hateful things to ourselves?

Satan is the master accuser, and he accuses us before God day and night (Revelation 12:10). When we identify accusing thoughts about God, somebody else, or ourselves, we need to understand it is the voice of Satan accusing us before God. Satan throws "fiery darts" into our mind (Ephesians 6:16). We must constantly test our thoughts, and examine whether they are good or evil. Well-developed discernment identifies if these thoughts come from God or from Satan; are they the truth or a lie?

It is a fact that Satan will bring accusations. Knowing this, we must guard our faith and prevent Satan from stealing it. Romans 16:20 says, "...And the God of peace shall bruise Satan under your feet shortly." When? Shortly, not instantly. God's bruising of Satan will take time, but it is coming. This thought provides hope. Take this promise to heart.

The key to winning the war in our thought-life is found in II Corinthians 10:4-6: "For the weapons of our warfare are not carnal, but mighty through God to the pulling down of strong holds; Casting down imaginations, and every high thing that exalteth itself against the knowledge of God, and bringing into captivity every thought to the obedience of Christ; and having in a readiness to revenge all disobedience, when your obedience is fulfilled."

First, we don't have to fight this war in our own power. Our weapons are not carnal — of man — but of God. We possess the full power and authority of Jesus in this war, and all authority has been given to Him. We must learn to rely on and use His power and authority, not our own.

Jesus' power and authority gives us the ability to destroy Satan's strongholds. Through Christ, we have the ability to defeat Satan in every area of our lives.

Secondly, we must cast down imaginations. To cast down something means to shatter it, demolishing it. The Greek word for "imaginations" means reasoning and thoughts. We are to demolish all reasoning and thoughts that run contrary to sound Scriptural teaching. We demolish the reasoning, or theories, of humanistic philosophers and their vain, empty speculations that attempt to nullify Scripture and the Gospel. We demolish cultural influences in our lives that run contrary to sound teachings. We destroy Satan's reasoning and lies. Jesus came to destroy the works of Satan and gave us His authority and power to do likewise.

How many of us, when confronting difficult attitudes or behaviors, get into debates within our minds, instead of trusting and believing Scripture? Before long, Satan plants a seed of doubt or discontent. "Maybe evolution is true or partially true. Maybe God did not really mean that we can ask anything in His name," Satan whispers. This negative thought then builds toward destroying our peace and confidence. We meditate on it and progress to unbelief, doubt and fear. This leads to rationalizing God's truth and adversely affecting us.

Sometimes our lives are controlled by lies that we heard as children: "You will never amount to anything," or "There is the right way and your way," or "This happened to you because you are bad." Do you believe these types of statements come from God's truth or Satan's lies? Applying faith, our minds need to absorb truth and apply that truth in our experiences.

Isaiah 26:3 says, "Thou wilt keep him in perfect peace, whose mind is stayed on Thee: because he trusteth in Thee." God wants us to live in His peace.

Philippians 4:7 says, "And the peace of God, which passeth all understanding, shall keep your hearts and minds through Christ Jesus." Victory in these spiritual battles bring God's peace as its reward. God guards our hearts and minds and lets His peace settle in us. Our struggle with Satan's lies ends when Jesus Christ is victorious in our lives.

Discernment is a powerful battle weapon that starts with bringing into captivity every thought, so that all our thoughts are obedient to Christ (II Corinthians 10:5). We demolish all kinds of wrong and evil thoughts through our use of God-directed discernment. All thoughts that are contrary to virtue, purity and righteousness are demolished. Like begets like, so that impure thoughts result in impurity, hateful thoughts result in hatred. In today's vernacular we say "garbage in, garbage out." To be victorious, our minds must remain vigilant, sensitive to God's truth so that we will not allow Satan any fraction of a victory over us.

Firmly implanting God's Word in our minds requires that we meditate on it daily (Joshua 1:8). Meditation is like mentally chewing on God's Word so often that it becomes part of us. How does it become part of us? Here's an example. If you refuse to forgive someone their sin against you, God will not forgive your sins against Him (Matthew 6:14-15, 18:35). Suppose we take this Scripture, tear it apart word by word, phrase by phrase, and "chew" on it, break it down into its smallest parts, "swallow it" into our minds and apply it to our lives. It becomes so much a part of us that we no longer need to quote it; we simply live it. It becomes part of our nature to forgive others as an automatic response to their actions or attitudes.

After having digested this idea of forgiving others, we are no longer concerned when somebody hurts us, rejects us, or insults us. Our humanity still feels the insult, but inside, suddenly, instantly, the hurt is quenched. It is gone, and in its place there is love and compassion for the person who harmed us. We see them as under the devil's influence. This is a powerful teaching, and I want you to understand it.

When somebody hurts us, we don't just blank out our hurt feelings saying "Well, God, You're just going to have to deal with this." No. God asks us to deal with our own unforgiveness. We forgive others as an act of obedience to God, and it accrues to our own benefit. Do you see the difference?

In contrast, Satan would have us think, "I'm just going to blank out the hurt that so-and-so caused and, God, I'm just going to give this to you. I'm just going to blank my mind out; I'm just going to let you fill me up, Lord." Or worse, "That so-and-so will get his someday. I'm done with him. It's the last time he'll hurt me!" Satan may bring to mind other hurtful experiences in which you failed to forgive this person, making the most recent hurt even more painful... and self-destructive.

The Bible teaches that forgiveness begins with *you*, and it starts in your heart. If *you*, from your heart, don't forgive your brother his trespass, God will not forgive *you*. This requires action on our part. God doesn't just erase the hurts in our life. He wants to meet with us after we choose to obey Him. Then He speaks to our heart and heals it. Forgiveness does not set the other person free, it sets you free from the bondage of bitterness.

Ask yourself how you are dealing with the thoughts and reasoning that come into your mind day and night. Do you find yourself thinking about someone who hurt you, or about a situation where you lost out to someone who harmed you? Do these thoughts sometimes come so fast you can't really think them through? Do thoughts of certain people or events cause you emotional pain? Do you harbor unforgiveness or resentment about your past? Do your own thoughts put you down? If you experience these kinds of thoughts, then Satan's lies are present in your mind. The good news is that you can win victory over Satan.

Ephesians 6 says our battle is not against "flesh and blood." This means our battle is not against people. We might think most of our conflicts are with our mother, father, brother, sister or someone else who has hurt or rejected us. We meditate on these negative thoughts and in so doing, we see their face and remember what they did to us. Satan runs this projector in our minds and whispers in our ear interjecting past hurtful feelings into the present. All too often, we buy the lie!

That person is *not* the one who really wronged you! Let Ephesians 6 give you the answer. Our battle is not with flesh and blood — people that hurt us. Satan wants to hide behind or inside these people. But to be healed, we must begin separating the person from their sin. We must separate the lie from the truth.

When did God offer you salvation? Did He ask you to get yourself all cleaned up first, or to purify yourself before coming to Him? Or did He save you when you still lived in the filth of your sins? Do we still struggle with sin today? Yes, we do. Are we still saved? Yes, we are! God did not require you to be perfect to save you; He saved you so you could be perfected.

God looked down from heaven and He loved you. He said, "That's My son," or "That's My daughter. Satan, that's enough, they belong to Me." He sent the Holy Spirit as our Helper and we responded. Right? Then are you greater than God? Am I? No, of course not. This means we, just as did God, must accept the sinful people around us who hurt us and realize the battle is with Satan, not them.

When we sin, who is it we sin against: others, God, or ourselves? In Psalms 51, what did David say about his sin with Bathsheba? Did he say he sinned against Uriah? That seems logical since he had Uriah killed in order to steal his wife away. Psalms 51:4a says, "Against thee, thee only, have I sinned, and done this evil in thy sight...." You see, all sin is against God, and we are the victims of sin just as was David's son. What does God do with us when we sin? He forgives us. Then we should do the same with others.

If we fail to forgive others, our unforgiveness is a sin against God. Unforgiveness is an act of disobedience against God that involves arrogance, pride, and self-exaltation. Matthew 18:21-22 gives us Jesus' instruction about forgiveness. "Then came Peter to Him, and said, Lord, how oft shall my brother sin against me, and I forgive him? till seven times? Jesus saith unto him, I say not unto thee, Until seven times: but, Until seventy times seven." Seventy times seventy is four hundred and ninety times in the same day for the same thing. Jesus meant for us to forgive others moment by moment, because that is how he wants to forgive us. In the manner that we forgive others is the same manner that He will forgive us (Matthew 6:12).

It doesn't matter what someone's debts against us may be. As mature believers, we need to cast down the imagination and reasoning that keeps us from forgiving others (I Corinthians 10:5). We cast down destructive thoughts because harboring unforgiveness gives the devil a place in our lives. An evil spirit of bitterness takes root and speaks through us.

John 8:32 says, "And ye shall know the truth, and the truth shall make you free."

The purpose of forgiveness is to set us free to become Christ-like. God wants us set free in Christ. I want to be free, and I want you to be free also. I am tired of having Satan steal my life and I hope you are, too. This is why it is so vital that we learn to recognize the wiles and devices of the devil.

Read II Corinthians 10:5 again: "Casting down imaginations, and every high thing." "High things" are Satan's demons that bring "spiritual wickedness in high places" (Ephesians 6:12). Spiritual wickedness exists in high places. What forms the various components of spiritual wickedness? Bitterness, for one thing. Others are unbelief, doubt, and fear. Still other spiritual wickedness in high places includes unforgiveness and resentment. I pray the Holy Spirit is speaking to your heart right now as He spoke to mine about this important matter of discernment.

Retaliation is another spiritual wickedness in high places. "I'm going to get even if it's the last thing I do. I'm going to get them for what they did to me."

What are some other forms of spiritual wickedness in high places? Anger, rage, panic, violence, murder, rejection, inferiority, self-hatred, and guilt.

What is a "high place"? The highest place in our body is right between our ears — the brain that houses our thoughts and directs our emotions. So what if somebody gets angry with us? So what if they tell lies about us? We must have the discernment to realize that it's the devil committing spiritual warfare against us through that person.

Ephesians 6 says that our battle is not with flesh and blood, but with principalities and powers, and spiritual wickedness in high places. Through the eyes of the Spirit, we can look directly at a person who is victimizing us or putting us down, and we see what is really happening. We look past the person talking to us and see the demonic spirit in high places that controls them. We realize it's not them talking to us, it's "spiritual wickedness in high places" inside them talking to us through them.

II Corinthians 10:5 instructs us to cast down every imagination, reasoning, thought and high thing that exalts itself against the knowledge of God. What is "the knowledge of God"? I believe that the most important practical application of the knowledge of God for a Christian is: "For if ye forgive men their trespasses, your heavenly Father will also forgive you: But if ye forgive not men their trespasses, neither will your Father forgive your trespasses" (Matthew 6:14-15).

Our own healing begins with forgiving others.

At any moment, when those who are driven by spiritual wickedness in high places offend us, we must remember that the knowledge of God instructs us to forgive them. We forgive because we are God's sons and daughters. He forgave us, set the example, and asks us to be obedient by forgiving others.

What did Jesus do on the cross? He exchanged bitterness for compassion. What did He say? "Father forgive them, for they know not what they do" (Luke 23:34). What did Jesus mean by that? He knew that the men who crucified Him were sinners. Jesus separated them from their sin. He knew the battle was not against flesh and blood. Just as Jesus did, we must replace bitterness with compassion.

Jesus used a shield of forgiveness to deflect the insults hurled against him. These insults were the "fiery darts" of the devil, not human accusations.

Satan has caused more fear, rejection and rebellion than any other creature. It's his nature to do so. The number one attitude that plagues mankind today is fear and its companion demon, rejection. Fear and rejection are the causes of many human diseases, mental or physical. Since Satan's sin caused God to totally reject him, Satan uses fear and rejection as his primary tactic to attack us. Satan knows that ultimately, God intends to reject him forever, casting him down to the abyss.

So, the knowledge of God involves both the power of forgiveness and knowing who is the real target of our spiritual warfare. It's not flesh and blood, but principalities and powers in high places.

In II Corinthians 10:4 we are taught that our weapons of war are not carnal or human in nature, but are of God. We don't have to rely on our power to fight this war, but we rely on God's power and, properly appropriated in our lives, nothing is more powerful.

Can you now take that thought captive when somebody blasts you, puts you down, rejects and ignores you, or tells you you'll never amount to anything? Who really says such things, a human? No, the source of such talk lays in spiritual wickedness in high places.

After you take such a thought captive, what do you do with it? You expose it to the obedience of Christ and the truth of His Word. What did Jesus say? When someone slaps you on one cheek, turn the other (Matthew 5:39). If someone asks you for your coat, give him your cloak, too. Exposing a thought to the obedience of Christ means bringing that thought into agreement with God's Word, thereby discerning truth from lies.

If our thoughts do not line up with God's Word, then we cannot receive God's blessings. God blesses us in our obedience. What did Christ do? As He was being murdered, He forgave. God wants to heal our broken hearts, but He will not do so if we continue to harbor resentments against other people. Our thoughts must line up with His.

We need to line up with God in both our thoughts and deeds. Many people can read about the thoughts of Christ, but they don't act like Him. James 1:24-25 says, "For he beholdeth himself, and goeth his way, and straightway forgetteth what manner of man he was. But whoso looketh into the perfect law of liberty, and continueth therein, he being not a forgetful hearer, but a doer of the work, this man shall be blessed in his deed."

The Bible is very clear: We are to be not just "a hearer of the Word," but we are to be also a "doer" (James 1:23-25). We can possess all knowledge and still not please God. The Pharisees had a tremendous knowledge of God, but they didn't live out these truths. Their spiritual pride and arrogance caused them to miss enjoying intimacy with God.

The reality is that we continue to struggle with many of the same issues over and over. This is not victory. Even though we know the truth, our behavior shows we have not yet let it master us. It proves we need to get to the root of Satan's lies in our lives.

So often we react to today's situations with emotional responses from our past. Instead, we need to examine the responses to see if they line up with the truth. We must ask God to tell us where these automatic emotions come from and tell us the truth about them.

Are we experiencing changes in our nature each day? Are we becoming more Christ-like each day? Why Christ? Because He is the perfect human being, the perfection of creation — of everything. And He is the Living Word. Our thoughts and words should match His. Our speech should match His. Our deeds should match His. We should be so much like Him that what we think, say and do, is Him. I Corinthians 2:16 says, "For who hath known the mind of the Lord, that He may instruct him? But we have the mind of Christ."

We need to understand and apply what Christ has done for us. He gave us victory over Satan. But we need to surrender to Him and His nature, the result of choosing to believe in and trust Him.

II Corinthians 10:6 says, "And having in a readiness to revenge all disobedience, when your obedience is fulfilled." We must stand ready at all times to take authority over sin, and to execute God's judgment against sin in our lives. We must quit letting Satan steal from us. We must quit cowering in the corner and instead, appropriate the power and authority God gave us to deal with Satan and sin. Sin opens the door for Satan or a demon to influence us and show himself through us.

II Corinthians 10:6 adds, "...when your obedience is fulfilled." We cannot ever expect to defeat the evil spirits in our life unless we are prepared to be obedient to God. We may strongly desire to be free of an unforgiving spirit, but unless we actually take the step to forgive others, we will still be held its slave.

Sometimes, we put ourselves in a position to agree with evil, becoming one with it. Sometimes bitterness even feels good, and unforgiveness feels justifiable. When these things happen, we have become one with sin.

We cannot cast down unforgiveness or bitterness until we are ready to break away from what they represent and choose to defeat them in our heart. This is the first step to becoming free from our diseases: We must be in agreement with Almighty God. We cannot be in agreement with, justify, or defend any sin in our lives.

For instance, if we struggle with bitterness, we must choose to confess the sin of bitterness and right ourselves with God, in spite of the influence of the demon of bitterness. We cannot be delivered from the spirit of bitterness if we are in agreement with bitterness in our lives.

We cannot be delivered from self-hatred without preparing our hearts to accept love. An evil spirit may scream accusations at us that we are "awful, and nobody loves us, that we are a piece of junk," but we must choose to believe God's truth that we are not junk. We were created in His image.

God created us. He described His human creation as "very good" (Genesis 1:31). We must come to a place of agreement with God about who He says we are, or we will not be able to defeat self-hatred, because our obedience hasn't been fulfilled.

One of our most powerful tools in this spiritual warfare is recognizing Satan's devices and by so doing, not allow him to manifest his nature through us. When a spirit of lust overtakes you and tries to grip your body, you recognize it and say, "Wait a minute, I can't revenge all disobedience until after my obedience has been fulfilled.

I recognize this thought as coming from Satan, and I cast you down, devil. I'm not going to act out this sin; I'm not going to fantasize with you, demon." As we choose to rebuke the demon of lust, and stand in the victory that is ours in Jesus Christ, our obedience is fulfilled. We receive victory.

There is a power from God that gives us victory over any demon. Satan doesn't want us to recognize it, because he doesn't want us to be able to separate ourselves from our sinful nature. He wants us to become one with him in rejection, and he wants us to become one with him in hatred. He deceives us to think that we are filled with "righteous" anger when, instead, we are filled with bitterness, resentment and jealousy. He wants us to become one with lust, and he wants us to become one with unforgiveness. Satan wants us to become one in agreement with his thoughts so he can get us to participate with him in sinning. Then he uses our sin to prove to us that we are powerless to defeat him. He lies to us, saying that we have sinned so much that God cannot possibly forgive us. It is a lie straight out of the pit of hell!

Why can't we defeat the devil? Because our obedience has not been fulfilled. Some lies are deeply embedded in childhood and are very difficult to discern. But, the Holy Spirit is our teacher. Ask Him for his help to identify these lies, and ask Him to tell you the truth, giving you the power and courage to cast them down.

As we learn to identify the influence of evil spirits in our lives, we get sick and tired of them. As we get tired of hating, and living in the hurt and pain of the past, and choose not to listen to Satan's lies anymore, the Spirit of God brings us complete healing!

After we have taken captive every thought and cast down evil, it doesn't matter who speaks against us or rejects us. It doesn't matter who ignores us, because it has nothing to do with who we are! When we have fully comprehended this powerful truth, we have achieved true spiritual discernment.

Why is spiritual discernment so important? Because it is the means by which we can free ourselves from Satan's snare.

II Timothy 2:24-26 says, "And the servant of the Lord must not strive; but be gentle unto all men, apt to teach, patient...."

This is what I am doing — teaching with gentleness and compassion, as Scripture has instructed me.

"...In meekness instructing those that oppose themselves; if God peradventure will give them repentance to the acknowledging of the truth."

How many of us actually oppose ourselves? How many of us practice self-rejection, put ourselves down, refuse to forgive ourselves, or live in self-pity? Our only true enemy is Satan, but our biggest battle is with ourselves. We need to discern what in our lives is not of God, and then repent and accept God's truth.

"...that they may recover themselves out of the snare of the devil, who are taken captive by him at his will."

Satan has taken us captive at his will. God's plan is for us to have the knowledge and understanding required for discernment. Then we can repent and line up in agreement with Him. We can be freed from Satan's snares. Why? I John 4:4 gives us the answer, "... because greater is He that is in you, than he that is in the world."

These teachings give us an understanding of the spiritual roots of disease. There is a legal reason why Satan has us bound down with diseases. Satan has every right to our life if we harbor unconfessed sin. We can not lay the blame anywhere we wish. We must accept the responsibility for our own choices. We must take personal responsibility and understand that we have been opening the door of our lives to Satan. Ephesians 4:27 says, "Neither give place to the devil." Now is the time for discernment.

Hebrews 5:14 says, "But strong meat belongeth to them that are of full age, even those who by reason of use have their senses exercised to discern both good and evil."

A mature Christian, by reason of the exercise of his spiritual senses, can tell the difference between good and evil, and then chooses to do good. Do you know the meaning of "reason of use have their senses exercised to discern both good and evil"? It is a practical idea of applying God's truth in our life; it happens when, having learned by experience, hard work, and serious study, we defeat the devil.

James 4:7 says, "Submit yourselves therefore to God. Resist the devil, and he will flee from you."

We defeat the devil by first submitting to God. This gives us the right and ability to resist the devil who no longer has a place in our lives. God will do His part by making Satan flee. Satan will no longer have any authority over us.

Each time we fail, we need to get back up! We need to confess our failure, repent and go on. It is in this practice and exercise of our senses that we learn to have discernment. What are we to discern? Whether our thoughts are from God or Satan; whether they are good or evil; the truth or a lie.

DOES GOD ALLOW EVIL?
The New Testament equates God to love and names Him as light, the rewarder of those who diligently seek Him, the giver of every good and perfect gift, and the beginning and the end. The Old Testament names Him the Creator, Redeemer, Shepherd, Savior, Provider and many other positive names. His names also describe His nature. If His nature consists of these attributes, how can there be evil in the world?

"God allowed this cancer (or other negative event) to happen," is a timeworn cliché. Insurance companies label large storms as "acts of God." Philosophers and theologians ask if God "allowed" Hitler to kill millions of Jews during World War II? Did God "allow" all the male babies under age two in Bethlehem to be murdered by Herod in his vain effort to kill the baby Jesus?

While ministering to people, we find many that go through life angry and bitter at

God. They blame Him for a family tragedy or personal loss.

Why do so many people see God as arbitrary and capricious, as someone that walks around carrying a big stick ready to punish them? Why are so many people afraid of God?

I have heard pastors and other Christians confidently say that God in His sovereignty "allows" evil, but He uses it for our good as an opportunity for Him to demonstrate His grace and mercy. This verbal salve is supposed to make it all better, make it okay that God "allowed" evil to happen.

Are any these statements accurate?

What does the word "allow" mean? Does it mean that if we choose to allow or not stop something from happening, that to some degree we approve or condone that action? If we choose to allow our children to do something, are we then responsible to some degree for the consequences of that action?

If God really allows evil to happen, does that imply that to some degree He approves or condones it? Would it make Him responsible for that evil action?

To be responsible for evil requires the commission of a sin. Does God ever sin? Of course not! Something is wrong with our human reasoning when we allege that God allows evil to happen.

Isaiah 45:7 says that The LORD created evil. What does this mean? The Hebrew word for "create" is *baw-raw* (HSN-1254) and it means to bring about; bring into existence. The Hebrew word for "evil" is *rah* (HSN-7451). It is never translated "sin." It is translated in the following ways: "evil" (Isaiah 45:7, Genesis 2:9, 17, Genesis 3:5, 22); "calamity" (Psalms 141:5); "adversity" (I Samuel 10:19; Psalms 94:13; Ecclesiastes 7:14); "grievous" (Proverbs 15:10); "sorrow" (Genesis 44:29); "trouble" (Psalms 27:5, Psalms 41:1, Psalms 107:26); "distress" (Nehemiah 2:17); "bad" (Genesis 24:50, Genesis 31:24, Leviticus 27:10-14); "affliction" (II Chronicles 20:9, Zechariah 1:15); "misery" (Ecclesiastes 8:6); "sore" (Deuteronomy 6:22); "noisome" (Ezekiel 14:15, 21); "hurt" (Genesis 26:29); and "wretchedness" (Numbers 11:15).

God created the law of sowing and reaping, and those who sow sin will, for certain, reap evil. God decreed that misery, wretchedness, sorrow, trouble and distress will result from sin (Galatians 6:7-8). The Hebrew word *rah* (HSN-7451) is translated "evil" 442 times, and it is never with the idea that God created sin. People sow their own sin and reap their own evil. The responsibility for both is theirs. God gave the law and it provided penalties for breaking the law. In light of this, we all should examine what we have been taught, or what we believe. Who is really responsible for evil?

Scripture is replete with references to the two kingdoms all mankind inhabit. Satan is called the "god of this world" and the "prince of the power of the air" (II Corinthians 4:4, Ephesians 2:2). He heads an earthly kingdom.

We also know that God the Father, God the Son, and God the Holy Spirit live in our lives. Jesus sits at the right hand of God in the third heaven, but His spirit lives within us. His is in a heavenly kingdom from which He rules the universe.

Satan's goal is to destroy us. He employs clever lies and principalities with their demons to persuade us to participate in evil and sin. God comes to us through the Holy Spirit and His Word, and wants us to embrace the truth and be set free from Satan's power.

In God's manifold wisdom, He created all of us with a free will. Our free will allows us to choose how to live. We have the option to follow God and His precepts, or Satan, the god of this world. These are the only two choices.

The ability to choose is valuable to each of us, but in order to choose there must be choices. Though God created good and evil, evil is not a sin until it results in an action.

Our free will is also very important to God. He wants each of us to freely choose Him as He has already chosen us. This reveals the heart of God. God is Love.

Have you ever been able to make someone love you? No! Has anyone ever tried to make you love him or her? Love requires an act of our free will. Love is an action and a choice. God wants each of us to choose a love relationship with Him, where we remain faithful to Him. It is the only kind of relationship that has any meaning to it. It is an intimate fellowship that only God can have with each of us.

The word "fellowship" found in Ephesians 3:9, means a partnership or joint effort. This type of fellowship can only happen if both parties voluntarily agree. God wants us to choose to love Him as He has already chosen to love us! "And to make all men see what is the fellowship of the mystery, which from the beginning of the world hath been hid in God, who created all things by Jesus Christ; To the intent that now unto the principalities and powers in heavenly places might be known by the church the manifold wisdom of God" (Ephesians 3:9-10).

Does this understanding of choosing to love God cast a different light on our relationship with Him? Does this cast a different light on our responsibility to properly exercise our free will?

Everything bad that has ever happened to us on earth was planned in hell and executed by one of Satan's demons. These bad consequences happen because of one or more of the following three aspects.

First, because this is a fallen and cursed world, things will go wrong — bad things will happen. There are natural disasters, diseases and other calamities that result from the curse. An example is the blind man in John 9. But these are still the result of sin and Satan. This was a perfect world before Satan's temptation of Adam and Eve led them to sin, and it will be again when God provides the new heavens and the new earth.

Second, exercising their free will, people choose to follow Satan and thus commit evil acts. These evil acts hurt innocent people. This is what Hitler, Herod and many others have done throughout history. In our choices to follow Satan and not God, each of us has also hurt innocent people.

Third, we suffer the consequences of our own sins. These consequences are something evil that enters our lives. As a result of our sins, God turns us over to our own devices (Proverbs 1:27-30). We will reap what we sow; in this God will not be mocked (Galatians 6:7).

God never allows evil. Mankind allows evil by making wrong choices. If we choose to practice evil, then we alone are responsible for the consequences. We cannot blame God for evil or any calamity in this life.

II Corinthians 10:6 says, "And having in a readiness to revenge all disobedience, when your obedience is fulfilled." Are you ready to "revenge all disobedience"? When you revenge (i.e., stop being) disobedience then your obedience is fulfilled.

We cannot blame God when we choose to disobey Him. Romans 5:12 says "By one man [Adam] sin entered into the world [mankind]." Sin did not enter this world by God. The verse goes on to say "all have sinned." Thus, all of us are just as guilty of sin as was Adam. However, we cannot blame him for our problems since we have the same choice he did whether or not to follow God or Satan.

Romans 5:18-19 says, "Therefore as by the offence of one [Adam] judgment came upon all men to condemnation; even so by the righteousness of one [Jesus] the free gift came upon all men unto justification of life. For as by one man's disobedience many were made sinners, so by the obedience of one [Jesus] shall many be made righteous."

God the Father loves us so much that He gave His only begotten Son that we might have life! By our disobedience we deserve death, but His love grants us life if we choose to accept it.

Sowing sin reaps evil. The decision of what to sow — God's good or Satan's evil — is each person's. God never allows evil. Allowing evil violates His Holy nature. We alone must bear the responsibility for sin and evil.

One of Satan's greatest tactics is to blame God for that which he is responsible. In Genesis 3, we saw how Satan falsely blamed God for withholding something good from mankind.

If we have been blaming God for some event or attitude in our lives, now is the time to recognize who is really responsible. Our enemy is not God. Our enemy is not ourselves. Paul said in Romans 7:17, "Now then it is no more I that do it, but sin that dwelleth in me." Let's recognize Satan as our true enemy and stop blaming God and ourselves.

Discernment comes from learning to know the difference between good and evil, and then making the choice to agree with God by doing good. This is the mark of a mature Christian. Let's use Godly discernment to destroy the lies of Satan that give him a foothold in our lives!

The bottom line is that God is Love. All of His acts, even those we don't understand, are motivated by His love.

CHAPTER THREE

Accusing Spirits

DESCRIPTION OF ACCUSING SPIRITS

In the first chapter of this study, we defined sin. We learned that sin entered the world through one man, Adam. The serpent (Satan) spoke words accusing God of withholding something good from Eve: the fruit on the tree of knowledge of good and evil. Satan lied to Eve.

Ephesians 6 showed us that we are engaged in spiritual warfare and verse 12 taught us that we battle not against flesh and blood, but against principalities and powers, and spiritual wickedness in high places. These verses confirm what happened to Eve in Genesis 3.

The "body of sin" (Romans 6:6) refers to Satan and his demons, the old nature, the flesh, or the Adamic nature. A study of the nature of Satan, the old nature, the flesh, or the Adamic nature, reveals that they all share the same characteristics. In reality they are synonyms. When we sin, we open the door for a demon to act out its nature through us.

Satan's attack began right after God created the first humans, Adam and Eve. Satan really is not very creative; he is predictable. What he did in the past, he will do in the future. Revelation 13 tells us that Satan will continue to lie and deceive mankind as time winds down.

In the previous chapter, we learned that discernment is the primary weapon of the mature Christian in spiritual warfare. Mature Christians discern between good and evil, and choose to do good. II Corinthians 10:5 teaches us to take captive all of our thoughts to see if they line up with Jesus Christ and the teachings of His Word.

I want to get into what constitutes our thoughts, their origins and effects. We discussed previously that the thoughts and voices we hear in our minds are not always our own. There are three sources for these thoughts and voices: they are either ours, from God, or from Satan. But the nature of our thoughts will always reveal whom they line up with: God or Satan.

The Bible implies about the second heaven as the place or sphere where Satan resides with his evil spirits, principalities and powers. These evil entities have access to our thought life. I don't believe that evil spirits can read our minds because only God is omniscient (all knowing). However, I know one thing: evil spirits size us up, then set us up, watch our reactions, and keep attempting to influence us to walk the wrong road until we have walked so far away from God that we think there is no way back.

We are under no obligation to accept or obey every thought that enters our mind.

The mature Christian knows that every thought is not necessarily for our Godly edification.

Have you ever heard yourself ask, "Where on earth did that thought come from?" Have you ever had a conversation with yourself? Conversations occur in our thoughts, and we do this frequently. To take captive our thoughts, we need to discourse with them, identifying and exposing them to the knowledge of God to verify their authenticity.

If we purpose to take the time to think during the process of thinking, we will see that some of our thoughts could not be our own. Some thoughts come in the first person, making us think they are our own. If we teach ourselves to think while we are thinking, we will find many of our thoughts come from someone or something else, even when they are in the first person. We have learned that we have the authority to command, in the name of Jesus, that Satan's demons only talk to us or tempt us in the second person. This greatly helps with discernment.

Some of our thoughts are good and wholesome, while others are dark and evil. Have you ever noticed that? We drive down the street and think, "What a beautiful spouse God gave me. Praise God." Or, "He didn't have to treat me that way. Sometimes I wish he'd die." We can have thoughts like these about the same person within moments of each other.

We need to be able to think about our thoughts and not allow them to randomly follow their own lead. We need to stop every thought and examine it to know whether it is from the devil or from God, determine whether it is a truth or a lie.

Examining each thought doesn't mean that we have become paranoid, nor should it indicate confusion. Actually just the opposite is true.

This process of examining our thoughts is powerful, preventing mental illness, and banishing sin and disease from our lives. It can keep us from being "double minded." James 1:8 says, "A double minded man is unstable in all his ways." Stability is one of the observable and measurable fruits of the Christian life.

Some people lose the thought war before they begin to fight by believing that every thought is their own. They have not learned to discern all the voices or thoughts, accepting truth and discarding lies. Often, doctors tell them they are schizophrenic or manic-depressive, thus labeling them with a horrible and usually false diagnosis that haunts them. The diagnosis itself brings additional condemnation, or provides an excuse so they never face the demons that actually cause their disorder. The only solution doctors offer is to prescribe mind-altering drugs that mask the real problems. The truth is that all humans hear or perceive voices in our minds. For some they are much stronger than others.

Grab hold of this powerful idea. Learn to stop and think about what you are thinking. This is the Scriptural principle taught in II Corinthians 10:5: "Casting down imaginations, and every high thing that exalteth itself against the knowledge of God, and bringing into captivity every thought to the obedience of Christ."

God wants us to develop and use discernment. If discernment were unnecessary, then all our thoughts would come from God and benefit us. If every thought entering our minds or every word spoken were truthful, we would have no need for discernment. Experience, however, has taught us that our thoughts and words, and those of others, are not always from God. They are not always good or true.

So, why do we need discernment to know what is of God, and what is not of God? We will never know the peace of God without Godly discernment and the subsequent rejection of ungodliness in our lives. We must learn to reject the thoughts that come from Satan.

Satan not only lies to us but he also accuses us. Revelation 12:10 says, "And I heard a loud voice saying in heaven, Now is come salvation, and strength, and the kingdom of our God, and the power of his Christ: for the accuser of our brethren is cast down, which accused them before our God day and night."

All day and night, Satan stands before God accusing us. As he does so, he plants thoughts in our minds that accuse us to ourselves, accuse others, and God. We know that Satan cannot be everywhere because he is not omnipresent. He can't accuse all of us at the same time, but he employs a host of demons to do this dirty work. These demons put thoughts into our minds that accuse God, accuse others to us, and accuse us to ourselves. It is these thoughts driven by these accusing spirits that we want to expose in this chapter.

Thoughts that enter our minds create energy resulting in saying, doing or thinking something about others, God or ourselves. Discernment puts a governor on our brain, slowing us down to stop and examine the thoughts and actions to determine what is appropriate.

Discernment gives us an "on and off" switch. It allows us at times to be quiet when otherwise we might strike out at someone. It stops us from doing something that later we would regret. Sometimes discernment works to stifle a thought altogether, disregarding our feelings. Discernment will keep us from committing many destructive actions, as well as prod us toward healthy ones.

Discernment works like a traffic signal, with a red, yellow and green light. It provides a way to mentally sit and observe our thoughts, as if waiting for a traffic light to change, to see whether or not it is safe to proceed down the street through a particular intersection of thoughts and actions.

We often show more sense while driving on a highway than we do in our personal lives. On the highway we are forced to obey the rules of the road. On the highway of our Christian life, God's Word provides the rules, but our obedience is our choice; God gave us a free will. Still, He wants us to make right decisions and gave us all the tools we need to do so. He wants us to grow into mature discernment. Hebrews 5:14 says, "But strong meat belongeth to them that are of full age, even those who by reason of use have their senses exercised to discern both good and evil."

Mature Christians are those, "who by reason of use, have their senses exercised . . . ," know the difference between good and evil, and chooses to do good. In Hebrews 5:14, the word translated "senses" is the Greek word *aistheterion*. It describes the organs of sense: the eyes, ears, nose, tongue, palate, fingers and the nervous system. With all our spiritual sensory organs properly exercised and employed, we develop our ability to thoroughly distinguish between good and evil. This implies a tremendous amount of responsibility and hard work.

In Matthew, Mark, Luke, and John, there are many examples of demons that speak through a person, making it seem as if the person were actually speaking. One of the gifts of the Spirit, taught in I Corinthians 12:10, is the ability to discern whether a spirit or the person is actually doing the speaking.

God wants us to develop discernment to be able to decide between good and evil, the truth or a lie. We exercise and enhance our powers of discernment by acquiring knowledge of the Word of God and applying it to our lives.

The Word of God delineates good and evil. Romans 3:20 says that through the law came the knowledge of evil. We need to know what evil is to help us recognize what is good. That is why we study Satan's nature so that he cannot ensnare us through our ignorance of him. This is also why we must understand God's nature. When we know God, we will be able to recognize the counterfeit.

One of Satan's tactics is to show us something that looks good, when in fact it is evil and counterfeit. To recognize the counterfeit object or thought, we must know what the real thing looks like.

Accusing spirits can operate in our life when we don't know what the real Spirit looks like. Accusing spirits build on our ignorance of who we are in Christ. They tempt us to misunderstand who other people really are.

They confuse our thinking about God's true nature.

Accusing spirits' goals are to bring us down, to bring others down, and to bring God down. They seek to separate us from God, others and ourselves. Satan uses an old military tactic of divide and conquer.

Evil is the counterfeit of good. Evil shows itself in a range of deception from outright lies and rebellion to those sometimes gray areas between truth and error. The only way to understand error is to understand truth. Unless we know the entire Word of God we will be deceived.

Evil does not always express itself as the total opposite of good. If we only look for opposites, Satan will use subtleties to deceive us. We will find ourselves accepting ideas that are ninety percent truth and ten percent lies, eventually being drawn into accepting a deeper level of lies. Accusing spirits routinely use this tactic of a ninety percent truth and ten percent lie as they seek to seduce and deceive us.

Accusing spirits hand us a generous portion of truth with one hand, and use the other hand to slip us a lie that begins to break down our value system. An accusing spirit will say, "Yea, I know I'm born again, I know the Word of God, I love Jesus and it's a wonderful thing that I'm a Christian, and hasn't God done wonderful things with me." The accusing spirit will build you up like this and then instantly, in a flash of thought, "but I still don't measure up to others. I'm still inferior to my brothers and sisters. It's wonderful where I've come from; it's wonderful who I am in Jesus, *but*...." Accusing spirits love to "but" in, to plant doubt that will us destroy our vibrant faith.

An accusing spirit will say things to you about your pastor. "The pastor is wonderful. I've heard wonderful things about his ministry. He's a good pastor. He's full of mercy and longsuffering." Then the accusing spirit will "but" in, saying, "But he's still just a man... he has feet of clay... why, look how he's stumbled in such and such an area." "Well, he is a Godly man, but...." And that "but" leads us to doubt and error, separating us from God, our pastor, our family and Christian friends. These kinds of thoughts can drive us to abandon our churches and leave our families.

Satan's nature is to destroy; it is the only aspect of his character that you can count on. He has no integrity. He will use every possible device to lead us down the wrong path away from God.

Matthew 10:16 says to be wiser than a serpent but harmless as a dove. We need to be wiser than Satan and his demons, but in our own actions as harmless as a dove. Serpents are always alert to movements in their environment. So, too, must we be always on the alert and ready to strike! There is never a good time to be spiritually asleep, because the moment we are, we give Satan an opening. Accusing spirits constantly strive to destroy Christ's work in the lives of believers and to create havoc in God's kingdom.

Revelation 12:7 says, "And there was war in heaven: Michael, the Archangel, and his angels fought against the dragon; and the dragon fought and his angels. And prevailed not; neither was their place found anymore in heaven. And the great dragon was cast out, that old serpent, called the Devil, and Satan."

The Greek words translated "Satan" or "devil" mean "accuser." Satan's name describes his nature — he accuses. His battleground is in human minds and his greatest power comes from lying accusations.

It's no wonder that we are buffeted by negative thoughts about ourselves, others and God. Satan deceives using both false and true accusations.

Revelation 12:9-10 says, "And the great dragon was cast out, that old serpent, called the Devil, and Satan, which deceiveth the whole world: he was cast out into the earth, and his angels were cast out with him. And I heard a loud voice saying in heaven, Now is come salvation, and strength and the kingdom of our God, and the power of His Christ: for the accuser of our brethren is cast down."

In these verses we see the whole of Satan's nature. Yes, he is a powerful deceiver and an effective accuser, but by appropriating Christ's power, we can still cast him down. By allowing Christ to live through us we win the victory.

Accusing spirits possess definite characteristics that result in certain manifestations. One is suspicion. Others include bitterness, mistrust or always believing the worst about someone. Presence of these in our thought life should sound a warning shot that an accusing spirit is at work. The same is true of suspicion, being easily offended, or easily offending others. These all give evidence that an accusing spirit is at work.

Exaggerating offenses and failures is evidence of accusing spirits. If we observe someone falling short of the glory of God and our thoughts become filled with bitterness, that's the work of an accusing spirit.

Galatians 6:1 says, "Brethren, if a man be overtaken in a fault, ye which are spiritual, restore such an one in the spirit of meekness; considering thyself, lest thou also be tempted." God's way is for us to gently restore a fallen believer, not condemn them in bitterness.

In Matthew 24:10, Jesus talked about the end times, saying in addition to wars, pestilence and famine, that many shall be offended and they shall betray one another and shall hate one another. During the end times it will be common for people to set themselves against other people. Sometimes we hear people say, "Well, Martha didn't treat me right," "Dad doesn't care," or "Pete stole my happiness." This is the kind of thought Jesus described in Matthew 24:10 when He said, "many shall be offended."

If we become completely honest with ourselves, we would admit that much of what we consider as offenses against us actually have their root in jealousy. Do you know what jealousy is? Jealousy hates another person because they possess something that we would cling to and admire if we had it. If we had it we would flaunt it, because jealousy and pride go together.

Jealousy promotes a sense of unworthiness. We become afraid that someone else will have more or better things than we do. We fear that somebody else will do more, be in better shape, or be faster than us. The spirit of jealousy says, "I don't want you to progress faster than I do," or "It's not fair that you got that job," even when we never applied for it.

In our ministry, we even see jealousy when someone else is healed. Jealousy asks, "Why them and not me?" "Why did God use you to help that person, instead of helping me?" Even though it is their best friend who has been healed, they don't like it. Instead of rejoicing with their friend, jealousy drives them to sulking and bitterness.

We've seen pastors get jealous because God used someone else to bring healing to one of their parishioners. Some pastors and church leaders become jealous because healing upsets their theological apple cart. They have been taught that the gifts of the Spirit and the miraculous works of the New Testament are not for this age. So when they witness healing, rather than rejoicing, they become suspicious and jealous, allowing accusing spirits to take root in their souls.

Matthew 18:7 says, "Woe to the world because of offenses for it must needs be that offenses come but woe to that man by whom offense cometh." If you allow accusing spirits to rise up in you and they are set in motion against another person, you bring a curse on yourself. The woe falls on you. Don't allow this to happen. Bite your tongue, govern your thoughts, even if what you want to say or think might be true.

Read Galatians 6:1-2 again. "Brethren, if a man be overtaken in a fault...." That refers to a true, verifiable situation, not mere speculation or a false accusation. This refers to a situation where we know a person really blew it. What does God have us to do? "...ye which are spiritual, restore such a one in the spirit of meekness; considering thyself lest thou also be tempted. Bear ye one another's burdens and so fulfill the law of Christ."

We are to restore that person to fellowship, not drive them away through accusations. To do this requires understanding and care, so that we don't become the judge and jury. God is the judge and jury. We must cut others and ourselves a little slack.

Let's take a look at how accusing spirits do their evil works.

ACCUSING OTHERS

I John 1:7 says, "But if we walk in the light, as He is in the light, we have fellowship one with another, and the blood of Jesus Christ His Son cleanseth us from all sin." Accusing spirits say, "I can't have fellowship with you and you can't have fellowship with me because we don't agree on the use of worship choruses." Accusing spirits attempt to separate us from God and our friends and family. But the truth is that we will have fellowship if we "walk in the light, as He is in the light."

What does verse 7b say? "And the blood of Jesus Christ, His Son, cleanses us from all sin."

We need to make sure that we understand I John 1:7. Here we are walking together in the light, as He is in the light, and it brings us together in fellowship. Along come accusing spirits to try and separate us. There are two ways that they try to do this.

One way is to bring a false accusation. A second is when there has been sin and the accusation is true. In either case, accusing spirits will tell the sinner he or she is not worthy to have fellowship with us, or that the righteous person cannot associate with a sinner, even after they have received forgiveness. Fellowship is severed because we don't walk in the light as He is in the light, but instead allow the demons of darkness to distort our paths.

I John 1:7b says that if we choose to walk in the light, Jesus' blood will cleanse us from all sin. This means that if there is a breech in our human relationships, then by repenting and claiming the power of Christ's blood, we receive forgiveness. Our fellowship should be renewed and restored.

Accusing spirits will keep us from walking in the light with our brother even after repentance and forgiveness. We continue to be reminded of his sin against us and against others. Accusing spirits will seek to keep us from forgiving. Accusing spirits encourage us to keep a record of wrongs. They seek to nullify the work of the cross to keep us from fellowship with each other, and bind us with self-condemnation. "I can forgive Pastor Dean, but I can never forget what he did. I can't wait until he leaves our church." This is a very destructive thought that brings joy to Satan and sorrow to our Savior.

God's will is that believers should be united, not separated. We should walk together as one body. When the flesh dominates one of us as a result of yielding to accusing spirits, a breech develops in Christian fellowship. God heals the breach when we repent and forgive each other.

Accusing spirits seek to prevent God's healing from occurring. Satan wants to hold us responsible for our sin forever, thus creating permanent breaches in our fellowship with other believers.

This teaching describes a very real problem in the Church. Many of our local churches are, at best, quite spiritually dysfunctional. Applying God's precepts within the walls of our churches is the starting point. If we do so and heal the breaches in our fellowship, we would attract more of those on the outside. Our churches should be safe havens where life's toughest issues can be dealt with in private, applying God's truth and love, where forgiveness happens naturally.

Of course, the world outside the Church is also Satan's target. Apart from God, nobody has immunity from the devil or his accusing spirits. Despite the prevalence of great world religions — Buddhism, Islam, New Age, Judaism, Christianity — there are still forty to sixty wars going on at any one time somewhere in the world. So much for "light and love." This reality reveals a problem.

The problem is that Satan is on the loose and he accuses the brethren, stifling their faith and spiritual effectiveness. He wants to destroy us. To do so, he seeks to separate us from each other and from God. He will use every means at his disposal. Accusing spirits are the powerful instruments of destruction Satan uses with great skill and intensity.

JUDGING OTHERS

Romans 2:1 says, "Therefore thou art inexcusable, O man, whosoever thou art that judgest: for wherein thou judgest another, thou condemnest thyself; for thou that judgest doest the same things." Accusing spirits love to get us judging each other. How often have you heard someone judge somebody else for the negative behavior they do themselves? It's seems easy to judge another's behavior, but not so easy to judge ourselves.

Romans 2:2-3 says, "We are sure that the judgment of God is according to truth against them which commit such things. And thinketh thou this, O man, that judgest them which do such things, and doest the same, that you shall escape the judgment of

God?" That's pretty tough talk! God doesn't pull any punches. We need to exercise extreme caution as it concerns accusations toward others. Our purpose must be to restore fellowship not to tear each other down through accusations. We are to carry one another's burdens, not place burdens on one another.

Ecclesiastes 7:2-6 says, "It is better to go to the house of mourning than to the house of feasting: for that is the end of all men; and the living will lay it to his heart. Sorrow is better than laughter: for by the sadness of the countenance, the heart is made better. The heart of the wise is in the house of mourning, but the heart of fools is in the house of mirth. It is better to hear the rebuke of the wise, than for a man to hear the song of fools. For as the crackling of thorns under a pot so is the laughter of the fool: this also is vanity."

God wants us to take our behavior seriously. Instead, He sees too much foolishness and a striving toward entertainment that distracts us from applying His precepts to our lives. All work and no play may make Johnny a dull boy, but all play may cause him to live a lonely, unfulfilled life that ends in eternal damnation. That is the message of Ecclesiastes.

Satan constantly points out our weaknesses and flaws to others. Let me emphasize this: we must always guard our hearts against seeing wrong in others. This is a constant necessity. It must be our nature to look beyond other people's flaws and failures. We need to practice mature discernment. We need to learn to separate people from their sin. We must love others and ourselves and hate sin. And we must take responsibility for our own actions.

Satan constantly reminds us why we should not have fellowship with others. Have you ever entertained these kinds of thoughts? "Well I'd like to be a friend with Sally, but I just can't. She gets under my skin."

These types of thoughts often find their root in mistrust. Mistrust comes from accusing spirits who give us no legitimate reason, just a vague sense of uneasiness. Accusing spirits speak lies to us, giving us reasons why we should not have fellowship with one another or why we cannot believe one another.

Their goal is to separate us from each other, from our spiritual leaders, and from the church. There are many people who refuse to go to church simply because they listen to accusing spirits who give them plenty of reasons to stay away. "Elder Smith is a hypocrite. Pastor Jones is so arrogant and drives a fancy car. They won't let me teach Sunday School. The music is too boring. My needs are not being met. Why go?"

ACCUSING GOD

Accusing spirits will tell us how wonderful God is, and praise His provision for others and then add a twist saying, "But not for you. He provides for others but not for you." They'll ask, "Why did God 'allow' your daughter to get sick? If God is so powerful, why didn't He stop..." insinuating that we cannot trust Him and causing us to have an unholy fear.

In our ministry it is common to hear, "I do believe. I have faith in healing. I have faith in salvation. I have faith in God's deliverance for everybody but me." "If God really cared about me, He would never have allowed all those bad things to happen." These are examples of an accusing spirit in action.

If we can't discern truth from lies, then we are in serious trouble. The accusing spirit will always work against us in just such a sly way. He desires to pit us against ourselves, others and God. Since we know these attacks will come, we must be prepared to repel them through the power and authority we have in Christ Jesus.

Fear and mistrust result from the work of evil accusing spirits. They have no place in the Kingdom of God.

Satan accused God early in the book of Genesis. He told Eve that God didn't really mean what He said. Genesis 2:16-17 records this. "And the LORD God commanded the man, saying, Of every tree of the garden thou mayest freely eat: But of the tree of the knowledge of good and evil, thou shalt not eat of it: for in the day that thou eatest thereof thou shalt surely die." Satan accused God of being a liar when he told her, "You won't die, Eve." Who did Eve believe? Satan, the father of all accusing spirits.

Satan constantly tells us that God doesn't care about our suffering. This is one of the most common issues we deal with in our ministry. We hear, "If God cared for me, then He would take away my suffering. If He cared for me, my child wouldn't be suffering." Are these true statements?

Satan always blames God for his own actions. Satan creates a dilemma that leads to suffering and then blames God for not stopping it, or worse yet, accuses God of creating it.

Here is a list of some of Satan's other common lies that we hear quite often:
- "God won't help me out of my problem. All is lost, I can't win anyway."
- "Why even believe God for it? God's not interested in me. He's got more things to do in this world besides notice me."
- "Hey, I've got a 'small' problem compared to others — its no big deal. What's the use in asking Him?"
- "He doesn't love me anyway; after all, He didn't help me yesterday."
- "I talked to Sue last week, and she complained for an hour about what God didn't do for her. Besides, He's no respecter of persons, so if He hates her, He must hate me too."

Do you recognize any of these lies?

ACCUSING OURSELVES

Satan uses self-condemnation to accuse us to ourselves. Let's face it, it is relatively easy for us to make peace with God when we have been wrongly accusing Him. And it is relatively easy to forgive others and accept others if we have been wrongly accusing them. But it is very difficult to cast down those accusing spirits that suggest that we are no good or that we don't deserve forgiveness.

The primary goal of accusing spirits is to steal our faith and confidence in God, and to make us feel like second-rate citizens in God's Kingdom. If Satan makes us feel like we are a "nothing," we will be a nothing.

We really need to understand who we are and who we are not in Christ. This is a profound truth: We are everything that God said we could be, provided we are living it.

Some people "live it" correctly and yet still feel unworthy, guilty, unclean, and unacceptable to God or man. If you feel that way, you have accusing evil spirits operating against you. It is not you.

We need to learn to separate ourselves from the demons that accuse us. If we fall to their accusations and begin to believe them, then we will act out their lies. We will say, "Well, since I feel that way, what's the use?" We begin acting sinful even though at the start, we weren't sinning.

Does any of this sound familiar? We begin to believe a lie, and then we find ourselves acting it out. We find ourselves powerless to stop the sinful behavior that results from the lie. These lies often are told to us as children and we continue to act on them even as adults. Because we feel unclean doesn't mean we are unclean. Because we feel unworthy doesn't mean that we are unworthy. Because we feel guilty doesn't mean that we are guilty. Because we feel condemned doesn't mean we are condemned.

Don't trust your feelings; trust what God has said about your relationship with Him.

Satan accuses us to God and to ourselves all the time. Satan and his accusing spirits focus on our weaknesses, sins, faults and failures. They focus on sins for which we have already received forgiveness, but they accuse us as if those forgiven sins were still part of our lives. One of the most successful tools of accusing spirits is to accuse us of confessed sins from which we have already turned away. They harass us as if we were still sinning, trying to discourage us so that we will sin again. They want us to think, "That's the way I am. I must be that way because I feel that way."

Romans 8:1 says, "There is therefore now no condemnation to them that are in Christ Jesus who walked not after the flesh but after the Spirit." If you have confessed your sin and have turned away from it, and you are now walking after the Spirit, there is no more condemnation or guilt. If you still feel condemnation and guilt after you have repented of a certain sin, and you have quit practicing that sin, then the condemnation and guilt bears evidence of the work of accusing spirits who want to drag you back down. Nail them! Stick Romans 8:1 under their noses!

Feeling like we don't fit in is another of the lies of an accusing spirit. We self-talk saying, "Well, I don't want to go to this church any more, I just don't fit in. Everybody seems to be having a good time praising God and so on, but I just don't seem to fit in.

Nobody really likes me here; they just ignore me." Or, "They don't like me for myself, just for my (talent, money, service, etc.)." These are examples of the attacks of accusing spirits who try to separate us from fellowship with other believers.

When self-accusation is present, understand that this is an evil spirit attacking you. It is not you! If you are accusing yourself in any way, or putting yourself down, go before the Lord and deal with it. If you still sense self-accusation, know that it is not you, but an evil spirit accusing you. Total victory happens when we understand this totally and kick the accusing spirit(s) out of our lives.

A Partial List of Accusing Spirits
  1. Refusing fellowship with a person who has changed
  2. Holding people to their past behaviors
  3. Keeping a record of wrongs
  4. Bigotry
  5. Competition, not feeling whole unless we win
  6. Mistrust
  7. Establishing non-Biblical standards for others to attain
  8. Heaviness
  9. Gossip and innuendo
 10. Being easily offended. Easily offending others
 11. Self-exaltation
 12. Envy
 13. Jealousy
 14. Resentment
 15. Misunderstandings can be the work of an evil spirit
 16. Suicide
 17. Judging another for the same behavior of which we are guilty, while excusing ourselves
 18. Not walking in or accepting forgiveness
 19. A scapegoat mentality
 20. Blaming others for problems
 21. Self-condemnation
 22. Self-accusation
 23. Trying to become The Holy Spirit in another's life
 24. Judging others
 25. Becoming one with accusation
 26. Focusing on another's weakness
 27. Anger
 28. Bitterness

29. Depression
30. Fear
31. Hate
32. Low self-esteem
33. Perfectionism
34. Rejection
35. Vanity
36. Worry
37. Suspicion.

How do we receive victory? God has the answer, but there are standards we must attain. Remember that in Christ, we have everything we need to gain victory. But we must allow His power and authority to work through us.

One powerful tool to use when we are under attack is to quote the Bible.

We need to master James 4:7-10 because it holds the key to success and receiving God's blessing in all areas of our lives. It produces answers to prayer. The conditions for receiving answers to our prayer are stated very plainly in James 4:7-10: "Submit your-selves, therefore, to God." The first condition is submitting to God. That's my motiva-tion for teaching this material.

We cannot submit to God if we don't know Him. All the ministry and deliverance this world, or even the church, offers does little good if we don't know and accept the truth. It all starts with knowing God personally because He is the one that brings healing. Submission requires obedience to God. We submit when we forgive others and ourselves.

Scripture says to resist the devil. Do you believe the devil is real? If you don't, you have bought into the ultimate deception. The Bible says the devil is real, and that settles it for me. Don't doubt the reality of Satan and his demons. The Bible teaches it, and teaches it, and teaches it. Satan is real and so are evil spirits.

The Bible says, "Resist the devil and he will flee from you." It means we must test every thought to know if it is of God, Satan or us. The devil manifests his nature through people. He uses people's bodies to manifest his sin nature (Luke 11:24-26). But he can only do this if we allow him to.

It's our right and responsibility to obey God and resist! Resist! Resist! Do you know what "resist" means? It means "to put up a fight." Just say no! "When you resist, he shall flee from you." If we don't resist, he won't leave us alone. When we resist, God steps in and the devil flees.

James 4:8 says, "Draw nigh to God and He will draw nigh to you." This verse requires us to do something: draw close to God. He will respond. God has told us to seek His face (I Chronicles 16:11, Psalms 27:8, Psalms 105:4).

Many people have the attitude, "I have given this up to God, it is now up to Him." Then they continue to live in their sin, waiting on God to do something. They wallow in the accusation of self-pity and pride and wonder why they never receive deliverance.

God promises to meet with us; He is moved by our faith. Hebrews 11:6 says, "Without faith it is impossible to please Him." John 20:29 adds, "...blessed are they that have not seen, and yet have believed."

James 4:8 tells us to "Cleanse your hands, you sinners, purify your hearts, you double-minded." A double-minded person doubts God and mistrusts himself.

James 4:9-10 says, "Be afflicted, mourn and weep: let your laughter be turned to mourning and your joy to heaviness. Humble yourselves in the sight of the Lord and He shall lift you up." If we want to receive God's promise of deliverance, now is the time to give up ourselves and lay down our lives.

Matthew 16:25 says, "For whosoever will save his life shall lose it: and whosoever will lose his life for My sake shall find it." Lay it down. No matter your status or self-image, lay down your life on His altar.

This is a time to fast and pray, to seek the meat in the Scriptures. When we fast and pray we go before the Lord in tears. When we have humbled ourselves, God will lift us up. That's what happened with King David.

David fell prostrate before God wearing sackcloth and ashes, weeping and crying. He confessed his sins to be released from them and have his joy restored. We, too, need to humble ourselves before God, and seek His mercy and His grace to be released from sin's power over us.

James 4:6-9 speaks of defeating the devil, and receiving God's grace. It says to cleanse our hands and purify our hearts. This process requires us to come to a place of tears and mourning for sin, and repentance. Remorse and repentance are necessary, because all of us have fallen short of the glory of God (Romans 3:23).

While coming before God, we need to resist the devil. Yet in humility, we are to seek His face. "Draw nigh to God and He will draw nigh unto you." Resist the devil; draw nigh to God. It's a formula that works because it is an eternal Scriptural principle.

There is a price for us to pay called "circumcision of the heart." Few people fast and pray these days, much less mourn and cry before God. Not many people take time out from their busy lives to seek God's face. It's time to change.

This is the key to receiving God blessings and healing: We must die to ourselves. We must die to everything we are. We've got to lay ourselves down at the foot of the cross, prayerfully confess our sin, and let it go.

Let me suggest that you pray the following prayers of deliverance from the accusing spirits.

Prayer of Release

Dear Heavenly Father, in the name of Jesus I repent for all of the ways that I have accused others in my life and in my generations. I forgive myself and release myself from this bitterness. In the name of Jesus I cancel all of Satan's authority over me in this bitterness because God has forgiven me and I have forgiven myself. In the name of Jesus I command the accusing spirit that accuses others to me to go. Holy Spirit please come and heal my heart and tell me your truth.

(Listen to the Holy Spirit and write down what happens.)

Dear Heavenly Father, in the name of Jesus I repent for all of the ways that I have accused myself in my life and in my generations. I forgive myself and release myself from this self-bitterness. In the name of Jesus I cancel all of Satan's authority over me in this self-bitterness because God has forgiven me and I have forgiven myself. In the name of Jesus I command the accusing spirit that accuses me to go. Holy Spirit please come and heal my heart and tell me your truth.

(Listen to the Holy Spirit and write down what happens.)

Dear Heavenly Father, in the name of Jesus I repent for all of the ways that I have accused you for what Satan has done in my life and in my generations. I forgive myself and release myself from this bitterness toward you. In the name of Jesus I cancel all of Satan's authority over me in this bitterness because God has forgiven me and I have forgiven myself. In the name of Jesus I command the accusing spirit that accuses God to me to go. Holy Spirit please come and heal my heart and tell me your truth.

(Listen to the Holy Spirit and write down what happens.)

CHAPTER FOUR

The Major Strongholds,
or Principalities, of Satan

In prior chapters we learned much about Satan: how he and his demons entered this world, how he conducts spiritual warfare against God and us, how he attacks us through our thought life.

Now we move to the aspects of Satan's major weapons that he carries with him. He uses these every day through his minions: bitterness, self-bitterness, jealousy and envy, rejection, fear, unbelief and the occult. We believe that each of these forms a "principality of Satan," as they are referred to in Ephesians 6:12. I believe that all of Satan's powers (demons) answer to at least one of these six principalities.

It's rare to find any teachings about these aspects of Satan. I have heard that we should not have a root of bitterness, but I wondered, what is bitterness? What is self-bitterness? What is jealousy and envy? What is rejection? What is fear? What is the occult? What is unbelief? Moreover, how do these principalities or sins affect our lives and how do we deal with them?

We have been taught to forgive, but what is forgiveness?

God says that His people perish for lack of knowledge (Hosea 4:6). That is what was happening to me. If you had told me just a short time ago that I had a root of bitterness, I would have strongly denied it. I knew that I had resentments about some of the tougher things that I had experienced, but I never felt that I was bitter. When I explained this to people who understood what bitterness really entails, they'd laugh. They knew resentment is a part of bitterness. I was bitter but didn't know it. I didn't have a clue.

As we explore Satan's principalities, we will discover many ways that we have been allowing Satan access to our lives. We need to come honestly before God, and earnestly ask Him to search out any wicked way within us, just as David did (Psalms 139:24).

Since our hearts are deceitful and wicked (Jeremiah 17:9), we cannot trust our feelings. As we study Satan's strongholds, the Holy Spirit will begin to reveal many ways that we have become separated from God, others, and our own best nature. As we go along, write down every area of unforgiveness in your life that comes to mind. To be able to cleanse our hearts before God, we must deal with all these areas of unforgiveness. Together, we will learn how to deal with and have victory over Satan.

I pray for each of us that we will come to understand the primary need for daily sanctification. I appeal to you to put God first in every area of your life. If you will do this, God will meet all your needs in Christ Jesus.

CHAPTER FIVE

Principality of Bitterness

DEFINITION
This chapter explores one of Satan's principalities in his evil bureaucracy: bitterness. We will look into the invisible world of the second heaven, from where Satan seeks to rule and control us.

We will explore a group of demons (devils, evil spirits) that answer to a principality, or higher authority. There are differing levels of authority and power in Satan's realm. Each specific evil spirit answers to another spirit higher up the line of authority. Just below Satan in this pecking order are his principalities. It is through this hierarchy of evil spirits and principalities that Satan continually seeks to draw us into captivity, taking control of our lives.

The evil spirit who presides at each step up in the hierarchy of a principality is more evil than the ones below him. Luke 11:24-26 says, "When the unclean spirit is gone out of a man, he walketh through dry places, seeking rest; and finding none, he saith, I will return unto my house whence I came out. And when he cometh, he findeth it swept and garnished. Then goeth he, and taketh to him seven other spirits more wicked than himself; and they enter in, and dwell there: and the last state of that man is worse than the first." (Also see Matthew 12:44-45.)

The original house refers to mankind — us. Even if we are "empty and swept clean," the evil spirits try to come back, and bring along seven more who are even more powerfully evil than the one who left. To prevent these spirits from moving in, we must be continually filled up with God's Word, and the knowledge of God, "precept upon precept, line upon line" (Isaiah 28:10). Being filled with God's Spirit is the antidote to Satan's ploys. This is why it is so essential to teach, and teach, and teach, and study, and study, and study and apply, and apply, and apply God's Word.

When, not if, the enemy comes back to attack us in areas where God has already delivered us, we need to be prepared for him. When that evil spirit comes knocking on the door of our minds with a seductive temptation — a feeling, a thought, a mental picture — seeking to lead us back into captivity we need to say, "Get behind me, Satan. I know you." Tell him, "I've been there, and I'm through with that thought and action. I order you leave me alone because I belong to Jesus Christ and speak in His authority."

We must be prepared to fend off evil spirits and order them out of our lives. I know what I've been delivered from . . . but . . . do you? I purposed to rid myself of every thought and action that's not of God. I want my "stinkin' thinkin'," my old nature, to be changed. I want to replace all of Satan's lies with God's truth. How about you?

We have been created to glorify God and enjoy Him forever. The question is, are we enjoying daily fellowship with God? Do our lives honor God, freed from the power of Satan's principalities?

Luke 11:21-22 says, "When a strong man armed keepeth his palace, his goods are in peace: But when a stronger than he shall come upon him, and overcome him, he taketh from him all his armor wherein he trusted, and divideth his spoils."

The strong man referred to here is one of Satan's principalities. He is armed. What does this mean? The Greek word means to fully equip with armor. The strong man is fully equipped, and this brings him peace.

The one stronger is Jesus. Since we have been granted Christ's power and authority, we also are the one stronger. Many times Scripture grants believers the right to use the name of Jesus. Mark 16:17-18 says, "And these signs shall follow them that believe; In My name shall they cast out devils; they shall speak with new tongues; They shall take up serpents; and if they drink any deadly thing, it shall not hurt them; they shall lay hands on the sick, and they shall recover."

As the one stronger, through Jesus, we will strip the strong man (the principality) of all his armor. He will be left standing naked and weak, unable to war against us. Of what does the armor of the strong man consist?

A principality is a ruling demon that has several lesser demons answering to it. Bitterness is a ruling demon. Answering to it, giving it protection and providing its armor are: 1) Unforgiveness, 2) Resentment, 3) Retaliation, 4) Anger, 5) Hatred, 6) Violence, 7) Murder.

In the hierarchy of the principality of bitterness, resentment is worse than unforgiveness; unforgiveness answers to resentment. Retaliation is worse than resentment; resentment answers to retaliation, and so on. Each lower demon protects and provides armor for the next higher demon.

Hebrews 12:14-15 says, "Follow peace with all men, and holiness, without which no man shall see the Lord: Looking diligently lest any man fail of the grace of God; lest any root of bitterness springing up trouble you, and thereby many be defiled."

To "follow peace with all men" means to actively seek for peaceful and healthy relationships with others. If we cause trouble, slander, stir up gossip, or are resentful, we are not following peace; we have serious issues with which to deal. This Scripture is very clear. If we don't seek peace and holiness we won't see the Lord, because we will have failed to receive God's grace. (The original Greek translation indicates that we'll "be late for" His grace.)

We are commanded to be holy, as He is holy (Leviticus 11:44). Holiness requires removing sin from our lives. Vessels of honor fit for His service remove all iniquity

PRINCIPALITY OF BITTERNESS / 63

from their lives. Vessels of dishonor do not (II Timothy 2:20-21). God has given us the tools to become overcomers in this life if we will do His word. Great rewards are promised, in this life and the next one, to those that overcome (Revelation 2-3). I hope we are each at a point where we actively seek after God and His righteousness as our first priority. Our salvation is at stake.

What does Hebrews 12:15 say? That we should look casually when we feel like it or when somebody's nice to us? No! It says, "looking diligently." This means active searching, the kind that requires constant effort. Scripture goes on to say, "lest any man fail of the grace of God."

What does "fail of the grace of God" mean? Galatians 6:1 defines it. It says, "if man be overtaken in a fault...." What's a fault? A spiritual defect. If another believer is overtaken by a spiritual defect, those who consider themselves spiritually mature are to restore that person in a spirit of meekness. They are to guard against falling into the same spiritual defect, the end result of which will be falling away from faith. This is "the knowledge of God" in this matter.

In Romans 2:1, Paul says that the very thing of which you accuse another, you are also often guilty. You accuse another of having a spiritual problem but excuse the same problem in yourself. Romans 2:1 says, "Therefore thou art inexcusable, O man, whosoever thou art that judgest: for wherein thou judgest another, thou condemnest thyself; for thou that judgest doest the same things."

We need to be very careful to build and restore relationships, not to tear them down. We are to restore one another in gentleness and love. Galatians 6:2 says to go one more step by bearing a brother's burden. How many of us ever even come close to doing this? We carry one another's burdens by leading them to Jesus so He can take the burden.

If we ignore this sound advice, we will be contaminated by a demon, and a root of bitterness will spring up to trouble us (Hebrews 12:15). When this root takes hold it not only defiles us, but branches out to affect every one around us. It is highly contagious.

Have you spent time with a bitter person? Have you ever been bitter? Are you able to discern bitterness in yourself, or in others?

Usually, when we encounter a bitter person, we cop our own attitude. Bitterness begins to flow from our spirit toward them. We play a game of bitterness ping-pong with them. It becomes my bitterness against their bitterness. We both become defiled. Does this sound familiar? It should. It's a common daily experience.

Bitterness gains its entrance to us through unforgiveness, the first piece of the armor surrounding bitterness. That evil strong man banks on unforgiveness to be an active part of our life. He counts on us never forgiving others or ourselves so that he can have his place, his habitation, within us. Once taking up a home in us, he can act out his evil nature through us and give his boss, the devil, a victory.

Unforgiveness whispers in our ear, "No, you're not going to forgive them, you don't need to forgive them, there's no way you need to forgive them." Unforgiveness keeps a record of wrongs against another person. Satan banks on the spirit of unforgiveness to remind us of the bitterness that somebody else has toward us. Unforgiveness reminds, rehashes, projects and torments us with past negative events. It reminds us of what others have done to us, and what we have done to others.

The strong man, the principality, uses the spirit of unforgiveness to constantly accuse us. But, unforgiveness is a smaller entity, a lower spirit. It's just the beginning.

After unforgiveness has done its work, the strong man sends out the spirit of resentment. Resentment builds on the foundation laid by unforgiveness. The record of wrongs ferments, and resentment begins to grow.

Resentment generates a feeling of ill will toward a person who has wronged us. Resentment says, "I don't like Mary," or "I will never forgive Alex," or "I don't trust my neighbors." Resentment constantly reminds us of past events, seeking to stir up negative sentiments that stew and ferment within us.

Unforgiveness formed the first piece of armor to provide protection for bitterness. Now Satan is trusting that resentment will gain a foothold. Resentment feeds off of unforgiveness. Resentment is a stronger evil spirit, because unforgiveness supports it. And it is more dangerous than unforgiveness.

Satan employs millions of evil spirits in his attempt to control or tempt us. This is why resentment can exist in many people at the same time. It can multiply its growth and so defile us that it can completely take over an individual, a family or a church.

Because of the work of resentment, families and churches become dysfunctional. They maintain their own records of wrongs that generate stronger resentment. One person shares their resentment, and soon, everybody is doing the same. Then, the church splits or the family ends up in divorce, and the devil has won a battle in his war against good.

Unforgiveness is like instant replay, replaying the words, voices, sights and sounds of wrong events from our past. Unforgiveness flashes negative thoughts and images of everything someone ever said or did to us. Have you ever had that happen? The accusing spirit continuously replays a record of the evil music of our lives to reinforce itself, so this strong man of bitterness can find a home in us. Resentment adds fuel to the fire.

Resentment and unforgiveness stem from thoughts. They find their homes in our memories.

After unforgiveness and resentment have gained a foothold in our minds, the strong man sends out the spirit of retaliation. Now it's time to get even.

I remember a bumper sticker I saw a few years ago that said, "I don't forgive, I just get even." Retaliation projects these kinds of sentiments: "Bill should pay for what he did to me," or "I am going to make Jane pay for what she said." "I am going to make sure Bob gets what he deserves, if it is the last thing that I do!"

The spirit of retaliation is much more dangerous than the spirits of unforgiveness and resentment. Retaliation's presence shows progressive demonization. Each spirit is much more dangerous than the previous one.

In ministry, when we see someone who wants to get even, and they say, "Well, they're gonna pay," we know immediately that a spirit of retaliation is speaking. We also know that the spirits of unforgiveness and resentment are present, and we know that the strong man of bitterness is behind it all. We know that this person is harboring a record of wrongs against others or themselves.

When you see evidence of any of these spirits, you know that all the others down the line are present as well. So, if we're going after the spirit of retaliation in ministry, we're going to go after the spirits of unforgiveness and resentment as well.

As we see evidence of higher orders of spirits, we know that the underling spirits are there as well, reinforcing the one just above it. What reinforces retaliation? Resentment fuels retaliation. What fuels resentment? Unforgiveness. And at the top of this principality is bitterness.

There exists an entire kingdom of evil spirits, and we name each spirit by the word that describes its nature.

Bitterness is the strong man; he wants to occupy the house. He trusts in his armor. To help people achieve healing, we have to strip this armor off of them. Bitterness will remain until its entire armor is stripped away. We have learned that the pain in a memory is evidence that there is bitterness. We have learned that we need to take every emotional hurt to the Lord in forgiveness or repentance and then he heals the broken heart and the pain (anger, resentment, hatred, guilt, shame, etc.) is gone. We see this happen over and over again in ministry. Every bit of the pain must go or there is still bitterness.

As unforgiveness gains a foothold, then resentment gains a foothold. Next, retaliation gains a foothold. Each of these manifests itself in ways that are progressively worse than the prior spirit.

When retaliation wins its foothold, bitterness sends out anger and wrath.

Anger and wrath are outward expressions that remind others that we are not going to forgive them, that we resent them, and that we plan to get even. With anger, we have crossed a line. Anger gives the evil spirit a voice. Unforgiveness, resentment, and retaliation can be kept unspoken, eating away at a person's own spirit through self-deception.

Once the line is crossed to anger and wrath, the demons start to show themselves physically. Have you ever seen anger in a person's eyes? It is very real and very observable. This is anger caused by the root of bitterness, because of unforgiveness, resentment and retaliation. Maybe you have experienced this yourself. We all have.

We need to understand, when our anger buttons are being pushed, it is the strong man of bitterness fighting to gain a foothold. Bitterness puts on the armor of anger and wrath to protect himself. You have sensed it yourself, when resentments fester over time, anger isn't far behind. Anger and wrath never occur without the first three spirits being in place.

We get angry when a trust has been breached, resulting in hurt. We feel victimized. Then unforgiveness, resentment and retaliation well up and overflow with the fourth spirit, anger and wrath.

After anger and wrath have gained their foothold, hatred moves in. Bitterness gains fuel from unforgiveness, resentment, retaliation, and anger and wrath. Now hatred starts a process of elimination. Hatred says, "I live on this planet and so do you. And one of us has to go and it ain't going to be me." Maybe hatred says, "This church ain't big enough for both of us. I think you'd better leave." Hatred seeks to eliminate the other person.

Retaliation ferments anger on behalf of bitterness. Anger vocalizes bitterness, and next comes hatred to act out of bitterness.

Hatred reveals your feelings toward an offender, tells them that they don't belong in your world, and you absolutely hate their guts. Hatred says, "I will do what it takes to get even."

Hatred provides the fuel for our final victimization by Satan. When we observe hatred in someone, we know that anger, retaliation, resentment and unforgiveness are there as well. And we know that bitterness is in the driver's seat, trusting in the armor provided by these lesser evil spirits.

What makes up the armor of bitterness? It is the seven levels of spirits who fall under his principality. Bitterness banks on the fact that when we are finally ready to forgive, unforgiveness will show us flash cards of voices, sights, sounds, and smells reminding us of how someone harmed us. Resentment joins in saying, "Now, let me help you really feel it right here, deep inside you."

You may try to argue against resentment saying, "But, I'm trying to forgive Ruthie," but resentment answers, "No, you really resent her." Retaliation joins in, saying, "Yeah, besides you never did get even with Ruthie, did you? She needs to pay for what she did to you."

Anger rears up, saying, "Yeah, and I'm going to go tell Ruthie just what I think, and if I don't tell her, then I'll tell somebody else."

You're getting emotional now, and hatred says, "Yeah, I'm not only going to get even, I'm not only going to retaliate, but I know how to hit her where it hurts. I hate Ruthie."

We see this scenario repeated daily in the lives of families, businesses and churches. This is evidence of how progressively more evil influences break up human relationships; the strong man, bitterness, causes it all.

The sixth level of bitterness is violence. Violence is anger and hatred set into motion. Our emotions erupt into physical or sometimes hate-filled verbal attacks. At this point, we see pots and pans thrown across the room, wrenches fly and punches being thrown. Fights erupt. Physical, sexual and verbal abuse result.

The seventh and worst spirit in the principality of bitterness is murder. Just as Cain slew Abel because of his bitterness, so we see others murder their children, spouses or friends in fits of rage.

The spirit of murder includes more than taking someone's physical life. God's Word teaches how we can murder someone with our words. Murder starts in the heart, because the ultimate level of the spirit of bitterness is the elimination of someone's person-hood. I John 3:15 says, "Whosoever hateth his brother is a murderer: and ye know that no murderer hath eternal life abiding in him."

Murderous hate-filled speech, driven by bitterness, kills a person's own spirit. Whether it is the person who is doing the screaming and his speech crucifies his own sense of decency, or a person who receives a verbal attack, whose spirit shrinks in fear, the end result is the death of a Godly, peaceful spirit.

Satan was the first murderer, and introduced murder to the world through Cain (John 8:44, I John 3:12). Cain's murder of Abel illustrates the progression of the root of bitterness, starting with an unwillingness to forgive, to resentment, to retaliation, to anger, to hatred, to violence, and then to murder during a short period of time (Genesis 4:1-9).

As we have been reviewing these levels of bitterness, have you sensed any bitter-ness in your spirit? Have you reflected on others who have failed to forgive you, or identified unforgiveness that you have toward someone else? Have you experienced resentment, a desire to retaliate, and anger directed at others, or even at yourself?

Have you hated others, or been hated? Have you had violence committed against you, or committed violence? Have you angrily cursed others, or yourself, or had others curse you?

Does your heart ache because these things have happened to you? Can you sense these spirits interacting with your spirit right now? Are you recalling someone or some-thing that has happened to you? If there is pain in this and other memories, there is bit-terness. The solution is to forgive and repent. Then the Lord will heal your broken heart.

What do you want to do about all this? You can choose to continue on as you are, or you can face these things and cast them out of your life. You choose.

Before anything else can be resolved, bitterness must be expelled from your spirit. If you harbor any bitterness against others or yourself, God will not forgive you of your sin. In Mark 11:25-26 Jesus says, "And when ye stand praying, forgive, if ye have ought against any: that your Father also which is in heaven may forgive you your trespasses. But if ye do not forgive, neither will your Father which is in heaven forgive your trespasses."

In Matthew 18:34-35 Jesus says, "And his lord was wroth, and delivered him to the tormentors, till he should pay all that was due unto him. So likewise shall My heavenly Father do also unto you, if ye from your hearts forgive not every one his brother their trespasses."

I see the tormentors of Matthew 18 as stress, anxiety, fear, depression, bitterness, etc., and the physical diseases that can follow. Bitterness and its supporting spirits form the root of many of our diseases.

Hebrews 12:14 says that we are to follow peace with all men, and pursue holiness. Achieving holiness is tough. We self-talk, "God is perfect. I'm rotten. How can I be holy as He is holy?"

Isaiah 35:8 calls holiness a highway to be traveled. What does this mean? Holiness comes through a progressive process of identifying the lies and sins in our lives and replacing them with God's truth. As we become holy, our nature is transformed from the old man — Satan's nature — into God's nature. This process is called sanctification. The way we think, talk and act is changed to conform more and more with the image of the living God. We regain what we lost in Adam's fall from grace: the nature of God. We are holy, as He is when we are manifesting His nature through us. In the time that love, joy, peace, long-suffering, etc. is manifesting through us, we are holy as He is because His nature is being displayed.

Genesis 1:26 says, "Let Us make man in Our image." The image of man was the image of God's nature, but even more than this. God gave us a soul, spirit and body. We lost the ability to assume God's nature because of sin. That is why our spirit needed to be born again, so we could come alive to God. Our nature had been dead to God.

Once we are born again, our spirit desires to conform to God's image because that is who we are spiritually in our creation; it is what constitutes the real person. This is the person with whom God wants to spend eternity in heaven.

It's amazing that we accept and expect God to be perfect, and yet we don't think He asks the same of us. The true believer is on a journey toward Godly perfection that is called sanctification. And it is available to every believer who appropriates the power and authority of Christ.

As we become sanctified, we know that Satan stands ready to condemn us using our weaknesses against us. He finds any opening he can to thwart our progress or cause us to backslide. Despite this reality, we still are responsible to live each day according to God's precepts. He does not leave us alone in this, giving us the power of Christ and the prodding of the Holy Spirit to defeat Satan's wiles.

What is human perfection from God's perspective? The Greek word for "perfect" is *teleios*. As it concerns our knowledge and application of Christian principles, it describes mature, full-grown people, not children. These are believers who, through thorough instruction and deep experiences, walk in the light with Christ. Hebrews 5:14

describes maturity as knowing the difference between good and evil, and choosing to do that which is good: Godly discernment. Being perfect, we live in a state of forgiveness where God declares us righteous because we have close, personal communion with Jesus Christ.

Being holy, as He is, is to abide in Christ. It is to manifest His nature. The high calling of God that Paul strove for all of his life was to manifest the nature of God one hundred percent of the time.

God commands us to forgive. To defeat an unforgiving spirit, and prevent a root of bitterness from springing up, we must learn to forgive moment by moment, offense by offense. We must give up our hold on the offender and hand them over to God (Matthew 18:21-22).

As we forgive, we also defeat resentment. We have released all the ill will formerly directed at others or ourselves.

Jesus said the thought of retaliation comes from an evil spirit. When James and John sought to rain fire from heaven on the Samaritans who rejected them, Jesus rebuked them saying, "Ye know not what manner of spirit you are of" (Luke 9:55).

The Word of God forbids us from seeking retaliation or revenge. We are told not to avenge ourselves, or to bear grudges (Leviticus 19:18). Proverbs 24:29 tells us not to ponder doing to our neighbor what he has done to us. Paul taught us not to repay evil with evil, but instead we are to give the offender over to God (Romans 17-19).

There is such a thing as "righteous anger," but it flows from a sense of an offense committed against God, not our own unforgiving spirit. A righteous anger is never expressed at a person. It is always expressed at evil. Revenge is never the motive behind righteous anger. Whatever the source of our anger, we are taught not to sin as its result, or retain anger in our spirit overnight (Ephesians 4:26). We are taught to be slow to wrath because man's wrath never brings forth the righteousness of God (James 1:19-20).

According to Galatians 5:20, hatred is one of the works of the flesh, our evil nature. The natural condition of all unregenerate people is to be "hateful and hating one another" (Titus 3:3).

Satan is the author of violence (Ezekiel 28:16). Satan used the spirits associated with bitterness to introduce violence and murder by influencing Cain to kill Abel. Cain's life illustrated the progression of bitterness as it grew from an unwillingness to forgive, to resentment, to retaliation, to anger, to hatred, to violence, and finally, to murder during a short period of time (Genesis 4:1-9).

Employing the spirits of bitterness, Satan brought so much violence to mankind that God destroyed all the people, save Noah and his family (Genesis 6:11-13).

These evil spirits seek to separate us from God and from His peace. They also destroy our peace, and separate us from living in peace with other people.

THE ANTIDOTE FOR BITTERNESS

First, we must recognize that we are bitter. This is harder than it sounds. A short time ago, I didn't see my own bitterness. If some one had told me I was bitter, I would have denied it.

"I have regrets in my life, but I'm not bitter." People who knew better would laugh every time I would say that, or they would politely smile knowingly. Ignorant, I didn't know that resentment formed a part of bitterness. Maybe that is what God meant in Hosea 4:6 when He said, "My people are destroyed for a lack of knowledge."

If there exists any evidence of unforgiveness, resentment, retaliation, unrighteous anger, hatred, violence, or murder in our lives, we have bitterness. If there is any pain in any memory, there is bitterness. If we go to bed at night leaving issues unresolved we will wake the next day with the root of bitterness already having budded in our spirit. I learned to accept this as truth and admitted that I did have bitterness. Admitting that we have bitterness is the first step to recovery.

Secondly, we must repent of the sin of bitterness. Repent means that we fall out of agreement and turn away from it. And we ask God to forgive us.

Thirdly, we must forgive others and ourselves. What does it mean to forgive? There are several aspects to consider.

FORGIVING OTHERS

Matthew 18:15-17 says, "Moreover if thy brother shall trespass against thee, go and tell him his fault between thee and him alone: if he shall hear thee, thou hast gained thy brother. But if he will not hear thee, then take with thee one or two more, that in the mouth of two or three witnesses every word may be established. And if he shall neglect to hear them, tell it unto the church: but if he neglect to hear the church, let him be unto thee as an heathen man and a publican."

Church leaders need to fully embrace and practice this Scriptural principle. It would eliminate many divisive problems.

What are we supposed to do when someone has offended us? We are to go to them personally and privately, seeking to regain their fellowship and friendship. Instead, we usually find somebody else to talk to first, involving someone who had nothing to do with the problem in the first place. We do this to win someone to our side, or build confidence that we are justified in being offended. But we seldom provide these confidants with all the facts. We load the gun with accusations and fire rumors at random. These spread and destroy any hope for restoration and reconciliation.

The correct principle is to go to our brother privately, telling him honestly, "We're not right together man, what's going on? I care about you and I want a good relationship!" If he doesn't hear us, we come back with two or three trusted brothers, saying, "Brother, we've got to resolve this." If that doesn't work, our spiritual leaders will go and ask, "Why didn't you receive your brother? What's the problem? Come with me and let's deal with it so we can have fellowship with you." If we fulfill the obligations of this system of forgiveness and reconciliation, not only will we have harmony in our churches, but our churches would attract more people.

But we're afraid of each other. We're afraid of losing somebody as a friend. Yet, if we don't deal with problems by seeking forgiveness and restoration according to this Scriptural formula, we will lose them anyway. Why not lose them over the issue of righteousness?

An open rebuke is better than a secret love (Proverbs 27:5). My part is to be willing to come and deal with you face to face. Are you willing to do that with others?

I don't know about you, but I want to release the power of love and forgiveness on the earth. I'm fed up with the hatred and bitterness that dominates human relationships. Are you?

If we handle forgiveness in the manner God intended, the result will usually be peace, if peace is at all possible. If the other person refuses to forgive or to stop their destructive behavior, we still can be set free from our own resentment and receive God's forgiveness.

The ultimate resolution of all human problems comes from God. If we say, "I'll give up bitterness when I have resolution with George," then George becomes an idol to us. We put him in the position of receiving our attention, and that is the place God desires to occupy. Bitterness places us in bondage to the one we are bitter at. God grants us spiritual freedom and forgiveness whatever of the outcome of our effort to reconcile with another person.

Still, God wants us to have a heart for resolution of differences and reconciliation with our brothers. But if their own root of bitterness keeps them from responding properly, if they're into unforgiveness, resentment, retaliation, anger and strife, that is not your problem. We can trust God to deal with their hearts through His Holy Spirit.

HOW OFTEN DO WE FORGIVE?

Matthew 18:21-22 says, "Then came Peter to Him, and said, Lord, how oft shall my brother sin against me, and I forgive him? till seven times? Jesus saith unto him, I say not unto thee, Until seven times: but, until seventy times seven."

Jesus said forgiveness is a moment by moment occurrence. With every breath, we are to forgive others and, of course, ourselves. Each minute of the day we are to forgive the same person for the same offense. Forgive them and then release them. If we don't, we give the strong man of bitterness a chance to come in and begin to build his stronghold in us. Our bodies are to be the temples of God, not Satan's stronghold.

The first spirit bitterness sends to accuse us of the breach in our relationship is unforgiveness. We must forgive! It is imperative if we ever desire to be healed. It makes no difference whether or not we feel like it. Forgiveness is not abut how we feel, it is about what we choose to do. We must learn to separate the person from their sin, just as God separates us from our sins and forgives us.

God forgave and accepted us before we were made right with Him, when we were still "in our sins." And do you know what? We still don't have it all together, yet He still accepts us and forgives us each minute of the day, doesn't He? Thank You Father, Thank you Jesus.

"If we confess our sins, He is faithful and just to forgive us our sins and to cleanse us from all unrighteousness" (I John 1:9). It doesn't bother me at all to confess my sins to God. Why should it bother me? He knows all my sins anyway. I can't conceal them from Him. I want to be clean (forgiven) before Him. But sometimes we need to confess our sins to others that we may be healed (James 5:16).

Matthew 18:34-35 says that we are to forgive from our heart, or we will be turned over to the tormentors. What does it mean to forgive from the heart? If we have forgiven from our hearts, the emotional pain from past hurts will be gone. I discovered that I had forgiven many times, but the emotional pain was still there. Satan still came and accused me day and night. I hadn't forgiven from my heart, just my mind.

Forgiveness is a matter of the will. We either choose to forgive or not to forgive. It doesn't matter how we feel.

One of Satan's favorite tactics is to accuse us in areas with which we had previously dealt. In our ministry, we ask people to make a list of every person they need to forgive. We want it to be a detailed list of people and the offenses they have committed. We want a comprehensive record of the wrongs these people committed against us.

James 5:16 says that we are to confess our faults to one another to receive healing. In our ministry, we put this verse to work.

At the end of this chapter is a "Bitterness Affidavit." We suggest that you use this form in making your list of those that you need to forgive.

Then we proceed through the list one item at a time, using the prayer printed at the end of the chapter. Some people have a hard time with this, but when we expose the bitterness to the power of Jesus Christ, the hurt, pain, anger, unforgiveness, bitterness, etc. are gone. And in their place is a peace and joy that passes all understanding.

As they finish this process of forgiveness, we ask them to date and sign the list as an affidavit that they actually have forgiven others from their heart. We sign the affidavit as witnesses to their forgiveness and as a means of silencing accusing spirits who fight the repentant person's desire to forgive. We always go through this exercise in the spirit of Galatians 6:1-2.

We have also learned that the emotional pain associated with past hurts is really a form of self-pity. People often ask, "why did this have to happen to me?" If we harbor self-pity very long, it can lead to full-blown depression.

I found in my own life that the emotional pain was the sin of self-pity. I repented and rebuked Satan, and the pain went away. God forgave me and was faithful to grant me His supernatural peace that passes all human understanding (Philippians 4:7).

THE BITTERNESS AFFIDAVIT

Make a list of all the bitterness you have against others. We need to confess and repent before Almighty God for holding onto this bitterness and believing it, instead of believing Him. The stronghold that bitterness has held in your life will be destroyed, and Satan's power over you will be legally cancelled. Be thorough, and pray through each bitterness individually. Do not give the devil any "legal" access to you. Here is an example of a prayer you can use to deal with bitterness, and eliminate it from your life:

Prayer of Release

*In the name of Jesus, I purpose and choose to forgive
(the person) from my heart for (what they did). In the
name of The Lord Jesus, I cancel all their debts and obligations to me.*

*Dear Lord, I ask You to forgive me for my bitterness
toward (the person) in this situation.*

*In the name of Jesus, and by the power of His blood,
I cancel Satan's authority over me in this memory
because I have forgiven.*

*In the name of Jesus, I command that all the tormentors
that have been assigned to me because of my unforgiveness to leave me, now.*

*Holy Spirit, I invite you into my heart, and to heal me
of this pain. Please speak your words of truth to me about
this situation.*

As the Holy Spirit speaks to you, write down His message in the space provided. This is God's testimony to you. When you have finished this prayer for each person or situation on your list, command the principality of self-bitterness to go in the name of Jesus.

As we work through bitterness toward others we often realize that we played a part in those situations. In the next chapter we will discuss self-bitterness. We will learn to identify and remove all the ways that we have belittled and cursed ourselves. In doing this we will become free of all shame, guilt, self-condemnation, regret and sorrow.

BITTERNESS TOWARDS (PERSON):   THE HOLY SPIRIT'S ANSWER (TRUTH):

CHAPTER SIX

The Principality of Self-Bitterness:
Unloving Spirits

Next to God, we should be our own best friend, enjoying and accepting ourselves. We should love ourselves. Perhaps self-love is a novel concept to you.

Pastors, teachers and parents often teach us to consider ourselves "as nothing." Most of our "Christian" schools and colleges teach that we are depraved and that we are to count ourselves as nothing. Sadly, many of us were even told as children that we were stupid or ugly or garbage, or that we would never amount to anything, or "never be as good as Billy Smith." We saw God as unreachable and ourselves as insignificant.

Self-love, though, is an important Biblical principle. Jesus taught that we are to love our neighbors as ourselves (Matthew 22:39). If we condemn, hate, and belittle ourselves, and we are to love our neighbors as ourselves, does this mean that we should treat our neighbors, spouses, and families just as negatively? Of course not.

Matthew 22:36-40 says, "Master, which is the great commandment in the law? Jesus said unto him, Thou shalt love the Lord thy God with all thy heart, and with all thy soul, and with all thy mind. This is the first and great commandment. And the second is like unto it, Thou shalt love thy neighbour as thyself. On these two commandments hang all the law and the prophets."

In this passage Jesus was asked, "Master, which is the great commandment in the Law?" This was the required test to see if the teacher was a true or false prophet. Jesus fully understood the intent and purpose of the question and His answer proved that He is geniune. Jesus said that we are to love God the Father with all our heart, soul and mind. In other words we are to have no other gods before Him. We are also to love our neighbors as our selves. This means that we must love our selves or we cannot love our neighbor.

These two commands are so important that Jesus said all the law and the prophets hang on them. These two commandments are the sum of all divine revelation and responsibility. We have learned that if we do not love ourselves, we cannot love others or God. In ministry we explore our relationships with others, with ourselves, and with God the Father. In these broken relationships we find the cause of our problems in life. If the Bible is not working for you, you will find the answer in the healing of these relationships.

In contrast, being "stuck on ourselves" is prideful. Pride means having an unrealistic high opinion of one's own worth: conceit. Scripture warns us often about pride.

Proverbs 16:18 says that "Pride goeth before destruction, and an haughty spirit before a fall."

Praise God, there is balance between pride and self-hatred. The Bible lays out this balance and God desires us to grasp hold of it and apply it in our daily lives.

Before we get too far into this discussion, I want you to consider this: I can teach what God has said about us, but you can reject it. Rejecting God's teaching about self-love is, in essence, telling Him that He made a mistake when He created us. Calling Almighty God a liar is serious business, yet when we curse ourselves we also curse God. To be successful in finding the peace of God and His healing power, we need to agree with God about this matter of self-love.

Anything that disagrees with God's Word flows from an anti-Christ spirit. So, not accepting and loving ourselves is the result of the influence of an anti-Christ spirit living in us. How do I know this? Lets take a look at what God's Word says about His children. Psalms 139:14 says that we are "fearfully and wonderfully made." Before we were ever knit together in our mother's womb, God knew us. Before our bones, eyes, hair and the rest of our body were formed, God knew us.

In Jeremiah 1:5, God told the prophet that He knew and sanctified him while he still lay in the womb. In Zechariah 2:8, God says we are the "apple of His eye." In Isaiah 49:16 we're told that we are engraved on the palms of His hand. God took a special interest in each one of us even before we were born. We are not the product of some accident of nature. When God sent His only Son to die for us and His Holy Spirit to convict and teach us, this was the ultimate expression of love. He considered us so valuable that Jesus died for us to make our salvation possible. John 15:13 says, "Greater love hath no man than this, that a man lay down his life for his friends." Jesus is our Creator, Savior and Friend.

Genesis 1:27, 31 says that "so God created man in His own image, in the image of God created He him; male and female created He them. And God saw every thing that he had made, and, behold, it was very good. And the evening and the morning were the sixth day."

We are created in the image of God and He says that everything He created is very good. If we curse ourselves we curse our maker. If we say anything that portrays us as less than very good, we are calling God a liar. It is true that we have sinned, but we learned earlier in this study we are not what we do. We are responsible for our sins, but we are who Christ made us to be.

Genesis 1:28 says, "And God blessed them, and God said unto them, Be fruitful, and multiply, and replenish the earth, and subdue it: and have dominion over the fish of the sea, and over the fowl of the air, and over every living thing that moveth upon the earth."

God blessed man and delegated sovereignty to us over every living thing on this earth. He also gave us sovereignty in our ability to choose. He gave us a free will. Does this sound like we are totally depraved and worthless? Does this sound like we don't have the ability to make a decision?

Additionally, Psalms 8:5 says, "For thou [Jesus] hast made him [man] a little lower than the angels, and hast crowned him with glory and honour."

The word translated "angels" is *Elohiym* which is Jesus. Jesus created man a little lower than Himself. Are we nothing? Are we trash? Of course not. We are the children of the Most High God. We are joint heirs with Christ. So let's act like it.

Why, then, did humans begin hating themselves and those around them, all of whom were created in the image of God? Because Satan came into the world and brought along his lies and accusations and man believed him. We must take responsibility for believing these lies and destroy the works of the devil in our lives. This is another reason we need to be fully informed of Satan's wiles.

DEFINITION OF SELF

Let's start by defining the term "self." The dictionary definition is "one's own person, an individual."

In Romans 7, Paul teaches about the two different parts of self. Paul said that there was a part of him that was good, and a part of him that was sin. Romans 7:18 says, "For I know that in me (that is, in my flesh) dwelleth no good thing: for to will is present with me; but how to perform that which is good I find not."

These are strong words: "In my flesh dwelleth no good thing." Paul speaks here of his carnal, sinful Adamic nature.

He adds, "for to will is present with me." The verb used here is "to will." It means to choose. What he describes is making a quality choice, a choice with which Paul admits he struggles. "For to will is present with me, but how to perform that which is good I find not" (Romans 7:18).

Romans 7:19-20 says, "For the good that I would I do not: but the evil which I would not, that I do. Now if I do that I would not, it is no more I that do it, but sin that dwelleth in me." It's vital to understand this. Verse 21 says, "I find then a law, that, when I would do good, evil is present with me." Does Paul's self include both the good and evil parts? Do you think that Paul claims that he is partly good and partly evil? No! Paul plainly states that it is not I that sin, but that the sin dwells within me.

The sin that dwelt within Paul was the flesh or the Adamic nature. It was not Paul nor you or me that is sin. Sin is not part of our original creation or nature, it was added by Satan at the fall. We are not evil. When we sin we must take responsibility for our actions but we are not those actions.

What is a law? Romans 7:7 says, "What shall we say then? Is the law sin? God forbid. Nay, I had not known sin, but by the law: for I had not known lust, except the law had said, Thou shalt not covet." God's law has never been nor will ever be a curse if it is applied as He intended. His laws have been given to show us our sin. Thus we are able recognize our sin, and then we are able to sanctify ourselves by forgiving others and asking God to forgive us. This is the process of purging ourselves of all iniquities (II Timothy 2:20-21).

Verse 16 says, "If then I do that which I would not, I consent unto the law [of Satan] that it is good." In other words, when I choose to do something evil, even though I know it is evil, I am calling evil "good." In verse 21 he says, "I find then a law that when I would do good evil is present with me."

Paul is saying that there are two laws working within him. One is the law of sin, and the other, the law of God.

A Biblical law is a precept or concept by which one ought to live: a standard. Paul says that residing within him are two opposing ways of thinking. One way loves God and desires to serve Him and righteousness. The other way responds to a different law than God's law. It presents a different word, precept, concept, or suggestion that entices me to follow it instead of God's law. By following this law of sin, I am saying to the law of sin, "you are good." I am saying to the law of God, "you are evil."

Both laws establish within us a code of thoughts, words and actions. Attitudes are defined as habits of thought, so both legal codes promote their own set of attitudes. We follow one or the other. This is how spiritual warfare plays out in our lives.

Do we follow God's law or a law that is anti-God, the law of sin?

Paul emphasizes this, writing, "I find then a law that when I would do good, evil is present with me, for I delight in the law of God after...." After what? After the inward man. The inward man is a very real part of him; it was part of his original creation. It is the nature of God that was born again in Paul when He made Jesus his Lord and Master. The inward man, or his new nature, is why the New Covenant is better than the Old Covenant.

There is, however, another part of him described in verse 23. "But I see another law in my members, warring against the law of my mind, and bringing me into captivity to the law of sin which is in my members." He sees another (different) law in his members that wars against the law in his mind, bringing him into captivity to the law of sin. He places the location of the law of sin in his members. This should be the real teaching in Psychology 101, not the pagan notions one usually hears. There is a battle between good and evil inside of each of us, but they are not equal.

Paul's explanation provides the truth-based alternative to psychotherapy. Man struggles against two kingdoms: the kingdom of God, and the kingdom of sin. This is a clear statement about the need for mature spiritual discernment. Understanding and applying this truth brings victory over mental disorders, panic attacks, depression and all manner of struggles that war in our minds and bodies.

When we learn to wage this war in our minds and bodies with God's tools, we have victory. Jesus came to deliver us from the bondage of sin. But obedience is required on our part.

The dictionary further defines "self" as "by its self" or "separate." A self is a separate, unique identity. Each of us is separately and uniquely different, and we stand alone as individuals.

Psalms 139 says that God made each of us "fearfully and wonderfully." Even before conception, God saw how our parts and our pieces fit together; this included our body, soul and spirit. "My substance was not hid from thee, when I was made in secret, and curiously wrought in the lowest parts of the earth" (Psalms 139:15). God knew our ancestry and our offspring before we ever actually came to be. God knows each one of us as unique individuals, separate and different from anyone else.

Believers know that their name is written down in the Lamb's Book of Life. Our separate individual identity is already recorded in eternity. This is further proof of our individuality in God's eyes. I Corinthians 13:12 says that in that day you shall be known as you are known. To win our battles against disease and Satan, we need to truly understand how important each of us is to God.

When exercising our free will, we need to make decisions that are pleasing to the Lord. We will carry memories from our life on earth with us into eternity in heaven. Have you ever realized that we will remember that David had Uriah killed and that Peter thrice denied the Lord? Since this is all written down in Scripture I am sure we will all remember it. We'll know our relatives, and we'll remember all our good and evil deeds for all of eternity. Knowing this, how should it affect our lives here on earth?

So, just who are we? Do we have a split personality, multiple personalities, or have we fabricated a personality? Have we created fourteen or fifteen different internal entities, some of which do good and some of which do evil? No! The real "us" is made up of the one person described in Psalms 139. We are the person God saw at the foundation of the world. *Some people never realize who they truly are.*

Paul wrote that God had ordained him to be an apostle to the Gentiles (I Timothy 2:7). God told Jeremiah, before you were ever conceived, I ordained you to be a prophet to the nations (Jeremiah 1:5). Paul and Jeremiah provide historical proof that God sees each of us as separate and distinct individuals with a God-ordained purpose in this life. God planned for each and every one of us individually from before the foundation of the world. He knew each of us before we were conceived or born. His sense of time is one of eternal perspectives, not temporal like ours.

When Satan entered the world through Adam, another nature became added to our original nature: the sin nature. Self now had a hyphen after it, and became the target of unloving spirits.

SELF-HATRED (UNLOVING SPIRITS)

What is an unloving spirit? It's a spirit that attaches to and attacks us, seeking to make us feel self-rejected, unclean and unworthy. It tells us that we don't measure up, that we are no good. Unloving spirits make us wretch at the sound of our own voice or the contents of our words: "everything I say is so stupid." When we look at ourselves in the mirror, unloving spirits tell us, "You sure are ugly." As we watch others, we become sure that they hate our guts, because unloving spirits tell us that we can see it in their eyes.

Under their attack, unloving spirits cause us to debate whether or not we even belong on this planet. We look in the mirror and see uncontrollable hair, wrinkles, sags and old tired eyes, and we hear, "Face it, you're no prize except maybe the booby prize."

Our days are spent feeling like we always fall short of others' expectations. "Not even God could like me. I can't stand myself. Why was I born?"

We find ourselves focusing on every negative thing we see and hear that makes us less of a person. "My sister never should have said anything about my kids. If she only knew the trouble they have been." "Every time I'm with Bob, he's gotta rub it in that I don't have a college degree."

We replay old memory tapes that keep us from enjoying fellowship. "I'd go to choir, but the director teased me about my high F last year." "Sure, going bowling with the folks from Sunday School would be fun, but that jerk Gary will just tease me again."

These unloving spirits continue their assault so that self-rejection becomes the norm in our life. The conflict wears us out.

A constant or high level of this type of self-accusation and rejection is evidence that unloving spirits have taken up residence in us. In order to do their evil work, they need to use us to express themselves. An unloving spirit wants to use us like a puppet on a stage. It wants to be the hand that pulls our strings.

The unloving spirit uses its armor to keep you from discovering the real you. It uses weapons of self-pity, self-abuse, self-rejection, self-hatred, competition, self-pride, self-enthronement, false piety. It thrives on the I: I will, self-exaltation, attention getting, excessive talkativeness, insecurity, self-mutilation, excessive eating and bingeing. It fires self-comparison, self-idolatry, perfectionism, and self-torment at us. It pushes us to be defensive, and filled with self-doubt, unbelief, self-bitterness, self-resentment, self-unforgiveness, self-retaliation, self-anger, self-violence, and suicide. These are but a few of the arms with which unloving spirits attack us.

In this warfare, it is essential to decide which law will rule our lives: the law of God, or of the kingdom of Self controlled by Satan.

The Unloving Spirit — Kingdom of Self — is the principality of self-bitterness, and it is protected by strong armor (Luke 11:24-26). Once again, to defeat Satan we must be able to recognize and deal successfully with all of his evil ways, and that includes defeating his principalities. Each principality is protected by layers of armor. Let's study the armor in this principality of an unloving spirit.

Turning back to our dictionary, we notice that following the immediate definition of the word "self," self includes many modifiers:

- Self-abandonment: disregarding all self-interest.
- Self-abasement: humiliation of oneself.
- Self-absorbed: focusing on oneself to the exclusion or consideration of others.
- Self-abuse: comes in many forms, i.e. obesity or anorexia; sleep deprivation or too much sleep; lack of exercise or pushing oneself to the brink; denial of normal sexuality or preoccupation with sex.
- Self-accusation: constantly finding fault with oneself.

Let's look more deeply.

COMPETITION OR SELF-COMPARISON

When we are preoccupied with competition it should be a clue that we have an unloving spirit. It tells us that we are not a whole person unless we win. In contrast, Luke 9:24 says, "For whosoever will save his life shall lose it: but whosoever will lose his life for My sake, the same shall save it." God has a different perspective about how we gain self-acceptance.

We need to stop worrying about who we are and comparing ourselves to others because we already know we are precious in God's sight — it's all that matters.

The Pharisees often compared themselves to others. Matthew records one such instance. Spotting a non-Pharisee, they pray, "Oh God, I thank you that I'm not like these worms that I have to associate with. I thank you that the good work that you've done in my life is so complete that I don't have to associate with these undesirable spiritual ones" (see Matthew 23:1-36). All of us, even a Pharisee, must learn to accept who we are in Christ, not in comparison to others. If we try to artificially build ourselves up in our own strength, using our own plan, we will lose our life.

Competition is rooted in self-pride or self-enthronement that forms another layer of Satanic armor. What is self-enthronement? Putting ourselves on the throne of our life so that we become the singular focus of everything that interests us. Me, me, me. Self, self, self. This is a piece of evil armor.

To be a candidate for greatness in God's kingdom we must quit trying to be the end of everything in this earthly kingdom. God's selection process works differently from ours. Luke 13:30 says, "And, behold, there are last which shall be first, and there are first which shall be last."

I Corinthians 12 provides a rich list of spiritual gifts made available to us by God. It teaches that these gifts of the Holy Spirit are God-given and that the Holy Spirit decides who receives which gift. Scripture teaches us to *desire* the best gift, not demand or take it. As we express our desire, the Holy Spirit fulfills our desire at His discretion. In this way, God's gifts are used for the right purpose: to bring Him glory and advance His Kingdom.

Many people like to claim to have the gift of prophecy. Yet, it is possible for a person to be prophesying from their own spirit, or worse, from an evil spirit of divination using them in self-exaltation. If the Holy Spirit gives a willing believer the gift of prophecy, that person couldn't help but prophesy. Then the gift will be used to bring glory to God, not to the prophet. The prophecy will increase our fellowship with God.

Matthew 25:14 gives us a glimpse at how God thinks. "For the kingdom of heaven is as a man traveling into a far country who called his own servants, and delivered unto them his goods." Whose servants and whose goods? These were the master's servants and his goods.

Matthew 25:15 says, "And unto one he gave five talents, to another two, and to another one; to every man according to his several ability; and straightway took his journey."

Does this Scripture teach that the person who got five talents was more important than the other two? Not at all. The Lord gave the talents according to each man's ability. It had nothing to do with trust or status. It had everything to do with the person's God-created ability. God gave them only what they could handle. The talent came from God, not man.

The first two servants invested the talents wisely, and doubled them. However, the servant who received one talent buried it, because he feared that the master would be angry with him if he lost it. When the master came back he called this last man an "unfaithful servant," saying, "The least you could have done is put my money in the bank to gain interest. At least you could have given me back a talent plus interest, but you didn't even do that. You hid it in fear" (Matthew 25:26-27).

Competition and self-comparison keep us from accepting who we are and leave us unfulfilled. It really shows that we have not trusted God's judgment. James 4:10 teaches us to humble ourselves in the sight of the Lord, and He will lift you up. It is time to learn to trust Him.

It is a fact: God is sovereign. If someone else seems to be doing more for God or seems more able than we are, even if it is true, it doesn't mean that we are a lesser person than they are. We are simply different. Competition and comparison always result in bitterness either toward another or our self.

An unloving spirit wants to steal your peace. It reinterprets the story, saying, "I'm really a nobody unless I can have the five talents or at least two. But I always get stuck with just one . . . or none." Self-pity has joined in the attack.

The truth is that God has created you with all the ability you will ever need to accomplish what He has called you to do. An unloving spirit attacks you to prevent you from using your God-given talents and spiritual gifts for any purpose.

Pride is an anti-Christ mentality. Pride drives a person to dishonesty about himself or herself. Pride says, "Everybody else has the problem, but I'm glad I don't."

Pride is the result of disobedience to the Word of God. Pride keeps a person from submitting to God, leaders, or the five-fold ministry of the local church (Ephesians 4). Pride never takes responsibility for anything, except when it flatters itself. And Pride never repents. Pride is the ultimate expression of Satan who thought himself to be so great he believed he was equal to God. We are expressing pride every time we choose to disobey God. In disobedience we are saying, "we know more than you do God."

There is another form of pride that says, "I am nothing." It is false humility. You hear it when a person responds to a comment, saying, "Oh well, it was nothing," instead of a simple "Thank you." False humility often finds its roots in a misunderstanding of the Bible's teaching about preferring others above oneself. It becomes, "No, you go ahead this time. I've had my chance," all the time hoping the other person will beg you to go ahead. It says, "Yes, the church does look beautiful. I'm glad God uses my gifts this way, even though it took a lot of time." That's false humility speaking.

Pride shows itself when a person finds a way to exalt himself or herself. That is false and unrighteous pride. It is self-centeredness and the wrong kind of self-love, rooted as it is in making oneself seem greater than others.

Self-effacement happens when a person purposes to hide in the background, minimizing their actions. They deliberately choose to exhibit modest, retiring behavior. This is often the wallflower in the group. True humility can, of course, be good, but not when it results from an unloving spirit showing itself in deliberate behavior. This is the kind of behavior that refuses to accept thanks for a job well done, preferring to almost back out of the room to avoid it. It comes from false piety. These are some of the forms of pride.

We have chosen to call pride a form of self-hatred because of the disastrous fruit it bears in a person's life.

Another piece of the armor of an unloving spirit is "I and the I will." An anti-Christ spirit will always protect, develop and look to itself first. It sees the world in a sphere that surrounds self. But a spirit that's not of anti-Christ will look beyond itself to the bigger picture.

Learning to be free from an unloving spirit requires looking beyond ourselves, and really seeing others. It gives us the ability to look at those who have rejected or victimized us, and realize they have serious problems of their own. It is the ability to separate the sin from the sinner, and gives us the ability to forgive and have compassion on them.

We have to be able to look deep into our own nature and discern what we really are from what we are not. If we can see our true Godly nature, then we will not act ungodly. Satan will be left without a foothold.

Faith is the substance of things hoped for (Hebrews 11:1). What do you hope for? A different way of thinking? A different nature? A different way of living? We will never have a different way of thinking if we haven't changed our hearts. It's not possible. Why? Because the Bible says so. "As a man thinketh in his heart, so is he" (Proverbs 23:7).

Referring to Satan, Isaiah 14:13 says, "For thou hast said in thine heart, I will ascend into heaven, I will exalt my throne above the stars of God: I will sit also upon the mount of the congregation, in the sides of the north."

Here we see the operation of "I will." Satan said, "I will ascend into heaven. I will exalt my throne above the stars of God. I will sit also upon the mount of the congregation in the sides of the north." In verse 14, he continues, "I will ascend above the heights of the clouds; I will be like the most High." I will, I will. It is critical to understand the nature of Satan is that of self, of self-exaltation. Pride. I will. An unloving spirit always seeks to exalt itself.

I, I will. These form the crux of our problem in creation. The Bible says in both Genesis and Jude, that there are angels reserved in chains of darkness awaiting judgment because they left their proper state of habitation. How did this happen? They freely chose to sin.

This is a truth about all created beings, from archangels to people; God gave us all a free will. God gave us the ability to make quality decisions. None of us was created as a puppet or clone, or to simply vegetate. All of us have been given the ability to reason out a matter and come to a conclusion.

Deuteronomy 30:19 says, "I call heaven and earth to record this day against you, that I have set before you life and death, blessing and cursing: therefore choose life, that both thou and thy seed may live." Every created being has free choice. Joshua 24:15 says to "choose this day whom we are to serve." Did Jesus have a choice? He said, "Abba, Father, all things are possible unto Thee; take away this cup from Me: nevertheless not what I will, but what Thou wilt" (Mark 14:36). Why do you and I serve God? Because we choose to do so.

Because of a free will, every created being has the potential to be a Lucifer. That's why the human race is on probation; God continues to test our hearts. Why?

We were created to be kings and priests in God's kingdom. Before appointing us, God wants to know if we are just another Lucifer or one of his fallen angels. Are you trustworthy?

In His sovereignty, God already knows who will choose to be faithful. But the question for us is, "do we know?" This is a powerful thought. We must have confidence that He that is in us is greater than he that is in the world (I John 4:4.) Do we have the confidence that we can overcome Satan and be found worthy of being a king or priest in God's kingdom?

Lucifer tempted the other angels with self-exaltation, promising them power, supremacy, and rulership. We need to answer the question, "What does Satan use to tempt us?" One-third of the angels followed his lead, indicating his temptation is powerful.

Many Christians work to establish their own "kingdoms" within church bodies, and they do so on their own terms rather than God's. As they strive for power, they mask their motives with an air of pride and superiority: "Well, I'm the only one who really knows how to do this." Their real motive is spiritual pride and arrogance.

How can we observe the real motives of a leader? David's life gives us the key. When Nathan confronted him with his sins, he tore his robes and lay before God, begging forgiveness. Psalms 51 powerfully tells us the story. Because David repented, he was called "a man after God's own heart" (Acts 13:22). The key was repentance: in humility going before God, acknowledging his sin, asking for forgiveness and turning away from evil.

Lucifer never repented, and neither did the fallen angels, his demons. They remain arrogant and jealous of God today.

Making the right choice today sets us apart in both this life and for eternity. Choosing to live humbly and with a contrite heart, while taking responsibility for the times we fall short of God's will, sets us apart from the sons of the devil as sons of God. Choosing what is right separates the sons of light from the sons of darkness.

Why was David called a man after God's own heart? Two reasons: he loved God, and he took responsibility for his sin. Then he sought and received God's forgiveness. God's desire is that we do the same thing.

MORE ASPECTS OF UNLOVING SPIRITS

A person who has an unloving spirit often desires attention. A bully usually has both a spirit of rejection and an unloving spirit. He compensates for these evil influences through bragging, bravado and threats. Why? He thinks that getting attention will mask his spiritual deficiencies.

Excessive talkativeness is another piece of Satan's armor he uses to disguise the strong man of the unloving spirit. This is the person who always has something to say, talks non-stop, but really never says much of value. Such a person has deep struggles with insecurity.

Insecurity is a form of fear: fear of man, of failure, of abandonment, of rejection. The unloving spirit is a principality who often links arms with the principalities of fear, and rejection. Together, they present a formidable foe, but they cannot stand against the power of God in Christ Jesus.

I John 4:18 says that perfect love casts out fear. We defeat fear with perfect love. It all starts when we receive the perfect love of God, learn to love ourselves, and then love others.

When we have mastered loving God, self and others, fear doesn't stand a chance. To defeat fear, we must face him down by learning to love ourselves and to be prepared to deal with the armor of the unloving spirit. We must realize that fear is unbelief and therefore a sin against God.

Satan's earthly kingdom is a counterfeit of God's eternal kingdom. Ephesians 6:11 tells us to "put on the whole armor of God that we may be able to stand against the wiles of the devil." Putting on this armor protects us from the devil's "fiery darts." We put on the armor of God by learning His Word and then applying His precepts to our lives.

Satan protects his "place" (Ephesians. 4:27) in our lives with his own counterfeit armor. The principality of fear has a set of armor for protection (see the chapter on fear). The principality of bitterness is protected by unforgiveness, resentment, retaliation, anger, hatred, violence, and murder. The principality of self-bitterness or unloving spirits is protected and reinforced by all of Satan's demons.

Winning spiritual warfare carries a responsibility on our part to behave in a Godly manner. All of what I teach is predicated on each of us choosing to be a man or woman of God. This results in changed attitudes and actions. I Thessalonians 2:12 says, "That ye would walk worthy of God, who hath called you unto His kingdom and glory."

The responsibility the master placed on the shoulders of the person who received one talent equaled the responsibility placed on the person who received five. The number of talents received by each person said nothing about their value to God. This parable teaches us not to compare ourselves to others.

Unloving spirits often drive us to make self-comparisons. This is the behavior in which we compare our successes to another person's, putting the other person in the position as an idol, a false god. You hold them up — their behavior, looks, lifestyle — as a standard to which you aspire. This type of idolatry can lead us to despise and resent the person we idolize.

In the business world it is common for motivational speakers and books to admonish us to pattern ourselves after successful people. For the believer, this requires special care, making sure that we do not let some perceived success key divert us from Godliness. Some people who the world judges as successful are miserable failures in their spiritual and family lives.

The truth is that God often takes an obedient believer and gives him more success than the person he's emulating. We cannot allow ourselves to set our standards based on our perception of another person. Instead, we need to conform to God's image. By so doing, not only do we avoid idol worship, we gain true success. This does not mean that we cannot learn from successful people in our industry or as family role models. The key here is to compare their methods and measurements of success to God's Word.

Idolatry provides armor to the principality of an unloving spirit. It also leads to another piece of evil armor: perfectionism. Perfectionism allows no room for failure and you can be sure that if you are engaged in any aspect of life, failure will come at some time. When perfectionists experience failure, it produces self-accusation and self-condemnation.

These aspects of an unloving sprit make up its armor. These are the "goods" of Luke 11:21. This is another example of how the armed strong man fights to keep his palace.

How do we spoil the goods? We learn to discern each of the goods to determine which ones are of Satan, and then we begin unraveling them.

There is more than one way to defeat the power of a rope that binds us to something. We can cut it, or we can unweave it one strand at a time. As we work toward banishing Satan's influence in our lives, we may have to do it a little at a time, peeling layer from layer. At other times, we will have the power to cut his bindings in two.

Satan uses self-bitterness against us. Here, instead of being bitter toward others, we are bitter toward ourselves. Self-bitterness produces an inability to forgive ourselves. Have you ever struggled with unforgiveness toward yourself? I have. Our ministry experience is that many people cannot say, "I forgive myself."

Unforgiveness of our selves leads to self-resentment. It says, "I can never do anything right. The harder I try the worse things get. I never have been any good, never will be any good. I'm just a nobody. I don't like the way I look. Daddy was right. I'll never amount to anything." This kind of self-talk buffers and bruises us, leaving us too weak to withstand Satan's onslaught.

Self-resentment leads to self-retaliation. This will cause us to react strongly and negatively to someone who accuses us. Our negativity results in their rejection of us, which is what we expected in the first place. We go into these situations with our eyes wide open, because we have a need to be rejected. Then the unloving spirit starts accusing us, telling us that we're not loved, causing a spiraling down. The worse we are, the worse we get. Before long, we have developed a continual pattern of victimization.

What drives a battered woman back to a husband who beats her? She has developed a need to be beaten in order to reinforce her self-hatred. Self-retaliation results in self-hatred. Though she now truly is a victim, she needs the beating, or a threat of the beating, to fulfill her need to hate herself. That belief is an absolute lie, but the unloving spirit accuses her and drives her back to her abuser.

Victimization, oddly enough, is a type of control. It gains us attention and can win us support outside of our abusive relationship. We win membership in the victim's support groups. We do not have to remain victims.

When self-hatred that results in abuse by others becomes dominant, it is a force that takes over and we are unable to stop the craziness. The only way to break its hold is to totally remove ourselves from the situation, to gain space and cool off. But this presents a new set of problems.

When we remove ourselves from a violent situation, but fail to deal with our root problems, the next person we marry or move in with is most often an abuser. We recreate the same situation, and hear ourselves say, "Oh, no! Here I go again."

It is common that when a girl grows up being abused by her father, she marries someone just like dad. We deal with many women who say, "The greatest tragedy of my life is that I tried to get away from my abusive father, and I married someone just like him." It is common among ninety percent of women we deal with from abusive homes.

We ask, "What do you mean by 'you married your father'?"

"Well, I married a man with the character traits that I most hated in my dad." But most often, they never see these traits until after their marriage when the abuse begins.

It is essential that if the person you are dating or engaged to shows any evidence of verbal or physical abuse, you must honestly recognize that you are headed for trouble. If your betrothed fails to deal with the spirits that drive him to this behavior, when you get married you will find that you bought the whole package. If you see patterns of victimization, but hear good intentions that "I have changed," be suspicious. Statistically these sentiments have been proven to be untrue. God designed the husband to provide physical and emotional shelter for the wife. Any other behavior is not of God.

God is the only one who can change an abusive man. He needs ministry for deliverance. What has him by the spiritual neck is not some passing emotion. It's an unloving spirit direct from the pit of hell.

How do I know that it's an unloving spirit? Because the Bible makes it clear that a man who hates his wife hates himself. They became one flesh in marriage, and if the man is abusing his wife he is abusing himself (Ephesians 5:31). He hates what God loves.

The reverse is also true. Women can hate or dislike men. This usually occurs when their fathers or husbands have been weak and disobedient, and have not provided for their families. A daughter may learn this from her mother and transfer it into her marriage.

What should you do if you're already in an abusive relationship? Understand that living in an abusive marriage will reinforce the unloving spirits in us.

Romans 12:18 says, "If it be possible, as much as lieth in you, live peaceably with all men." Many pastors who deal with spousal abuse advise an immediate separation. They want to stop the abuse and deal with its causes. Both partners can benefit from this wise counsel.

People who are accused by an unloving spirit often pick fights just to get rejected. For instance, a wife with a black eye will parade it in front of others, saying, "Look at the black eye I got. Look at what he did to me." Who is actually speaking those words? Unforgiveness. Bitterness. Self-pity.

Some people seem to get up in the morning so demonized that they try to pick a fight all day long, until it happens. They set up their day and their relationships so that somewhere along the way there will be a big problem.

People accused by unloving spirits split churches, split families and ruin businesses. They seem bent on finding trouble. What did the Lord say? "If at all possible, live peaceably one with another." When two people cannot live together peaceably, it might be time to separate.

Have you ever experienced self-anger? "I just can't stand myself!" "See, here's more proof how stupid I am. I should just kill myself!" From where does this behavior come? It is the result of a successful attack by an unloving spirit.

In self-anger, we will find perfectionism, self-accusation, and self-condemnation. When these three come together, they will trigger anger like a flash fire. When self-anger wells up, we are wise to keep our distance from others because we are heading for territory where even angels fear to tread.

Self-anger is no respecter of persons. We see how it affects us well enough, but if we're not careful, this anger will spill over onto somebody else. The evil fruit of this demonic attack is to include others as victims, not just us. The devil is an equal opportunity oppressor.

Consider self-hatred. We don't get to self-hatred without self-bitterness accusing us. Self-hatred is the result of a process of working through self-unforgiveness, self-resentment, self-retaliation and self-anger, each stage being more dangerous than its predecessor. Self-hatred results from something that simmers and festers below the surface, often for days, weeks, months or years.

The next stage is self-violence. Self-anger spills over into committing some type of hurtful act against oneself. Our ministry has served many that have cut or mutilated themselves out of extreme shame or guilt.

The ultimate expression of self-violence is, of course, suicide. When we entertain thoughts of suicide, we have clear evidence of self-bitterness with its entire evil armor in full battle array, getting close to celebrating final victory over us. To defeat self-murder, we have to break the bond of the unloving spirit and eliminate self-bitterness.

It is characteristic of people who have reached this point to constantly entertain thoughts like, "I need to eliminate myself, I don't belong here." "Nobody would care if I died. In fact, the world would be better off." "The only way I can make Jane happy is to kill myself!" These are sick, irrational thoughts, but quite commonly seen in our ministry.

Self-murder is an anti-Christ mentality that comes from the armor of an unloving spirit. When you experience such thoughts, turn them around, saying, "I do belong here." "God made me. I'm precious to Him." I do belong here! We must repent for believing the lies of the devil, in the name of Jesus command his lying spirit to go, command the spirit of death to go, and then ask the Holy Spirit to heal and make us whole.

Here are some more ways that we self-destruct. Constantly defending oneself is rooted in the fear of rejection, but it's also tied directly to the unloving spirit. We desire to feel safe in our relationships, and if we perceive an attack we become defensive. So sensitized are we to these perceived attacks, that we fly off the handle even when we are not being provoked. An unloving spirit won't let us feel safe. Our need for security drives us to aggressively defend ourselves. All this is rooted in fear tied to an unloving spirit.

Profanity and an unloving spirit also walk together. The use of four-letter words degrades and cheapens us. We make excuses that the vulgar words are more descriptive than others we might choose, but this is just rationalizing. Profane language may be colorful, but it degrades us and those with whom we are talking.

Some people always seem to be trying to "fix" someone else. They marry the alcoholic or the abuser, suffer for it, get divorced and do it again. This, too, is driven by an element of the unloving spirit. Here we are drawn to others who "need us" so we can feel good about ourselves. We have an urge to help these people see that they are all right and worthwhile, but we fail to confront their real spiritual needs. The result is a continual spiraling down of our own sense of worth.

The Word says that we should love each other despite our fallen state. Galatians 6:1-2 says, "Brethren, if a man be overtaken in a fault, ye which are spiritual, restore such an one in the spirit of meekness; considering thyself, lest thou also be tempted. Bear ye one another's burdens, and so fulfill the law of Christ."

If someone disregards us because we commit an error or they think we have, they have also committed an error. In contrast, a person who walks in the spirit would forgive, restore, accept and come alongside us. They would help us bear our burdens.

Likewise, if someone sins against us, we are to come alongside him or her in a spirit of forgiveness with a desire to help. Our motivation is to aid them in recovering from their sin and be freed from "the snare of the devil" (II Timothy 2:23-26).

It is good and healthy to want to be at peace with someone with whom we have had differences. It's scriptural. The Holy Spirit will assist us in such an endeavor. However, when attempting to resolve these differences, we've got to be careful that the other person has dealt with their own sin. If they haven't, God's Word tells us to "restore such a one in the spirit of meekness," adding that we are to "bear one another's burdens." Is it risky to ask someone to forgive you when they are capable of eating you for lunch? Yes, it is. Is it worth taking the risk? Absolutely, because in taking that risk and seeking restoration, we fulfill the law of Christ (Galatians 6:1-2).

But if they reject you, calling fire down from heaven on you, get away from them. Don't be a victim! Don't let their sinful nature draw you in. Your approval does not come from man. No man serves as your judge. If you follow the Word of God and your motives are pure, then God will judge you righteous.

MORE AREAS OF CONCERN

Self-pity is the most dangerous of all of the unloving spirits because it binds us to past demons. This binding keeps us from God's future provision, binds us to what somebody has done to us or what we've done to ourselves. Self-pity says nobody really understands us, and even if they did, they don't really care. After all, if they did care, they'd love us more and show us more attention. They'd call us every day, come and see us, and want to do things together.

Because of self-pity, when someone does come we tell him or her to go away. We whine about being unloved and we can prove it with illustrations from our past. Their visit then becomes an irritation. Either we ask them to leave or, once they have left, they purpose to never again visit. After they leave, we rail against them for their insensitivity to our needs.

Self-pity is like a wet diaper. It feels good and warm at first, but the longer we sit in it the colder and smellier it gets, driving everyone else away.

Self-pity creates a vicious circle. We need to be loved and use our manipulating techniques to get someone's attention. Then we offend them enough that they leave us alone. This increases our self-pity and the cycle repeats itself. Self-pity is very dangerous, because it binds our freedom with a life sentence.

All kleptomania is rooted in a spirit of self-indulgence. A person who shoplifts gets fulfilled from the fix of thievery. Self-indulgence is rooted in an unloving spirit.

A kleptomaniac desperately wants to be caught stealing. They don't need what they steal, but they use it to fill an inner void. They want to be caught to attract attention. But, when they get that kind of negative attention, it brings on more guilt and self-hatred. It reinforces the unloving spirit in a debilitating vicious circle.

Cocaine acts in much the same way. Cocaine is not chemically addictive. It is psychologically addictive. Cocaine releases dopamine. Dopamine is the pleasure neurotransmitter. When a man takes his first hit of cocaine, he will never again experience that same rush because the body remanufactures dopamine very slowly.

A cocaine hit releases the same amount of dopamine as a sexual orgasm does. The dynamics of sexual addiction are the same as those of cocaine addiction. A sexual addict can never attain the same high again, or achieve the same satisfaction. In a vain attempt to do so, they both keep repeating their behavior, but it eludes them.

A compulsive spender needs the rush gained from buying yet another thing. It is his fix to help him feel good about himself.

Compulsive spending is very similar to bingeing. It attempts to satisfy its love void with material possessions. It flows from an unloving spirit. It says, "You know dad doesn't like you. He thinks you're a loser. Well, you show him! Buy that new car right now and everyone will see you're a winner!" You drive the car for a week and its newness wears off, your dad never sees it because you avoid him anyway, and within months, the finance company forecloses because you couldn't afford it in the first place. So you go out and buy something else.

Self-sabotage is very dangerous because it is tied closely with self-mutilation and self-destruction. Self-sabotage destroys our faith, because faith is the substance of things hoped for, the evidence of things not yet seen (Hebrews 11:1). Self-sabotage says that our faith will never work and on those occasions when we attempt to live by faith, we sabotage the results. Self-sabotage keeps us from ever achieving our hopes. Yet the Bible says, "hope deferred maketh the heart sick" (Proverbs 13:12). Now we're caught in a web with a sick heart and mind, yet still needing to be loved and to overcome. Self-sabotage rears up, saying, "I don't qualify," and "Everything good that happens to me needs to be destroyed." And this spiritual attack reinforces the unloving spirit that accuses us.

Vows are another form of self-sabotage. When we say, "I will never trust women (or men) again," because of how we have been hurt, Satan is there ready to fulfill those words, and every future relationship that begins to grow close is destroyed. The "I will never do this or that" statements set us up for failure in the future. When we say "I don't matter, I'm not good enough, I'd better be perfect, I'm just a doormat, I'm just a victim, men don't cry, I'm bad seed, I have to keep peace at any price," or other similar words, we curse ourselves. The words and fears that we speak against ourselves are self-fulfilling forms of prophecy. They will come true if we do not repent and break the curse we spoke against ourselves, in the name of Jesus.

False piety is another evil spirit. In the context of the Christian faith, piety means devotion to God, His Word and Biblical religious practices. It carries the element of loyalty and devotion to parents and family.

False piety is contrary to Godly piety. It sounds like, "Even though mom and dad abuse me, victimize me, and reject me, since the Bible says to honor your father and mother, I'll just have to submit, like it or not." This false piety preaches the stiff upper lip when confronting ungodly behavior in others.

Nowhere in the Bible are we taught to submit to this kind of evil. This is not suffering for your faith. When Paul suffered for his faith he was stoned, falsely accused, imprisoned or beaten because he served Jesus (II Corinthians. 11-13). Suffering because of our sin is not suffering for our faith.

When God says to honor your father and mother, He doesn't mean to submit to their authority if it is used in an evil way. I don't believe we need to submit to the authority of a mother or father who physically, verbally, or sexually abuses us or who habitually demonstrates other ungodly behavior. Neither do we attack them in return. We get out from under their evil influence and honor them differently, by trying to win them to submit to Christ and ban the demons that control their lives.

False piety might drive a wife to continue suffering verbal or physical abuse from her husband. The Bible teaches women to submit to their husbands, and abused wives often misunderstand this teaching. There is another side to it. The Bible also tells men to love their wives as Christ loves the Church. An abusive husband commits an evil act, and the wife must get out of the way. Yet by allowing the abuse to continue, the wife is saying that she's getting the treatment she deserves. In essence, she is agreeing that the abusive treatment is all she is worth. Since God created her in His own image, this false piety has her saying that God is of little worth.

False piety is closely related to codependency. Codependency is really calling evil good. In codependency we are allowing evil and sinful behavior to continue because we do not love or respect ourselves. We allow ourselves to be physically, emotionally and sexually abused because we think that is our lot in life. We believe that we deserve to be treated in those ways.

In reality, in codependency, we are calling evil good and in doing so have become accessories to sin. Verbal, physical, emotional and sexual abuse are sins, and they can also be criminal acts. If we allow these to happen, if we allow ourselves to be doormats, we are then agreeing that we deserve it. In not stopping this kind of behavior we are not loving, or respecting ourselves as God commands us to. When we allow ourselves to be treated this way it becomes our sin also. We stop the behavior by telling the person to stop. If they refuse, we remove ourselves from the situation.

God calls us to peace and to have a perfect hatred for evil. So why would we submit to evil? False piety and codependency produce martyrdom and martyrdom can be true or false. When we hear ourselves say, "My sufferings allow me to identify with the world's pain," or "Ungodly people beat and killed the Savior; I should count it a blessing to be beaten by my evil husband," this is evil thinking. True martyrs suffer for the sake of the Cross, not to raise their own self-image or to give them an excuse why they should do nothing to correct a bad situation.

My experiences have taught me that the two most common occurrences of false piety are found in wives and in pastors.

Pastors get clobbered by their flock or their board and then go back for more. Once clobbered again, they retreat into false piety, asserting that they are suffering for the Lord. What they're really doing is teaching that inappropriate, non-Christian behavior is acceptable. Pastors need to appeal to their flock based on the authority of the Scriptures. Allowing their flock to continue in sin becomes their sin.

There are many ways that we show a lack of Godly self-love. We need to learn to accept our position in Christ and the extreme value God places on us, and begin a proper love relationship with ourselves.

GOD'S TRUTH

I Corinthians 12:14-31 reads, "For the body is not one member, but many. If the foot shall say, Because I am not the hand, I am not of the body; is it therefore not of the body? And if the ear shall say, Because I am not the eye, I am not of the body; is it therefore not of the body? If the whole body were an eye, where was the hearing? If the whole were hearing, where was the smelling? But now hath God set the members every one of them in the body, as it hath pleased Him. And if they were all one member, where was the body? But now are they many members, yet but one body. And the eye cannot say unto the hand, I have no need of thee: nor again the head to the feet, I have no need of you. Nay, much more those members of the body, which seem to be more feeble, are necessary: And those members of the body, which we think to be less honourable, upon these we bestow more abundant honour; and our uncomely parts have more abundant comeliness. For our comely parts have no need: but God hath tempered the body together, having given more abundant honour to that part which lacked: That there should be no schism in the body; but that the members should have the same care one for another. And whether one member suffer, all the members suffer with it; or one member be honoured, all the members rejoice with it. Now ye are the body of Christ, and members in particular. And God hath set some in the church, first apostles, secondarily prophets, thirdly teachers, after that miracles, then gifts of healings, helps, governments, diversities of tongues. Are all apostles? are all prophets? are all teachers? are all workers of miracles? Have all the gifts of healing? do all speak with tongues? do all interpret? But covet earnestly the best gifts: and yet shew I unto you a more excellent way."

Verse 14 says that the body is made up of many members. Take a look around; you'll see it takes many of us to make up the body of Christ. Verse 15 says, If the foot shall say because I am not the hand then I'm not part of the body. Is it therefore not of the body? Verse 16 continues, And if the ears shall say because I am not the eye, I'm not of the body. Is it therefore not of the body? Verse 17 says, If the whole body were an eye, then how could you hear? And if the whole body was an ear, then how could you smell?

Read verse 18 again, carefully. But now hath God, the Father set the members of the body. Every one them. The body of Christ is made up of individual members: you and me, and others. How did God choose where to place each member? "As it hath pleased Him." He willed it! It is His choice, not ours.

God has decided on the function of each member. If God called me to be an eye, then I will see for the body. If He has called me to be an ear, then I will hear for the body. Each part of the body is designed to function together in harmony. If you are a hand and another person is the mouth, don't reject yourself because he does all the talking and you do all the lifting. It is the way God designed the body to work together to accomplish His purpose.

Verse 21 says, "The eye cannot say unto the hand, I have no need of you." Which body part do you think is more important, the eye or the hand? God says they have equal importance. We cannot tell any body part that it is unneeded, even when we are a part that seems less desirable.

God assigns each one of us a function in the family of God. Our desire should be to function as God created us, not as the devil has recreated us. To be whole and mature, healthy and strong, we need to stand beside each other. Occasionally we might need to carry another person's burden, but our main purpose is to fulfill the function God assigned to us at our creation.

If God created you to be the foot, it doesn't do the whole body any good if you don't go anywhere. If God created you to be a finger but you never lift one, the whole body suffers. A healthy Christian Church depends on healthy body parts, each faithfully and humbly performing its function. This requires self-acceptance, accepting ourselves as God has created us.

One man received the spiritual gifts of caring and helps, and practiced them in his Christian walk, especially at his church (these are like the hands and heart of the body). He faithfully exercised these gifts for more than eighty years until infirmity (human weakness) overtook him. Yet he asked God to still use him in some way, so God had him stand by the exit doors at church each Sunday to greet people and show them that God cares. Though somewhat immobile and hard of hearing, he still did the work of a caregiver.

Verse 21 says, "the eye cannot say unto the hand I have no need of you. Nor again the head to the feet I have no need of you. Nay, much more those members of the body which seem to be more feeble...." I've heard people say, "Well I'm just feeble-minded lately." Or, "I just don't have any strength." Have you ever felt unimportant to the body of believers, like no one would really miss you if you simply left town? If so, you need to be on guard, because these are fiery darts from the enemy and they lead to self-unforgiveness, self-resentment, self-retaliation, self-anger, self-hatred, self-violence, and self-murder.

When God offered us His salvation, He paid the ultimate price. He did this because He loves us. Now is the time to accept God's truth.

The unloving spirit rushes alongside, saying, "Well, you don't know what my dad told me when I was thirteen." Does it really matter? First of all, you're no longer thirteen, but more importantly, we know what God said about us long before our parents were even conceived. Are we going to believe what our sinful dad said or what God has said from the foundation of the world?

Choose today to believe the Lord's promises. Do you really want to be well? Are you tired of the mess the tormentors bring into your life? You must love yourself as God loved you. You must quit listening to lies!

Satan's lies emanate from an anti-Christ spirit. They contradict what the Bible says. Repeat with me: "I am part of the body of Christ. I am important, I am special, I am valuable." Repeat it a few times. It is what God says about each of us. Each of us is incredibly important to God.

When we believe Satan's lies, God has been ripped off by the devil, and He doesn't like it. Because God created us in His image to glorify Him and enjoy Him forever, the only creatures that can bring Him joy are humans. And only forgiven, mature Christian humans, living victorious lives, bring Him the fullness of joy. Only mature Christians living victorious lives are vessels of honor fit for His service (II Timothy 2:20-21). Only Christians living victorious lives are overcomers that are promised to sit in the throne with Jesus (Revelation 2-3).

"I am not necessary, I am not important, I am not needed." These are phrases that have no place in a Christian's lexicon. These phrases belong to the devil.

What does the Bible say? All of us are important and necessary! Let's quit debating this with God! Tell the unloving spirits to "shut up!" Choose to go through the whole day blessing God, saying, "I am necessary, I am needed, I am important to my Creator." Don't believe me on this; believe the Bible; believe Christ!

An unloving spirit, or an accusing spirit might tell you that you are unnecessary, or that you are a failure. Tell him, "God didn't create me that way! And if God didn't create me this way, then I'm not the failure. You, Satan, are the failure. I no longer agree with you, Satan. Get out of my life now!"

We need to refuse to agree with failure. When a voice in our mind says, "Well, I'm not going to even try to do this, because I'm just going to fail anyway," we need to refuse to accept it. It's not from God.

Members of the body too often place undue importance on the role of some members of the body while disparaging the value of other members' roles. Which members of the body do you think are less honorable or important? Is the man who faithfully cuts the grass, tends the garden, and trims the trees any less important than the church treasurer is? Not to God he isn't.

If it is common for us to rank each function of the body by some scale of priority of importance, we know that this is not of God. God's system of priority starts with simple faith followed by obedience, not by who preaches or who polishes. Consider others as God did at creation. God said that Adam and Eve were very good.

Unloving spirits lie about who God created you to be, and urge you to rank your relative importance to others, and they tell you you're not worth much. Part of the armor of the unloving spirit is self-doubt, self-unbelief, and self-questioning. When we battle an unloving spirit, we always question our beliefs and motives, further eroding our self-confidence.

Verse 23 and 24 continue, "And those members of the body which we think to be less honorable upon these we bestow more abundant honor and our uncomely parts have more abundant comeliness. For our comely parts have no need, but God hath...." God put the body together, and He gave more honor to "that part which lacked."

It is really interesting to watch how God does this work of using the "dishonorable" to bring Him honor. Often we see God raise up some insignificant, uneducated "failure" of a human being, someone that has seen devastation in his life, and use him as a great warrior for the kingdom of God. As this happens, a seminary graduate stands by doing very little for the kingdom, befuddled because God would use this unwashed nothing of a man for such a noble purpose. Such a person, motivated by his God-given honor and strong in His love, will tear down Satan's strongholds with supernatural power.

Never discount your value in and to the body of Christ. You are important!

Verse 25 warns, "that there should be no schism...." The word "schism" means division. Part of an unloving spirit's armor is division. An unloving spirit seeks to divide and conquer by destroying unity. When an unloving spirit successfully accuses a person, they are not interested in peace; they're interested in war. Schisms produce or result from strife. When strife exists, a door for every evil thing is flung open.

An unloving spirit continuously promotes its agenda of disunity, trying always to create division in the body. Yet, we are commanded to love our Christian brothers and sisters.

For there shall be no schism in the body, but that the members shall have the same care one for another. And whether one member suffer, all the members suffer with it and when one member be honored, all the members rejoice with it (I Corinthians 12:25-26). Do you celebrate with your brother when something great happens in his life? Do you weep with him in his sorrow? These are examples of the act of bearing each other's burden.

Verse 28 says, "And God hath set some in the church." Who set them? God. "...first apostles, second prophets, thirdly teachers, after that miracles, then gifts of healing, helps, governments and diversity of tongues." In this one verse, God showed the range of functions from the greatest apostle to those who simply have the gift of tongues. But Paul lists also the gift of helps.

Helps is one of those gifts often disparaged by those who consider themselves a member of the spiritual elite. The ministry of helps means licking stamps, stuffing envelopes, cleaning the floor and the restrooms, holding the ladder, etc. To God, these jobs are just as important as the work of an apostle.

Verses 29-31 says, "Are all apostles?" No. "Are all prophets?" No. "Are all workers of miracles?" No. "Do all have all the gifts of healing?" No. "Do all speak with tongues?" No. "Do all interpret?" No. "But covet earnestly the best gifts and yet I show unto you a more excellent way." Paul spends an entire chapter laying out clearly what makes up this more excellent way.

Chapter 13 tells us the more excellent way is love. Godly love and charity, directed at others and ourselves, drives out an unloving spirit and all its armor. Without it, everything we do falls far short of God's desire.

In a body of believers that consists of people in love, when one person hurts, the rest of the body feels it. They identify and grieve, carrying each other's burdens. God created us to need each other.

Spiritual gifts were given for the edification of the body of believers, not to edify individuals. When Paul tells us to "desire the best gifts," we want to diligently seek to employ our spiritual gifts. The body of Christ needs our participation. The exercise of a spiritual gift brings responsibility and a lot of work, but it is joy-filled and rewarding.

God calls you the "apple of His eye." Do you know what that means? Deuteronomy 32:10 tells the story of how God preserved and tenderly cared for Israel. He found them wandering in a desert land, a howling wilderness. He put them in the position of the "apple of His eye," leading, instructing and protecting them.

The word "apple" is the Hebrew word *ishon*. It refers to the dark pupil of the eye, the hole, the gate, the door of the eye. God sees us as the gate or opening to His own heart.

Psalms 17:7-8 says, "Shew thy marvellous lovingkindness, O thou that savest by thy right hand them which put their trust in thee from those that rise up against them. Keep me as the apple of the eye, hide me under the shadow of thy wings." What a wonderful statement from God to which we can cling when we are under attack from the unloving spirit of rejection.

We may have an unloving spirit because our own family has rejected us. Who will keep us from those that rise up against us? The Lord will. Look at Psalms 17:8 again. The psalmist asks God to keep me as the apple of Your eye.

The Hebrew word *ishon* also means "the little man of the eye." It's an idiom meaning "that which is dearest to us, and that which must have extreme care and protection."

I Peter 3:12 says, "For the eyes of the Lord are over the righteous and His ears are open unto their prayers...." God focuses His attention on you. He is zealous for you. He loves you. He wants you completely.

Isaiah 49:15-16 says, "Can a woman forget her sucking child, that she should not have compassion on the son of her womb? Yea, they may forget, yet will I not forget thee. Behold, I have graven thee upon the palms of My hands; thy walls are continually before Me." God has written your name indelibly on His heart. He will never forget you.

In the first three chapters of Ephesians, Paul describes six doctrinal statements that define our position in Christ:

1. God chose us. Ephesians 1:4 says, "According as He hath chosen us in Him before the foundation of the world, that we should be holy and without blame before Him in love." When the enemy seeks to persuade you that you are cut off from God, hit him with this truth.

2. God saved us. Ephesians 1:7 says, "In whom we have redemption through His

blood, the forgiveness of sins, according to the riches of His grace." God redeemed us with the blood of His Son; thus we have forgiveness of sins. Satan no longer holds the power of death over us. James 4:7 tells us to resist the devil and he will flee from us. Jesus gave us His power and authority over Satan, but we must choose to use it.

3. We are sealed. Ephesians 1:13 says, "In whom ye also trusted, after that ye heard the word of truth, the gospel of your salvation: in whom also after that ye believed, ye were sealed with that Holy Spirit of promise." Satan tries to demoralize us and steal our hope. He wants us to doubt our security in God. The Holy Spirit gives us constant refreshment in our life in Jesus Christ, sealing us, guaranteeing our redemption.

4. Positionally, we are seated at the right hand of God. Ephesians 2:6 says, "And hath raised us up together, and made us sit together in heavenly places in Christ Jesus." When you are involved in spiritual warfare, where better could you be sitting than with Christ Jesus? There is neither a better nor more secure place than this.

5. We are secure. We will always be seated with Christ. Ephesians 2:19 says, "Now therefore ye are no more strangers and foreigners, but fellow citizens with the saints, and of the household of God." Ephesians 3:6 says, "That the Gentiles should be fellow heirs, and of the same body, and partakers of His promise in Christ by the gospel." We are citizens and full heirs of God, and a member of the same body in Christ.

6. Our position is one of strength. Ephesians 3:16, "That He would grant you, according to the riches of His glory, to be strengthened with might by His Spirit in the inner man."

Psalms 139 says that we are "fearfully and wonderfully made." We were created in the image and with the nature of God (Genesis 1:27). But we were tarnished by Adam's sin. The choice of how to live is ours. We can choose to believe God and be set free, or choose to continue in bondage to Satan's lies.

When we believe all of the unloving spirits that scream in our heads, we are saying that God is a liar!

I certainly don't want to stand before God and say, "Well, Lord, I know I'm fearfully and wonderfully made. I know I'm the apple of your eye. I know you love me with an everlasting love. I know I'm the righteousness of God through Christ Jesus. I know I'm a child of God. I know I'm a king and a priest I know you said all that, but I never really believed it."

I don't want Jesus to ask, "Why did you call me a liar when I said I loved you?"

I choose to believe the report of the Lord. Let God be true and every man, devil, angel and created being that preaches another gospel be accursed and be a liar (Romans 3:4).

What is the answer to unforgiveness? Forgiveness! We must learn to forgive others and ourselves. Thus begins the unraveling of the stronghold of bitterness.

THE SELF-BITTERNESS AFFIDAVIT

Make a list of all the bitterness you have had against yourself. We need to confess and repent before Almighty God for holding onto this bitterness and believing it, instead of believing Him. The stronghold that self-bitterness has held in your life will be destroyed, and Satan's power over you will be legally cancelled. Here is an example of a prayer you can use to deal with self-bitterness, and eliminate it from your life:

Prayer of Release

Dear Heavenly Father, in the name of Jesus, and as an act of my free will, I confess, repent and renounce my (specific sin of self-hatred). I ask you to forgive me for this sin. I purpose and choose to forgive myself for this (specific sin) from my heart. I release myself from any guilt or shame because of this self-bitterness. In the name of Jesus, and by the power of His blood, I cancel Satan's authority over me because of the self-bitterness of (name specific sin mentioned above). In the name of Jesus, I command this spirit of self-bitterness to go.

Holy Spirit, I invite you into my heart to heal me of self-bitterness. Please speak your words of truth to me about this situation.

As the Holy Spirit speaks to you, write down His message in the space provided on the next page. When you have finished this prayer for each person or situation on your list, command the principality of self-bitterness to go in the name of Jesus.

SELF-BITTERNESS IN THE AREA OF: THE HOLY SPIRIT'S ANSWER (TRUTH):

CHAPTER SEVEN

Forgiveness

Before we go any further, I want to repeat what I said early in this study. If I teach anything that doesn't conform to God's Word, throw it out! God expects each of us to study to show ourselves an "approved workman" (II Timothy 2:15). I'm accountable to teach truth. You're accountable to verify my teaching by comparing it to the Bible. But, when you see that our teaching conforms to the Word, you are also accountable to receive and apply it to your walk in the Spirit. Is that fair?

Throughout this book we have discussed forgiveness many times. But is such an important issue I want to cover it one more time.

Satan tries to deceive us in many ways. Ask yourself these questions:
1. Do you know in your heart that you are saved?
2. If you are sure of your salvation, have you ever sinned since coming to Christ?
3. If you have ever sinned since you were saved, do you believe that if you ask God to forgive you, He will?
4. Do you believe that He can and will forgive any sin?
5. Do you know that God h as set conditions on forgiveness? Do you know that under certain circumstances, God will not forgive because His holiness prevents Him from doing so? Our past, present, and future sin are not automatically forgiven.

There are two conditions that Christians must meet to receive forgiveness. First, we must forgive others. Second, we must ask God to forgive us.

THE FIRST CONDITION FOR RECEIVING FORGIVENESS
Matthew 6:9-12 says, "After this manner therefore pray ye: Our Father which art in heaven, Hallowed be Thy name. Thy kingdom come. Thy will be done in earth, as it is in heaven. Give us this day our daily bread. And forgive us our debts, as we forgive our debtors."

What does verse 12 say? Jesus says that we are to ask the Father to forgive us our sins, when or in the same way we forgive those that have sinned against us. Do you really want to ask God to forgive you in the same way that you forgive others? God gave us a requirement to fulfill before He will forgive our sins. Our forgiveness is directly tied to our forgiving others. It's profound that this verse doesn't say that God will always forgive us.

Matthew 6:14-15 makes the above statement from the Lord's prayer very plain: "For if ye forgive men their trespasses, your heavenly Father will also forgive you: But if ye forgive not men their trespasses, neither will your Father forgive your trespasses."

The manner or way that we forgive others set the standard by which God will forgive us. If we do not forgive, or in other words, judge others, we will be judged by God in the same way.

THE SECOND CONDITION FOR RECEIVING FORGIVENESS

We must confess all of our known sins, past, present and future. I John 1:9 says, "If we confess our sins, He is faithful and just to forgive us our sins, and to cleanse us from all unrighteousness." Notice that this verse begins with an "if." It is critical that we pay attention to the "ifs, buts, and thens" in Scripture.

James 5:16 says, "Confess your faults one to another, and pray for one another, that ye may be healed. The effectual fervent prayer of a righteous man availeth much."

What happens if we do not confess our sins and forgive ourselves? We are not forgiven and the guilt, shame, anger, regret, sadness, hatred, bitterness, etc. is still in the memory and in our lives.

If we harbor unforgiveness against anyone, including against ourselves, God will not — even cannot — forgive our sins. Does that trouble you? Let me see if I can make it even more troubling....

While doing ministry, I met a lady with whom I have spent a lot of time. Raised in a Satanist home, she grew up dedicated to Satan. Her parents baptized her with blood and urine and they repeatedly molested her. So did others. She became pregnant and was forced to have abortions as early as high school. She participated in the ritualistic murder of little babies and developed several personalities as defense mechanisms in her vain attempt to save herself. Assuming a different personality helped her avoid pain for a time, but in reality it was protecting her from the love and deliverance of Jesus.

We talked about forgiveness and I told her that she must forgive her father. She couldn't. And as awful as he had been toward her, I agreed with her. I wanted to stake him out on a hill of red army ants. No punishment seemed too harsh. But who actually was hurt by her unforgiveness? Her father? Not directly, but her husband, children and herself. To receive God's forgiveness and the blessing of healing, she had to start with forgiving her father.

If you have ever forgiven someone, yet the pain of your anger or resentment still persists, the bitterness is still there. Either you did not really forgive or at a later time you fell back into the bitterness. Either way you have allowed a root of bitterness to take hold and it prevents you from receiving God's forgiveness.

Do you think that Satan knows what the Bible says? Absolutely! He knows that forgiveness is conditional on our obedience to God's laws. Why do you think it is so hard to forgive others and especially hard to forgive ourselves? Satan fights this with all of his might because he knows that we are set free from him when we forgive others and repent for our sins.

If you bury a root of bitterness, what does it do? It grows. Satan's demons water and fertilize it, so that it will continue to grow. Our lives become so filled with pain that we believe we are unable to forgive. This is Satan's favorite weapon, the inability to forgive.

One woman dealt with her mother's constant harangues by saying, "I'm sorry, I'm sorry!" She said it so often and so ineffectively, that each time she repeated "I'm sorry," she became more bitter. There was no plea for or acceptance of forgiveness, nor did her mother give her any. "I'm sorry" served only as an attempt to bury her pain.

We have all been hurt. The church is filled with the "walking wounded," so medicated with a "forgiveness" that is really denial, that the root of bitterness destroys us from within. Instead of an outpouring of the power of forgiveness, we see Satan pouring fire on our differences.

Hebrews 12:14-17 says, "Follow peace with all men, and holiness, without which no man shall see the Lord: Looking diligently lest any man fail of the grace of God; lest any root of bitterness springing up trouble you, and thereby many be defiled; Lest there be any fornicator, or profane person, as Esau, who for one morsel of meat sold his birthright. For ye know how that afterward, when he would have inherited the blessing, he was rejected: for he found no place of repentance, though he sought it carefully with tears."

Verse 14 says to "follow peace with all men." In other words, if we consciously strive for peace with others — requiring mutual forgiveness — we will attain holiness. But if we have no peace, we will not have holiness. The moment we lose our peace, we lose our holiness. Unforgiveness causes us to lose peace by playing a record of wrongs in our mind, creating constant turmoil.

"Without which, no man will see God." This refers to us never knowing the quality of a true, close relationship with God. Without peace and the holiness it produces, we become spiritually blind, unable to see God. This sets us up for even more deception, costing us our ability to discern. We learned earlier that discernment is a primary weapon in spiritual warfare.

Losing our holiness leads to failure to experience the grace of God. Eventually, we will have no love or care for others or ourselves. Instead, we become focused on ourselves, but unable to find any relief for our self-pity. Our record of wrongs plays louder and faster, building into resentment, retaliation, anger, hatred, violence and murder. The presence of any of these indicates a root of bitterness. We need restoration such as is described in Galatians 6:1-2.

Bitterness is one of Satan's principalities and has seven evil spirits that provide its armor: 1) unforgiveness, 2) resentment, 3) retaliation, 4) anger, 5) hatred, 6) violence, 7) murder.

Each of these gets progressively worse, supporting and protecting the next one. Each of the lesser spirits is present in the greater ones.

Bitterness is Satan's wild card. A wild card is a card that can substitute for any other card in the deck. Even though it has no power of its own, it assumes the power of the card for which it is substituting. So it is with bitterness. It can bring any number of troubles, depending on which one it uses to accomplish its purpose. Its purpose is to ultimately destroy faith, ours and that of others around us.

Bitterness drives divorce, heart disease and digestive problems. Bitterness is an extreme form of anxiety and stress which effects every organ in our bodies. Most organic diseases are tied to bitterness, including cancer. All of the auto-immune diseases are tied to self-bitterness.

Do we really want to be bitter? Christians are taught to seek to forgive. We are told to do so to receive the sacrament of communion. And so we confess our sins and say that we forgive others. But if we still carry emotional pain after we have forgiven others, then we have not truly forgiven.

We need to learn how to forgive, not just that we ought to forgive.

The root of bitterness not only causes us trouble, it defiles many others as well.

By the time the devil plays this wild card, everyone we have touched is defiled. Have you ever been with someone that is angry, hateful, and who refuses to forgive? Maybe they carry grudges and brag about getting even. How does this affect you? Bitterness is very contagious.

Hebrews 12:16 mentions sexual immorality. Chisel this in stone. If we have bitterness, one hundred percent of the time it will invade our bedrooms, weaken our relationship with our spouses, and mess up our sex life.

Hebrews 12:16 also mentions profanity. To be profane means to desecrate that which the Lord has called holy. Paul illustrates profanity by the story of Esau who sold his birthright to satisfy his stomach. His foolishness was the result of an unholy — profane — chain of events. The chain of events continued to the point that Esau could not find a place of repentance or forgiveness even though he sought it with tears. I hope you are getting the picture that this is a serious issue.

Matthew 18 teaches about another unholy progression of events that surrounds unforgiveness. This story needs to be put into historical context.

The Romans occupied Jerusalem and oppressed the Jews. This dilemma started a dialogue between two rabbis that led two opposing views of thought about forgiveness. One rabbi was a conservative, the other a liberal. They debated how many times a day forgiveness should be offered to someone. Rabbi Hillel taught that we should forgive once in twenty-four hours, and then we could knock the tar out of them. Rabbi Shammai taught that we must forgive seven times in one day.

Simon Peter came to Jesus with a question designed to make himself look holy. He asked, "how many times must I forgive, seven times...?" (Matthew 18:21).

Simon Peter meant to manipulate Jesus with this question. But Jesus had an unexpected response. He said, to forgive seventy times seven times. What? 70 x 7 = 490.

If you sleep eight hours each day, you're awake sixteen hours. How many minutes are in sixteen hours? Nine hundred sixty.

Jesus taught us to forgive 490 times in 24 hours. 960 divided by 490 is 1.95. This means that we are to forgive the same person for the same offense once every minute and 50 seconds of every day. The principle is that forgiveness needs to be an ingrained attitude, occurring naturally all of the time. Forgiveness should be as automatic as breathing — and just as important.

Jesus then tells the parable of the debtor to a rich man. The debtor owed the rich man about fifteen million dollars, but couldn't repay him. The debtor begged for forgiveness of the debt and received it. While the debtor was leaving the king's house, he saw someone that owed him about twelve dollars. That person couldn't pay, so the newly-forgiven debtor had him thrown into prison, and turned over to the tormentors, until he could pay the twelve dollars, a common practice of the day.

The king learned of the debtor's foul deed and called him back in. As a result of the debtor's spirit of unforgiveness, the king reinstated his debt, threw him prison, and turned him over to the tormentors until he could pay the unpayable fifteen million dollars.

This seems like a good story and we sympathize with the king's decision until verse 35 gives us the punch line. Matthew 18:35 says, "So likewise shall My heavenly Father do also unto you, if ye from your hearts forgive not every one his brother their trespasses."

What is Jesus saying? What is the result of unforgiveness? First, our debt will be reinstated. Our debt is the debt that Christ paid on the cross. We will not receive this forgiveness of our sin-debt.

Secondly, we will be turned over to the tormentors. This is serious. Who are the tormentors? Demons. Some people consider demons to be imaginary, but the Bible teaches that they are very real and they cause tremendous suffering. Bitterness brings torment in many mental, emotional and physical diseases.

Thirdly, we are held in bondage to the memories and pain through the bitterness. In bitterness we are constantly remembering what has happened to us and these memories control our lives.

The Kingdom of God is not a democracy. We don't get to vote on how the rules are written. The Bible declares that if we harbor bitterness, we will be tormented by demons. The only way to rid ourselves of demons is to rectify the legal right they have to torment us (Ephesians, 4:27). This requires us to forgive our debtors, that is, those who have sinned against us, including ourselves.

The lack of forgiveness in local church bodies is a major problem. Satan and his minions craftily use bitterness and unforgiveness to stifle the work of the church, thereby limiting the spread and effectiveness of the Gospel. Any indication of the effects of bitterness and unforgiveness is direct evidence of Satan's influence.

Ephesians 6:10-12 says, "Finally, my brethren, be strong in the Lord, and in the power of His might. Put on the whole armor of God, that ye may be able to stand against the wiles of the devil. For we wrestle not against flesh and blood, but against principalities, against powers, against the rulers of the darkness of this world, against spiritual wickedness in high places."

What is a "wile" or "scheme"? It is a craftily laid plan. What does it mean to "wrestle"? We are most familiar with phony professional wrestling or the carefully controlled amateur versions in high school or college competition. The Greek or Roman wrestling of Paul's era was very different from these two.

In first century wrestling, two naked men entered the arena knowing that only one would walk out. The victor was required to kill the loser and desecrate his dead body. He poked out the eyes, pulled out the tongue, broke the jaw, and then either cut or tore off the genitals, stuffing them in his opponent's mouth. He cut open the abdominal cavity, and pointed at the body, ridiculing it as a writhing, dying mass of insignificance. The real person, lying dead at his feet, was now totally humiliated.

When the Bible says that principalities and powers wrestle with us, it is the picture of this struggle to the death that should come to mind. And the wrestling match has been brought to us. We have no choice whether or not to participate.

Jesus warned us that Satan comes to steal and destroy. It fits his character.

Nothing bad that ever happened in your life was an accident. Its details were planned in the highest council of hell. We are in a military struggle between two kingdoms, God and Satan's. Everything bad that has ever happened to you was executed by one of Satan's demons, a highly trained military specialist. Those demons that attacked my friend who was raised in a satanic home had committed the same warfare against others in the past. They are skilled and experienced warriors.

The Bible says that the sins of the father are passed on to his children to the third and fourth generations (Exodus 20:5). In my friend's case, her parents had probably been abused as children. If we have been abused, we will probably abuse others unless we deal with the effects of abuse in our own lives. Have you come to understand that the devil does this kind of thing to us? These abusive parents reaped the harvest sown by Satan's demons, and germinated it once again in the lives of their own children.

We cannot forgive until we have learned to intelligently hate Satan. Don't miss this important truth. The Lord gave us the keys to His kingdom. They are found in His Word. Using these truths allows us to unlock the door to Satan's rancid kingdom, and throw him out.

HOW DO WE FORGIVE?

We start with the sure knowledge that every negative thing that ever happened to us was planned in hell. Our parents, spouse, children, boss, siblings, peers — whoever has inflicted pain in our lives — served as a tool of the devil. Understanding this moves us toward forgiveness. Understanding this allows us to feel compassion toward others and separate them from their sins. God the Father is the giver of every good and perfect gift... if it is not good and perfect, it is from the devil (James 1:17).

In Ephesians 2:2, the Bible describes the spirit that is at work in the sons of disobedience. This spirit teaches disobedience. Is it the Holy Spirit, or an unholy spirit?

Ephesians 2:2

"Wherein in time past ye walked according to the course of this world, according to the prince of the power of the air, the spirit that now worketh in the children of disobedience."

This is obviously Satan. We have a choice to allow the "prince of the power of the air" to work in us or to allow the Holy Spirit of God to work in us. Through the Holy Spirit we can have power and dominion over Satan and his works. The choice is ours.

Next, we must learn how to intelligently hate the real culprit, Satan. Intelligently directing our hatred toward Satan opens a pathway to freedom by allowing us to forgive others. Not many of us have really hated the devil. Instead, we have hated each other. Galatians 5:15 says, "But if ye bite and devour one another, take heed that ye be not consumed one of another."

To intelligently hate Satan requires a change in the Christian mindset. We have been taught that anger has no place in our lives. As a result, we suppress anger or, when it occurs, we become self-accusatory.

Jesus got angry but He focused anger at the right culprit. I John 3:8 says, "He that committeth sin is of the devil; for the devil sinneth from the beginning. For this purpose the Son of God was manifested, that he might destroy the works of the devil." Since Jesus came to destroy the works of the devil, is it fair to say that He was angry with him?

The first time the Bible mentions anger is in Genesis 3:15. "And I will put enmity between thee and the woman, and between thy seed and her seed; it shall bruise thy head, and thou shalt bruise his heel." God tells the serpent (Satan), "I will put enmity," the strongest word for anger and hatred, between Satan and the woman, and between her seed and his seed.

What is the source of anger? God is. The devil just misdirects it so that we become angry with each other, ourselves and God, not him. He deceives us in this.

Consider your life. If someone treated you like the devil, how welcome would they be in your presence today? Yet we lay out the welcome mat for the same damnable devils that continue to torment us. We get angry with our spouse who is accused by a spirit of bitterness, thus opening the door to our lives to the same spirit. Getting angry with another person finds us bowing down to the same demons that caused their problem. It is an unholy conspiracy.

Am I being clear enough? How do we forgive? We dig out that root of bitterness and get rid of it.

The abuse my friend sustained was abominable, deplorable and damnable. There is no defense for it. She wanted to get rid of its hold on her, but first had to learn to intelligently direct her anger at Satan, not her parents. She had to learn to separate her parents from their sin, just as Paul separated himself from his sin (Romans 7:17, 20).

My first job in helping you win your freedom is to successfully prosecute the devil, and in doing so, defend God. To do so, you need to understand the righteousness of directing anger at the devil. God will bless correctly directed anger.

Let me tell you a personal story about my relationship with my mother. In my perception, no matter what I did, it was never good enough. I felt that she constantly told me I should have done this or that. But Scripture tells me to honor my mother.

I knew I needed to forgive mom, but I didn't know how. My bitterness caused a disease called multiple chemical sensitivity, or environmental illness. It made me feel miserable. For my own good, I needed to rid myself of bitterness and that meant forgiving mom and others.

Finally, I determined to work hard at forgiving her. I canceled her debts: anything that I thought she owed me. These included both her sins of omission and commission. I openly and honestly examined the record of wrongs I kept against my mother since childhood, and forgave her for each item on the list.

In my unforgiveness I had really judged my mother. Scripture teaches that we will be judged in the same manner that we judge others. This is the same principle as forgiveness. In the Lord's Prayer we are told to ask God to forgive us in the same manner as we forgive others (Matthew 6). I judged my mother for being critical and so I became critical of others. God's law of reaping and sowing will always apply. I had to go before God and repent, and ask for His forgiveness for my sin of judging others and then for my own critical spirit. As I forgave my mother, I broke the judgment that I had placed against her.

When my father and stepfather both passed away within short weeks of each other, I was forced to go home and spend a lot of time with my mother. I did not look forward to this, but I quickly sensed that something had changed in mom. It was my act of forgiveness. How is this possible?

Matthew 18:18 says, "Verily I say unto you, Whatsoever ye shall bind on earth shall be bound in heaven: and whatsoever ye shall loose on earth shall be loosed in heaven." The context of this passage is forgiveness. We are to loose, or let go of, unforgiveness, resentment, retaliation, anger, hatred, violence and murder, the elements of bitterness. And bind to the situation God's law of forgiveness, grace and mercy. When I forgave her and cancelled my bitterroot judgment, it released in the heavens God's principles of forgiveness, grace and mercy — instead of Satan's principles of bitterness.

When I forgave my mother, I played a part in winning her spiritual freedom. My act of faith allowed a release of forgiveness, love and understanding into our relationship. When we forgive others, the chains fall from them and us. Walls are removed. We both win.

Do you have debts to cancel? Is the Holy Spirit bringing anybody to mind right now? Do you have any buried roots? Let the Holy Spirit search you. Can you give God your pain and grief? Will you give them to God?

Would you like me to show you how to do it?

Think of the person that has hurt you the most during your life: an unfaithful husband, a rapist, a sexual abuser, or maybe a parent that rejected you or always put you down. Ask the Holy Spirit to bring to mind the one that hurt you the most.

With that person held in your mind's eye, pray this prayer:

> *In the name of Jesus, and as an act of my free will,*
> *I purpose and choose to forgive (the person) from my*
> *heart for (what they did).*
>
> *In the name of the Lord Jesus, I cancel all (the person's)*
> *debts or obligations to me. Lord Jesus, forgive me for my*
> *bitterness towards (the person).*
>
> *In the name of Jesus, I break and cancel Satan's power*
> *over me in this memory, and the resulting pain. I hate*
> *the devil.*
>
> *In the name of Jesus, I command that all the tormentors*
> *that have been assigned to me because of my unforgive-*
> *ness to leave me now. In the name of Jesus, I command*
> *the bitterness to go.*
>
> *Holy Spirit to come into my heart, and heal me of this*
> *pain and this hurt. Holy Spirit, please tell me your truth*
> *in this situation.*

(Pause quietly and allow the Holy Spirit to speak to your heart. Listen carefully for what He has to say.)

God is faithful to do His part and forgive, if we do our part. Our part includes forgiving every single person for everything they have done. It also includes repenting and forgiving ourselves for everything that we have done. The Holy Spirit will complete the work of forgiveness in your heart. The sin of unforgiveness will no longer stand between you and God, or between you and others. God will declare you righteous and blameless. You will become a vessel of honor and an overcomer if you will obey. You will regain your right standing as an heir of God with all the blessings it carries. The peace that passes all understanding will fill you.

Satan and his tormentors have no legal right in us when we confess our sins and forgive others and ourselves (Ephesians. 4:27). We are free. John 8:36 says, "If the Son therefore shall make you free, ye shall be free indeed." Praise God!

CHAPTER EIGHT

Principality of Jealousy & Envy

DEFINITION

There are two types of jealousy and envy. One is the righteous jealousy that God has for each of His sons and daughters, and the other is Satan's counterfeit.

The dictionary defines "jealousy" as "full of envy, grudging, resentful, or suspicious"; "envy" as "discontent or ill will at another's good fortune because one wishes it had been his." In both the Greek and Hebrew languages as used in Scripture, the words for jealousy and envy are interchangeable. In addition, they describe covetousness.

Hebrews 13:5 says, "Let your conversation be without covetousness." Conversation here goes beyond mere talk. Rather, it includes a wide range of personal interaction, describing the manner and conduct of those interactions. So, Hebrews is teaching that as we interact with others, our motive should never include coveting their goods or position. Someone whose conversation is always targeted at gaining an advantage over another has a problem with covetousness.

Covetousness results in an intense desire to own another's status or possessions. We envy our friend's fine wardrobe or position at the office. We may also covet his wife.

We may covet Cousin Kate's healthy, well-tuned and tanned body, while looking at our own as flabby and wrinkled. We may be jealous of Kate because she has better health than we do.

Satan adds lust to jealousy and envy. Here lust refers to an intense, unrestrained desire to acquire in order to "keep up with the Joneses," or to satisfy some emotional or physical void. It adds strong emotional energy to our thirst for self-satisfaction. As a factor of jealousy and envy, lust schemes to take something beautiful — for instance, someone else's spouse or child — and use it to satisfy a selfish pleasure. The assumption is that by so stealing away another's beautiful possession, we will gain their status or pleasure.

ENTRY ROUTES

There are two major routes jealousy and envy use to enter our lives. One is through comparison and the other is through competition with others. Either route results in bitterness at another or ourselves.

Competition drives us to say, "I don't care if Jodie has a new diamond ring. I'm worth at least as much as she is, so I think you should get me that diamond earring and necklace set. That'll make Jodie take notice." Competition does not care that the other person has something we just want more. This usually results in anger and bitterness directed at another. We become angry at others because they have something that we don't.

Comparison takes a different approach to jealousy and envy. Comparison says, "Oh that Jodie thinks she's really something with her fancy clothes and all. Now she's got this big ring. I can't stand her haughty attitude." Or we might compare our figure, intelligence, speaking abilities or other talents with others. Comparison results in bitterness toward ourselves. In comparing to others we degrade or belittle ourselves. We become angry at our selves because we do not measure up to others in some way.

As we study jealousy and envy, I don't plan on dissecting the difference between how competition and comparison express themselves. It may not even be possible to do so. But it is important to recognize how Satan attacks us.

Satan's kingdom applies the strategy of networking. Jealousy and envy are tied to bitterness. Until we defeat bitterness, we cannot begin to deal with jealousy and envy. We cannot successfully deal with rejection until we have dealt with bitterness and jealousy and envy. All of these sins support one another, tying themselves together in a bundle of evil. Don't lose hope, though, He that is in us is greater than Satan!

Jealousy and envy cause us to take our eyes off God and focus them on others. Instead of gaining value and fulfillment internally, from above, we attempt to do so externally, from around us.

Jealousy and envy employ hatred. "Yes, Axel's Lexus is beautiful. I appreciate that he's made millions in the stock market. He's got a lot of nice stuff. But I hate him because he got all the breaks and all I got is five kids in braces."

What makes jealousy so insidious is that we really love and want for ourselves what we hate in the other person. It's not that we don't like what they have, it's that we don't have it for ourselves. No matter how much jealous and envious people obtain, they are never satisfied. They will never have peace, because they always compare themselves with someone else.

We will only lose the comparison or competition game. There always will be someone that has more, or can do more. We must realize and accept our position in Christ. He does not compare us to others, so why do we?

Satan uses jealousy and envy to destroy our self-security and self-acceptance. We fail to see what God is doing in our lives because we are focusing elsewhere. Jealousy and envy seek to prevent us from becoming what Jesus Christ created us to be. They convince us that God doesn't provide what we really need. They say, "If God really cared, He'd see that we need a bigger house, like the Olsons.' "

The ultimate result of jealousy and envy is murder. If not controlled and eliminated, eventually jealousy and envy push us to get rid of someone from our lives. Almost none of us resorts to physical murder, of course. Instead we become verbally abusive, driving someone away, or we purpose to avoid someone, thereby "murdering" our relationship with them. So incensed do we become, that we find ways to sever our relationship with another person.

The root of most wars between nations is jealousy and envy. Why do many nations of the world hate America? Because we have great material wealth as a result of God's blessing.

Why do so many groups and individuals hate Jews? It is because they tend to be very successful people. Do you know why? Because of the covenant God made with Abraham and the giving of His law, Jewish people have a culture that drives them to be successful. If we apply His precepts, His blessing will follow. The rain falls on the just and the unjust.

In nations dominated by a Christian culture, material comforts and political liberties tend to be more abundant. This is a result of God's New Covenant with believers sealed by the blood of Jesus Christ.

Jealousy and envy are like the flames of hell that constantly torment sinners: they are never satisfied. Hebrews 13:5 says, "Let your conversation be without covetousnes." And, "be content with such things as you have. For He has said, I will never leave you nor forsake you."

This Hebrews verse is taken from an Old Testament passage. Joshua 1:5 says, "There shall not any man be able to stand before thee all the days of thy life; and I was with Moses, so I will be with thee. I will not fail thee nor forsake thee." In Hebrews 13:5-6 we read, "...for He hath said, I will never leave thee, nor forsake thee. So that we may boldly say, The Lord is my helper, and I will not fear what man shall do unto me."

Jealousy and envy steal our peace and contentment. They prevent us from being Godly. Without Godliness, we are like an unpainted, non-galvanized, metal pail. Over time, rust eats it away and creates holes. Everything we try to carry falls out and eventually the whole bucket collapses under its own weight. All the time, the rust quietly saps the bucket's strength.

Jealousy and envy steal our self-esteem, accusing us every day. We lack peace with God, and the peace of God, rendering us unable to get along with anyone, including ourselves. Instead of measuring our level of Godliness against the Bible, we measure our level of goods against the Bensons' — and the Bensons always have better than we do.

The first blessing God wants to give us is peace of mind and heart.

Have you ever felt fearful of another person or intimidated by them? Hebrews 13:6 says, "...so that we may boldly say the Lord is my helper and I will not fear what man shall do unto me." We fear rejection by the other person, or fear what they can do to us. Why? God says not to fear what man can do to us.

Too often we try to emulate people we fear, thinking that if we can only have what they have, or be like them, we will have peace. We always lose this game of comparison. There is always someone who has more or is better looking.

The bitterness that jealousy and envy fuel in us against others — and ourselves — ultimately leads to distrust and unbelief in God's provision. This will eventually lead to bitterness against God. As we sense a root of bitterness in our lives, we need to remember we were the ones who allowed it to be planted, not God. We chose to compare ourselves to others or judge a person's value based on their looks or appearance of success. God never participates in this game of comparison (Acts 10:34).

We say, "If I could just look like Mike, if I were just like him, then he'd accept me." God says, "I like the way you look. I made you that way and, even better than that, I can make you look more like Me. You want to be like Mike, or like Me? You choose."

Colossians 3:5 says, "Mortify therefore your members, which are upon the earth: fornication, uncleanness, inordinate affection, evil, concupiscence, covetousness, which is idolatry." To covet is to idolize. God says to put no other Gods ahead of Him. Idolatry is rooted in jealousy and envy, both of which are Satan's spirits.

Idolatry, with its link to covetousness, can be defined as looking at others, and lusting after them or their possessions. Lust links to bitterness.

Idolatry is the act of giving anything a higher priority in our life than God. If we value others' opinions more than God's, we are idolatrous. If we covet someone else's possessions instead of being satisfied with God's provision, we are idolatrous.

God is greater than everything else, individually or collectively. I John 3:20 says, "If our heart condemns us, God is greater than our heart and He knoweth all things." If we are fighting bitterness, self-bitterness, envy, jealousy, rejection, uncleanness and unloveliness, God is greater than all these. God is greater than any demon influence. God knows His plan for us, and He will lead us through it. Satan doesn't know God's specific plan for us, but he knows he hates God and will use jealousy and envy to divert our direction.

When Jesus began His public ministry, as recorded in Mark 1:14-15, He preached the Gospel in Galilee. He said the time is fulfilled and the kingdom is at hand. Repent and believe the gospel. Many people hear the Gospel preached, but fail to believe it or act on it.

James 1:22 says, Don't be a hearer of the Word only, but also be a doer. Those who hear without doing ought to just go fishing. It's as close to heaven as they will ever get. Does this seem like a hard statement? It's the truth. Believing the gospel is the issue and real belief is followed by real action. Action is driven by the tutoring of the Holy Spirit and God's Word. Belief is more than head-knowledge. Even the demons believe, and they tremble, but they do not obey God (James 2:19). Belief alone does not provide justification (salvation). Romans 2:13 says, "For not the hearers of the law are just before God, but the doers of the law shall be justified." James teaches us that faith without works is dead, being alone (James 2:17-18, 20, 26).

Jealousy and envy are rooted in a shallow and ineffective belief in the Gospel. The mature believer knows that all his needs are met in Christ, and has no room for jealousy and envy. He knows God loves him and will care for him. If we are still jealous or envious, we have fallen out of agreement with God, failing to accept that we are special to Him, and that He is able to satisfy all the needs of our life.

Bitterness, self-bitterness, jealousy and envy, rejection and fear are all networked. If we fail to successfully defeat them in spiritual warfare, we run the risk that they will become so entrenched that we will assume their nature. It is a sad situation when we know that God created us, yet we call ourselves bitterness.

For some of us, the root of bitterness has grown into a fruit-bearing vine. Our only escape is through the power of God, and He uses ministries such as ours to help bring deliverance.

The fruit of the vine of bitterness includes retaliation, cruelty, fury, malice, rage, sadism, screaming, spitefulness, treachery, control, bossiness, dominance, impatience, agitation, criticism, covetousness, greed, craving, curiosity, discontent, material lust, stealing, bitterness, anger, antagonism, contempt, contention, enmity, fighting, hatred, hatred of authority, hostility, irritation, murder, resentment, self-hatred, temper, unforgiveness, violence, wrath, strife, annoying, bickering, contention, discord, quarreling, sarcasm, and slander. All of these demons network with jealousy, envy and covetousness. They move together as worms in a bait bucket, feeding off each other.

Proverbs 6:34-35b says, "For jealousy is the rage of a man. Therefore, he will not spare in the day of vengeance. He will not regard any ransom. . . ." Jealous people aren't interested in reconciliation. Maybe you have been on the receiving end of such a relationship. You approach someone, pouring your heart out before them, but they have a jealous spirit. Instead of ransoming their jealousy, they ravage you. Instead of reconciliation, they seek advantage or even revenge.

Proverbs 9:8 says, "Reprove not a scorner, lest he hate thee: rebuke a wise man, and he will love thee." Have you ever had the pleasant experience of reproving a wise man? It seems almost contradictory, but even wise men make mistakes. Yet, when a mature believer (or even a novice) confronts the wise spirit-filled man, he receives back a smile, or a frown of real concern and repentance. He is offered a Christian hug. And when he is wrongfully reproved, he still seeks non-judgmental reconciliation.

The scorner, though, retaliates when reproved. His retort is filled with jealousy, envy and bitterness. He cannot accept reason. Each time you buffer your comments with kindness, he has an evil retort. When you're done with him, he tries to get even with you. It's not enough for him to win. He wants you to pay for what you did.

The reproved scorner will then slander you to every person who will listen. He will try to recruit others to his team. Others who likewise have a spirit of covetousness, jealousy and envy, and bitterness, identify with the scorner, and the reproof now becomes a divisive spiritual military attack. All that's left is to satisfy the vultures that hover above, waiting to swallow up the pieces.

Two pastors on the staff of the same church fell into conflict. The teaching pastor believed his job included only the tasks as specifically outlined on his job description, and when pushed by church members to launch something new, he responded angrily. The music and worship pastor believed he ought to go beyond his job description and do whatever the Spirit laid on his heart. He resented the lazy schedule of the teaching pastor and allowed a spirit of bitterness to take root. The senior pastor refused to resolve the conflict. Finally, the music pastor resigned. His followers attacked the teaching pastor who rallied his own troops. The church nearly split.

Months later, one of the men who tried to bring public reconciliation between the pastors, elders and members, was asked to teach. The elder who chose him appreciated his spirit of meekness and the wisdom with which he handled the teaching pastor's personal attacks against him. Weeks later, the teaching pastor pressured the elder to fire the man as a teacher, suggesting he deserved the punishment of Galatians 5:12. It talks of cutting such a person out of the fellowship, comparing it to a castration.

Two years later, after the member tried to win reconciliation with the teaching pastor, the teaching pastor resigned. The two years had been tough on him as he fought the spirit of bitterness that had been watered and nurtured by jealousy and envy. Satan nearly won a major victory in a fast-growing, Bible-believing and alive church.

You can see in this true example how jealousy and envy can lead a viscous attack when given a battlement within the body of believers.

Proverbs 27:3-4 says, "A stone is heavy, the sand is weighty, but a fool's wrath is heavier than them both. Wrath is cruel, anger is outrageous, but who is able to stand before envy?" Who is able to stand before envy? Proverbs 27:5-6 continues, "Open rebuke is better than secret love. Faithful are the wounds of a friend; but the kisses of an enemy are deceitful."

Song of Solomon 8:6 says, "Set me as a seal upon thine heart, as a seal upon thy arm, for love is strong as death, and jealousy is cruel as the grave. The coals thereof are coals of fire, which hath a most vehement flame." Wow, what a statement! "Love is strong as death, jealousy is cruel as the grave, the coals thereof are coals of fire, which hath a most vehement flame." Jealousy is a burning, demonic reality.

A person who has a spirit of jealousy is very dangerous. They are not content until everyone around them is destroyed, so they can stand there in victory. But jealous people never get the very thing they want. Jealousy is an unquenchable thirst. Because they can't have it, they seek to make certain that others will never have it either.

A man may be so jealous of his wife that she can hardly breathe without arousing his jealousy. She can't even talk innocently with another man, or look at him. Sometimes this type of jealousy and envy even results in abusive stalking. Occasionally, jealousy and envy rage so strongly they lead to murder.

Such a scenario shows that the love that might have existed in the beginning either was not really love, or became infected with a root of bitterness. Sometimes, love is not love at all, but a lustful fantasy. Impure love builds on a set of false expectations and it's not scriptural love. Jealousy and envy says, "If I can't have you, no one else will. I will kill you, and them too, if I have to." The media reports just such outcomes every day.

Infidelity can arise out of a spirit of jealousy. "My wife looks like an old sea dog. She doesn't care about satisfying me, anyway. Now you, you got all the looks and charm that a good-lookin' guy like me deserves."

Though both men and women can be adulterers, the breach caused by a woman's infidelity is more serious than the man's is. This is not to diminish his sin. Rather, it's because a man's blessing or cursing of his wife is of a special concern to God.

In God's order of things, He chose to give more permanent power to a man's curse or blessing than that of a woman. A woman can create a situation that the devil will use. But when the man in authority makes a declaration or a statement of intent, it has a greater potential for demonic abuse than the woman's statement. When the woman screams, "I hate you! I want to see you dead," it is serious. When the man screams out the same words, it stirs Satan's stewpot of demonic activity and evil intent often leads to evil actions. This is another one of the added responsibilities God assigned to men.

We see about ninety percent women in our ministry. Men tend to let emotional things roll off, and don't dwell on them to the same extent a women does. A man may vent his anger loudly and aggressively, but within minutes he's done with it. A woman tends to live in an angry stew for days. God created women to be responders to their husbands. Men who fail to unselfishly love their wives, who lash out and curse at them, bring devastation into their hearts.

Another reason we minister to more women than men is that women are much more willing to come humbly before God and deal with the issues in their lives than are men. Men usually have too much pride and arrogance to admit they even have a problem.

It is important to understand that God considers all sins equal. Even the smallest sin separates us from our perfect God. Adultery is no greater a sin than creating strife. In Jesus, all sin is forgiven, save one: the unpardonable sin. Matthew 12:31 says, "Wherefore I say unto you, All manner of sin and blasphemy shall be forgiven unto men: but the blasphemy against the Holy Spirit shall not be forgiven unto men."

In civil and criminal law, if we break one law we are called a lawbreaker, no matter the seriousness of our crime. But human law metes out differing punishments for different crimes based on how grave they are. The Bible teaches that if we are guilty of breaking one law, we are a lawbreaker, and as guilty as if we broke them all. This is because the penalty for breaking even one of God's laws is the same: eternal damnation.

Satan deceives us about this. Many adulterers are so filled with guilt that they have made adultery the greatest of all sins. Unable to rid themselves of guilt, Satan accuses them even more, and they abandon the hope of ever finding forgiveness for any sins. We need to understand that this is not scripturally true. Every sin has the same eternal consequence, though the consequences on earth can be quite different (a liar will not acquire a sexual disease by lying). Every sin opens the door for Satan to find a place in us, to produce disease in our body, and conflict in our soul.

Terminated male and female relationships, whether they ended in divorce or just a break up, produce flash points that ignite jealousy and envy. The spiritual dynamics are incredible. The Bible says that when a man has had sexual relations with a harlot, he becomes one with her.

I Corinthians 6:16 says, "What? know ye not that he which is joined to a harlot is one body? for two, saith he, shall be one flesh." This is called a "soul tie."

When the relationship is ungodly, it results in the transference of unclean spirits to both of the partners. Matthew 5:28 says, "But I say unto you, That whosoever looketh on a woman to lust after her hath committed adultery with her already in his heart." The soul tie is formed in any sexual relationship. We have also learned that they can be formed with emotional attachments to old boy or girl friends. If we find ourselves comparing our spouse to another person, there is a soul tie that we must repent for and break.

Genesis teaches that a man should leave his mother and father and cling to his wife. They become one flesh. When he lies with another woman, or she with another man, they tear apart their own flesh and throw wide open the door for the spirit of jealousy and envy to accuse them. They set themselves up for spiritual and physical disease.

Restoration of a marriage or of a healthy sexual life will only result when the spirit of jealousy and envy has been swept out of our minds. These are very strong forces that work insidiously.

Numbers 5:14 says, "And the spirit of jealousy come upon him, and he be jealous of his wife, and she be defiled: or if the spirit of jealousy come upon him, and he be jealous of his wife, and she be not defiled."

When a wife is caught in adultery, a spirit of jealousy often rules the husband. If there is a child born out of the illicit sexual relationship, the spirit of jealousy often transfers to the innocent child. Satan uses the father's spirit of jealousy and envy as grounds to attach himself to the wife and children.

The spirit of jealousy and envy is common between two or more females competing for male approval. The competition arises out of a sense of insecurity. Daughters compete with each other for dad's approval, or even with mother, jealous of the way he treats her as compared to them. Women competing to win the same suitor run the risk of developing deep-seated jealousies and bitter envying. This kind of jealousy often follows rejection by a father, husband or lover. Because of the rejection, the woman feels terribly insecure.

No foundation for trust exists in marriages or relationships dominated by jealousy. To resolve these conflicts and restore a loving relationship, we need time with the Lord to get our heart right concerning ourselves. We need to deal with our past as well as the present situation, and, if we need to forgive or be forgiven, it must take a high priority in our lives. Sometimes going back to an ex-husband or ex-boyfriend to seek forgiveness isn't possible. It may even be dangerous. Still, you do need to take personal responsibility for allowing the spirit of jealousy into your life, and for feeding it.

If we were an innocent victim in a sorry situation, we may not need to be forgiven. In these cases people usually internalize the situation and blame themselves for the sin of others. If we have believed this lie of the devil, we need to repent for believing the lie and forgive those that have hurt us.

Still, we can be plagued with temptation that comes because of the actions of our mother, grandmother, or someone else in our family tree. The spirit of jealousy may have been working in our family tree for generations. If tormenting thoughts plague us with temptations even though our own behavior has been clean, we may have inherited them. We may need to deal with several generations before winning this battle.

It is extremely important to identify and break generational curses to deliver our children from their consequences. Romans 6:23 says, "the wages of sin is death." This principle remains unchanged. Through Christ Jesus you will receive the power to break the bonds of the spirit of jealousy, and bring life to your family. Spiritual cleansing such as this greatly pleases God as evidenced in numerous Old Testament stories. There we read of entire families being blessed for the repentance of one member, or entire families being killed because of the sin of one member. Choose life for your family.

Proverbs 26:2 says, "As the bird by wandering, as the swallow by flying, so the curse causeless shall not come." If there's any evidence of an intergenerational curse in our life, today is the day to come before the Lord and break its hold. God will honor the integrity of our heart. Approach Him boldly with sincerity, plead for the power of Christ, and break those bonds in pieces!

GOD'S TRUTH

Let's change gears and look at jealousy from a different angle. In many Bible passages, God says that He is jealous, or that He is a jealous God (see Exodus 20:5, 34:14, Deuteronomy 4:24, 5:9, 6:15, Nahum 1:2). How can God be jealous?

Let's once again examine the definition of jealousy. There is another definition of "jealousy" in Greek, Hebrew and English that means "zeal" or "to be zealous." God is jealous, or zealous, and the focus of his jealousy is you. This is the positive side of jealousy. It is not possible for God to possess an evil spirit of jealousy and envy.

Deuteronomy 29:19-20 describes a common condition of man's disobedience. Verse 19 says, "It should come to pass when he heareth the words of this curse and he bless himself in his heart saying I shall have peace, though I walk in the imaginations of my heart."

In other words, "I've heard the word of God, I understand that taking this action could leave me open to the curse (evil consequence) but, I'm going to have peace no matter what my heart tells me, so just leave me alone, God!" This man has decided that he's going to disobey God by doing things his own way. He's even determined to define peace for himself, though doing this results in a curse from God as a result of the sin that will surely follow.

Verse 20 says, "the Lord will not spare him, but then the anger of the Lord and His jealousy shall smoke against that man and all the curses that are written in this book shall lie upon him, and the Lord shall blot out his name from under heaven." It's very serious when we hear the truth and decide we can ignore it. This behavior causes the Lord to come against us. We're saying to Him, "I'm going to have my own peace and my blessings. The devil's going to bless me. Lord, I don't need You, and I don't need Your opinion. I don't need the discernment. I'm going to do what I want to do."

In such a case, the Lord is jealous for us. He desires a relationship with us and doesn't want to share us with Satan. But because we have made up our minds to live our own way, He releases us to the consequences of our own devices (Proverbs 1:31). This is a tough Scripture, yet still true.

I Kings 14:22 says, "And Judah did evil in the sight of the LORD, and they provoked Him to jealousy with their sins which they had committed, above all that their fathers had done." God's jealousy is not from an evil spirit. It's God's zeal for us, and an expression of His love for His children. If you are a parent, you know what it means to be jealous over your children. This type of jealousy is an expression of God's desire to protect and care for us, to desire the very best in our lives. Picture a mother hen sheltering her little chicks under her wings, protecting them from the hawk that stalks them from above. It's the zeal of protection.

When God speaks to us through His Word or by His Spirit, it is a grave danger to refuse His counsel. Not only does it tell Him that we don't need Him, it removes us from His protection against Satan's wiles. God gives us over to our own devices (Proverbs 1:24-31), leaving us to battle Satan alone. None of us is that strong.

What does all this mean? For this "I did it *my* way" person, it means that Satan has become their "word." Satan has become their zeal and he is jealous over them. Satan's jealousy is destructive, and his ultimate goal is to see them destroyed.

God cannot have an intimate relationship with us if we choose to be a spiritual harlot, making Satan our spiritual pimp. Look at Ezekiel 8:3. It speaks of something called the "image of jealousy." Here it was a heathen God named Tammuz.

This Scripture teaches about yet another dimension of jealousy from which we need deliverance. This judgment comes from spiritual fornication. Without being delivered from spiritual fornication, we can never win freedom from the occult. This deliverance is vital to life, and comes only after repenting, seeking God's forgiveness and becoming His spiritual "wife" forever. God will never share us with false gods or mythological entities. He'll never share us with the devil, a cult or divination. He is jealous for us, and desires purity in His intimate relationship with us. His is a call to sanctification.

Ezekiel 8:1-3 says, "and it came to pass in the sixth year, the sixth month, and the fifth day of the month as I sat in my house and the elders of Judah sat before me, but the hand of the Lord God fell there upon me. And I beheld and lo a likeness as the appearance of fire and the appearance of his loins even downward, fire; and from his loins even upward as the appearance of brightness as the color of amber. And he put forth in the form of a hand and took me by a lock of my head and the spirit lifted me up high between the earth and the heaven and brought me in the visions of God to Jerusalem to the door of the inner gate that looketh toward the north where was the seat of the image of jealousy, which proveketh to jealousy."

This Scripture has nothing to do with the jealousy of man in matters of love or a man's jealous rage. It speaks of God's zeal for His people. God will never commit spiritual adultery, and He wants total fidelity in us as well. Tammuz was the "image of jealousy," and a symbol of idolatry, or giving one's affections to another god-spiritual adultery.

Ezekiel 8 tells a story about the Old Testament church, the Jews. They came to God's temple but gave their reverential affection to a different spiritual husband than God. Yet the Scriptures teach that the Lord is our spiritual husband forever. Isaiah 54:5 says, "For thy Maker is thine husband; the Lord of hosts is His name; and thy Redeemer the Holy One of Israel; The God of the whole earth shall He be called."

Despite our earthly gender or marital status, we are betrothed to the Lord Jesus as our spiritual husband. This is not in a carnal sense, but a spiritual sense. We are His bride and He is as the One to whom we look, our spiritual leader, the One whom we choose to follow above all others. Jesus provides the perfect pattern for a husband; there is no better example. He laid down His life for us.

Ezekiel presents a picture of the Lord looking down on His betrothed wife and spotting the image of jealousy in the door to her temple. (By the way, in Jewish custom two people who are betrothed must practice the same literal requirements as those who are married.) This is a type of spiritual harlotry.

One of our greatest concerns as Christians is not to be deceived by error. We cannot afford to follow a lie or anything that doesn't match God's Word; that would be spiritual harlotry. We must not serve any other gods. Yet false gods are very insidious and crafty. They seek entry to our lives in ways that we cannot even imagine and, the next thing we know, we're having fellowship with them. To protect against this, we must diligently study Scripture, know our enemy, and practice Godly discernment.

Ezekiel 8 is about the physical image of jealousy which "proveketh to jealousy." It was an idol of a pagan mythological god. God wasn't much concerned with Tammuz until His own "wife" (His people) began worshiping her. His people had "taken a different husband."

About our own spiritual harlotry, we need to confess, "Yes, Lord, I have done things in my life that showed me to be unfaithful to you spiritually. I have followed this, and I may have followed that, I may have gone here, and I have gone there. I was unfaithful to you, and I whored around on You, Almighty God. I am a harlot."

We must make peace with God about this, and take responsibility for our spiritual whoredom. This might include repenting of occultism, false religion, spiritual error, and worshiping gods, devils, and demons. We must confess both our own life and our ancestral line to break any generational strongholds of Satan. We must repent of any pagan activities with which our parents may have been involved, or false philosophies that have the effect of separating us from the love of God.

I know what I've been saved from, and I know what I've been saved to. I'm not going back! I understand that there is a hell to shun and a heaven to gain!

God desires fellowship with us far more than we desire fellowship with Him. We were created for His pleasure. He came to the Garden of Eden, and walked in the cool of the evening with Adam and Eve every day. And He wants to be our Best Friend. Jesus said, I no longer call you servants, but I call you friends (John 15:15).

Before we can have a close relationship with another person we must become friends. A marriage doesn't work unless we become friends. Jesus wants each of us as His friend. Friendship creates a foundation upon which He builds an eternal marriage.

The Bible is filled with information that brings God's desire for intimacy down to a level where we can understand it. We must understand and cling to the depth of the relationship, the depth of the commitment, the depth of the covenant, and the depth of the fellowship we have with Him so that nothing can ever separate us from God's love. Romans 8:39 reminds us of this. But if we are not diligent, we can allow ourselves to become separated from Him. Then the image of jealousy will bar the door of our temple and we will lose intimacy with God.

Have you made peace with God, the Lover of your soul? Have you asked Him to help you dispose of jealousy? He loves you with an everlasting love, and will not share you with another.

The spirit of jealousy seeks to destroy you forever, but God's jealousy, even after we have run off and committed spiritual adultery for a time, comes to woo us back to Him. Through the Holy Spirit's prodding, He seeks to receive our repentance and grant us full forgiveness and a reaffirmation of the marital vows. God delights in restoring us to a place of intimate fellowship with Him.

We will reap what we sow. If we sow jealousy and envy, we reap their rewards. If we sow hatred or bitterness, what will we reap? (See Job 4:8.)

That is the bottom line. Ezekiel 35:11 says, "I will do to you according to your anger, I will do to you according to your envy, and I will do to you according to your bitterness and your hatred." If we sow hell's garbage then we have no right to cry because we reap the bitter fruit of our immoral labor.

We need to have balance in our lives. Before God will hear our plea, He has set certain conditions we must meet. For example, if we have a disease and cry out to God for healing, but at the same time we want to ignore our problem with spiritual harlotry, God will not heal us.

If we cry out to God because of some major financial loss, but steadfastly refuse to share our resources with His work, He will not hear us. If our adult child is afflicted by drugs, illicit sex and alcohol, and we plea with God to heal him, but sit in front of X-rated movies drinking a few scotch and sodas every night, He won't hear our prayer.

On the other hand, if we cry out to God in humility as a response to the Holy Spirit's conviction, and we honestly seek the root cause of our devastation, if we repent and give up idolatry and harlotry, He will be faithful to deliver us. II Kings 17:39 says, "But the Lord your God ye shall fear; and he shall deliver you out of the hand of all your enemies."

Our ministry centers on teaching the truth about repentance and the restoration of a right relationship with God. We teach the process of sanctification as the antidote to spiritual and physical disease.

II Timothy 2:24-25 says, "And the servant of the Lord must not strive; but be gentle unto all men, apt to teach, patient. In meekness instructing those that oppose themselves; if God peradventure will give them repentance to the acknowledging of the truth . . ." What is our motivation to do this? Verse 26 gives us the answer. ". . . that they may recover themselves out of the snare of the devil, who are taken captive by him at his will."

God wants to heal, save and deliver us, but He cannot if we continue to rebel against Him. He wants to set us free. John 8:36 says, "If the Son therefore shall make you free, ye shall be free indeed."

Do you know why God wants to set us free? Because then we can teach others how to have the same freedom that we have found in Jesus Christ. In Psalms 51:13, David says, "Then will I teach transgressors thy ways; and sinners shall be converted unto

Thee." However, before he made this pledge, he prayed, "Create in me a clean heart, O God; and renew a right spirit within me. Cast me not away from thy presence; and take not thy Holy Spirit from me. Restore unto me the joy of thy salvation; and uphold me with thy free spirit" (Psalms 51:10-12).

David dealt with his own life before he attempted to help others. We need to clean out our spiritual house to such a degree that we will have the freedom and power to effectively minister to others. Jesus is more than sufficient to act as our cleansing agent.

Many churches today preach a gospel that ignores personal responsibility or accountability. They attempt to deliver the sweet message of God's salvation without teaching the need for repentance. They teach the blessings of being freed from Satan's curse, but fail to teach that with freedom comes the responsibility to walk away from Satan and toward God. "If, then, and but," are very important words to pay attention to in Scripture. Blessings from God are always conditioned on our obedience.

Some teach that obedience is legalism. I disagree. To not teach obedience is to teach rebellion and witchcraft. Not to teach obedience is to teach stubbornness and idolatry. I Samuel 15:22-23 says, "And Samuel said, Hath the Lord as great delight in burnt offerings and sacrifices, as in obeying the voice of the Lord? Behold, to obey is better than sacrifice, and to hearken than the fat of rams. For rebellion is as the sin of witchcraft, and stubbornness is as iniquity and idolatry. Because thou hast rejected the word of the Lord, He hath also rejected thee from being king."

Samuel said obedience is better than sacrifice. Some preachers say instead, that if we sing loud enough, long enough, and raise our hands high enough, God will accept our praise and heal our diseases. They say, "Just come down here and let me touch your forehead. God's power will heal you." They might as well add, "You can kiss your old wife goodbye. You can steal your neighbor's wife," because they present grace without obedience. Maybe they see momentary healing from an adrenaline rush, but never permanent healing from the rush of the filling of the Holy Spirit.

What is the source of murder? "Full of murder, debate, deceit, malignity, whisperers, backbiters, haters of God, despiteful, proud, boasters, inventors of evil things, disobedient to parents, without understanding, covenant breakers, without natural affection, implacable, unmerciful" (Romans 1:29-31). Have we ever seen any of these natures manifested in people we know or in ourselves? They need to go.

Christ came to win the eternal victory over sin and leave behind His Spirit. This makes it possible, despite the presence and power of Satan, for us to have a right spirit and to have spiritual understanding and discernment, to have victory over sin. I Corinthians 15:57-58 reassures us, "But thanks be to God, which giveth us the victory through our Lord Jesus Christ. Therefore, my beloved brethren, be ye steadfast, unmovable, always abounding in the work of the Lord, forasmuch as ye know that your labour is not in vain in the Lord."

There's an evil spirit that brings with it jealousy and envy, covetousness and contempt. It's a spirit of rebellion.

Ezekiel 44:23 says, "...teach My people the difference between the holy and profane, and cause them to discern between the unclean and the clean." Hebrews 5:14 says, "...even those who by reason of use have their senses exercised to discern both good and evil."

Contempt for our Christian brothers and sisters has no place in our lives. Isaiah 64:6 says, "But we are all as an unclean thing, and all our righteousness are as filthy rags..."

We are redeemed solely by the grace of God. Ephesians 2:8 says, "For by grace are ye saved through faith; and that not of yourselves: it is the gift of God."

I Corinthians 1:9 says it another way. "God is faithful, by Whom ye were called unto the fellowship of His Son Jesus Christ our Lord."

In John, Jesus taught that if the people refused to receive Him, they also refused to receive God. John 5:43 says, "I am come in my Father's name, and ye receive me not: if another shall come in his own name, him ye will receive."

There is a deceiver and his name is Satan. He presents himself as a false Christ. The word "Christ" means "the anointed one" or "anointing." In the last days (today) there will be many false Christs or those with false anointing. A spirit of anti-Christ goes out from him, claiming to have come in Jesus' name, and he deceives many Christians. It is because of this spirit of anti-Christ and his deceptions that we need discernment.

Paul puts it this way in I Timothy 6:4: "He is proud, knowing nothing, but doting about questions and strifes of words, whereof cometh envy, strife, railings, evil surmisings." What does "doting about questions and strifes of words" mean? It describes those believers who argue divisively over the most minute meanings of words that they miss the true spirit of those words. Their nagging arguments provoke friction in the body of believers and result in jealousy and envy, bitterness, rejection and division.

I Corinthians 13:12 says we all see through a glass darkly. We are not capable of seeing the entire, clear picture of God's creation. We learn and discern more every day. None of us has all the answers. Instead of insisting that we are right in a dispute over words, we need to admit that we don't know it all. Then, in a spirit of unity, take the time to open God's Word and have a Bible study, searching for God's answer. James 3:16 says, "For where envying and strife is, there is confusion and every evil work." When it comes to division in the body of believers, or in a family, we each have a responsibility to do our part, and that starts with admitting we don't have all the answers.

The Church is filled with error and divination through some very bad teachings. One of these is called "name it and claim it" giving. Some call this "name it claim it" theology." Following this teaching, a spirit of divination offers God's blessings just by appropriation, without any regard to personal responsibility. It says, "Joe, if you just give God a thousand dollars, He will bless you a hundred- or a thousand-fold." This is not the truth. God already owns all our money — He was the source of it in the first place. This false theology ignores teaching that God asks us to return a portion of our wealth to His work, or about being a faithful steward of what God has entrusted us with in this world. You see, we give to God first because He asked us to do so. He promises to meet our needs, or to give us a return that overflows, though His return is not necessarily monetary. It is a cause and effect relationship.

"Name it and claim it" giving appeals to greed and the "get it for nothing" or "get rich quick" attitude so prevalent in the world. Many Christians fall for it, thinking they're immune to Satan's ploys. Greed, covetousness, jealousy and envy open us up to these deceptions.

When we fall for statements like, "gain is godliness," we agree with the devil that worldly success is the only measure of God's approval. That's divination (i.e., witchcraft). It's a false teaching reaching up out of the pit of hell.

The blessings of God, found in both the Old and New Testament, are clear and easily understood. There is no inherent evil in receiving or enjoying material blessings. Indeed, God does bless some believers with a nice car, a nice house and a large bank account. There are many humble, Godly people who run fabulously successful businesses. We need discernment to know which spirit underlies these blessings: the Spirit of God, or an evil spirit of greed.

Scripture teaches that Christian leaders must abhor teaching divination. They must take care not to encourage in their people a slot machine mentality that suggests if we keep putting in nickels, eventually we'll win the jackpot. Instead, these teachers should focus on seeking God's righteousness as our first priority, and then the blessings will flow. Matthew 6:33 says it clearly: "But seek ye first the kingdom of God, and his righteousness; and all these things shall be added unto you." This is a conditional promise, and demands personal responsibility.

God wants us to recognize that we are, first and foremost, to be Godly people. Material prosperity is a blessing from God; this is Scriptural, but with a balance of personal responsibility and accountability on our part. We are called to walk worthy of God (Ephesians 4:1). God's blessings are a result of our obedience.

Church leaders who forget repentance, personal responsibility and Godliness bring on themselves a terrible curse, and cause untold suffering for those who hear and believe them.

The Beatitudes as recorded in Matthew 5:3-5 teach us, "Blessed are the poor in spirit: for theirs is the kingdom of heaven. Blessed are they that mourn: for they shall be comforted. Blessed are the meek: for they shall inherit the earth."

Psalms 84:11 says, "For the Lord God is a sun and shield: the Lord will give grace and glory: no good thing will He withhold from them that walk uprightly."

Matthew 6:33 says, "But seek ye first the kingdom of God, and His righteousness; and all these things shall be added unto you." With theses passages in mind, together we must ask, where do these prosperity preachers get their teachings? Certainly not from God's Word.

Here are some examples from Scripture of jealousy and envy:

Cain, of Abel (Genesis 4:4-8)
1. Cain hated Abel because God accepted Abel's offering and not his.
2. Cain's envy fueled anger and murder.

Sarah, of Hagar (Genesis 16:5-6, 21:9-10)
1. Sarah hated Hagar because Hagar gave Abraham a son and she could not.
2. Sarah's envy led to harsh treatment and expulsion of Hagar.

Philistines, of Isaac (Genesis 26:15)
1. The Philistines hated Isaac because of Isaac's riches.
2. Their envy led to filling Isaac's wells and asking him to leave the country.

Joseph's brothers, of Joseph (Genesis 37:4, Acts 7:9)
1. Joseph's brothers hated Joseph because of his favored position with their father.
2. Their envy led to plots to murder Joseph and they sold him into slavery.

Korah, Dathan, and Abiram, of Moses (Numbers 16:3-10, Psalms 106:16-18)
1. These men hated Moses and Aaron because of the leadership position that these men wanted for themselves.
2. Their envy led to evil speaking and rebellion against Moses and Aaron.

Saul, of David (I Samuel 18:8-11)
1. Saul became angry with and hated David because David was more popular and God was with him.
2. His envy led to many attempts to kill David.

Haman, of Mordecai (Esther 5:9-13)
1. Haman was indignant toward Mordecai out of pride because Mordecai did not consider Haman to be as important as Haman considered himself to be. Haman could not bear Mordecai being honored.
2. His envy led to his plot to have Mordecai hanged.

Chief Priest, of Jesus (Mark 15:10, Matthew 27:18)
1. The chief priest hated Jesus because Jesus performed miracles from God that he could not. He feared losing his position to Him.
2. His envy led to Jesus' crucifixion.

Consider for a moment the opposite of jealousy and envy by looking at the physical person of Jesus Christ. Isaiah 53:2 tells its readers what Jesus would be like when He came in the flesh. "For He shall grow up before Him as a tender plant and as a root out of a dry ground, He hath no form nor comeliness and when we shall see Him there is no beauty that we should desire Him."

Isaiah 53:3 goes on to say that He was "despised, and rejected of men." He is acquainted with, that is, understands experientially, our grief and sorrows. He felt the same rejection we experience. "He is despised and rejected by men, A man of sorrows, and acquainted with grief. And we hid, as it were, our faces from Him; He was despised, and we esteemed Him not. Surely He has borne our grief and carried our sorrows; Yet we did esteem Him stricken, smitten by God, and afflicted. He was wounded for our transgressions, He was bruised for our iniquities; the chastisement of our peace was upon Him. And by His stripes we are healed" (Isaiah 53:3-5).

The Isaiah 53 description of Christ is certainly different from some of the pictures that depict Him as a long-haired, effeminate man with a halo. The truth is that if we had a pre-crucifixion picture of Him, we'd probably walk right past it, because nothing about it would be prominent enough to draw our attention. (An actual rendition of His appearance during His crucifixion would be so horrible most of us could never look at it.)

"There is no beauty, that we should desire Him," Isaiah wrote. Jesus had no comeliness. He was not physically attractive. His face and physique would not attract women lusting after Him. He never wore thousand-dollar Armani suits or Florsheim shoes. There were no diamond studs in His ears or gold chains hanging from His neck. He walked almost everywhere, so He had no Cadillac to envy. In all of His outward appearance, there was nothing to provoke envy or jealousy.

Jesus of Nazareth was unique, but not for His looks. Still, He had immeasurable value. Do you see Him as a special man? John 1:18 quotes Jesus, "No man hath seen God at any time; the only begotten Son, which is in the bosom of the Father, He hath declared Him." Jesus' life declared, or was a picture of, God.

John 14:9 says, "Jesus saith unto him, have I been so long a time with you, and yet hast thou not known Me, Philip? He that hath seen Me hath seen the Father; and how sayest thou then, Shew us the Father?" "I and my Father are one" (John 10:30).

We need to take our eyes off others and focus them on the Christ of the Gospel.

God created us with much vulnerability. From this, through us, He shows evidence of His ability to forgive sin and heal diseases. This is especially true when He allows us to be in the presence of sinners, and we walk away unscathed after interacting with them. II Corinthians 13:9 says, "For we are glad, when we are weak, and Ye are strong: and this also we wish, even your perfection." God is strong when we are weak, and in this, He perfects the saints, making them stronger (Ephesians. 4:12). His Holy Spirit within us accomplishes this purpose.

Will you trust Him? Will you make yourself vulnerable today? Vulnerability might frighten you. Can you choose faith in God over your feelings? That describes a miracle, doesn't it? God wants to work a miracle of healing in you, but you must be vulnerable and ready to receive it.

All jealousy and envy must go. They prevent wholesome relationships with others and with God. Discernment allows you to see how jealousy and envy seek to act out their evil natures in your life. Malachi 3:18 says, "...discern between the righteous and the wicked, between him that serveth God and him that serveth Him not."

HOW TO BE FREE

On a practical level, to rid yourself of jealousy and envy, make a list of the specifics in your life where you have sinned in this area. Write across the top of the page, "People I've envied or been jealous of, and the reasons why." As you write out your list, be honest with yourself and God. Be vulnerable.

Next, renounce and repent of each instance of jealousy and envy in your life, and in past generations. Repent of all covetousness, idolatrous comparisons, discontent, not trusting God, competition, pride, self-conceit, strife, rivalry, and fear of man. Be sure to consider jealousy between you and your spouse, betrothed or others with whom you are close.

Develop a holy hatred of jealousy and envy. Just as there is a Godly counterpart to jealousy, there's a Godly counterpart to hatred (Genesis 3:15). Jealousy and envy are unacceptable in a believer's life. You must fall out of agreement with jealousy, envy, and covetousness, and purpose to have nothing to do with them. Pray for discernment to be able to recognize when you are being attacked. Recognize that these attacks are Satan's fiery darts. Resist them and the evil they seek to accomplish in your life.

Break the curse of jealousy in your life from prior generations. Then in Jesus' name command the spirit of jealousy and envy to leave you and all your generations, clear back to Adam!

Then ask God to come and heal your heart and restore your bones that sin destroyed. Why ask that He restore our bones? Because Proverbs 14:30 says, "A sound heart is the life of the flesh: but envy [is] the rottenness of the bones."

God wants to bless you in every area of your life. Agreeing with Him and appropriating the power and authority of Jesus Christ, you can rid yourself of anything in your life that opposes His will for you. John 8:36 gives the result: "If the Son therefore shall make you free, ye shall be free indeed."

FREEDOM PRAYER

Now you have identified the jealousies and envies in your life, and you can take them before the throne of God and confess and repent of them. The stronghold they have held in your life will be destroyed and Satan's power over you will be legally cancelled. Here is an example of a prayer you can use to banish jealousy and envy from your life:

Prayer

Heavenly Father, in the name of Jesus, and as an act of my free will, I confess and repent for the (specific jealousy/ envy). I ask you, Lord Jesus, to forgive me. I purpose and choose to forgive myself, from my heart, for this (specific jealousy/envy), and I release myself from any guilt or shame from this (specific jealousy/envy). In the name of Jesus, and by the power of His blood, I cancel Satan's authority over me in this (specific jealousy/envy). In the name of Jesus, I command this jealousy and envy to go.

Holy Spirit, I invite you into my heart to heal me of this pain and hurt. Please speak your words of truth to me about this situation.

As the Holy Spirit speaks to you, write down His message in the space provided. When you have finished this prayer for each person or situation on your list, command the principality of jealousy and envy to go in the name of Jesus.

MY JEALOUSIES/ENVIES
(PEOPLE, THINGS, CIRCUMSTANCES):

THE HOLY SPIRIT'S ANSWER (TRUTH):

_____   _____

_____   _____

_____   _____

_____   _____

_____   _____

_____   _____

_____   _____

_____   _____

_____   _____

_____   _____

_____   _____

_____   _____

_____   _____

_____   _____

_____   _____

_____   _____

_____   _____

_____   _____

CHAPTER NINE

Principality of Rejection

DESCRIPTION OF REJECTION

Feeling rejected is one of the most devastating of all human emotions, and it is usually ill-founded. But we can't defeat rejection if we have given bitterness, jealousy and envy a place in our lives. It's impossible, because bitterness is the root of all the unloving spirits that accuse us with rejection. To have freedom from rejection, we must have freedom from bitterness.

Herein lies a spiritual paradox. The spirit of rejection opens the door for bitterness, jealousy and envy, but you can't defeat rejection until you have defeated bitterness, jealousy and envy.

The most common reason for separation from God and others is unforgiveness. Unforgiveness is the first element of bitterness. To defeat bitterness and all its armor starts with defeating unforgiveness.

The dictionary defines "rejection," "to cast off, to rebuff or repulse. To throw away as useless or unsatisfactory. To put aside. To disapprove."

Rejection consists of several major aspects.

Rejection tells us we are unwanted, put aside and refused. It's a feeling of being unloved and not accepted either as a member of a group, by a friend or sometimes, even by the human race. Rejection places a wall around us that repels acceptance even when it is offered.

Rejection reminds us of our desperate need to be loved and, at the same time, we're convinced we're unloved. This causes emotional torment. Rejection drives love from us, and drives us from love. Even when someone does love us, we still feel rejected. "You're just saying that. I know better. You don't really love me. You only like what I can do for you."

This unloving spirit tells us that no one can ever really love us — we're unlovable. Any time someone begins to open love's door to us, unloving spirits slam it shut with accusations that we're unworthy of being loved.

As someone starts to show love toward us, rejection starts picking their affection apart. "Oh, you say you love me, but you won't go to my ball games." "I saw you looking at my dress. You think I dress stupid!" "See, you said it. You can't stand detail. You've never been able to tolerate someone who talks as much as me. This'll never work out." Rejection judges facial expressions and body language, or evaluates nuances, looking for a reason to feel more rejected.

Rejection drives us to pick a fight with the person who wants to love us. The result will be another sure rejection. Rejection says, "You're like everyone else. You're avoiding me. Well, I understand. I can't imagine anyone who'd want to be with me anyway." We speak our own words of rejection to others, and play a game of verbal ping-pong.

Rejection blocks our ability to reconcile differences with others over misunderstandings. It carries us into bitterness. We debate with ourselves about the rejection rather than going to the other person to resolve the misunderstanding. The hope of reconciliation rapidly disintegrates.

The fear of being rejected is fueled by the fear of man and by the fear of failure. Rejection, unloving spirits and fear work together. Rejection says, "I'm not accepted." Unloving spirits agree, saying, "There's a good reason for you being not accepted, because you're not worthy of being loved." Then fear says, "If he ever knew what I was really like, he'd hate me." We're afraid that no one loves us, not even God. Yet, as these spirits are talking to us, and we're under attack, it's time to go to God. He is the only one who knows the real truth about us and is big enough to forgive us. God accepts us as we are, provided we come to Him in faith.

Rejection drives us to reject love from others. Even though people offer love and acceptance to us, we're unable to believe them and receive it. Giving and receiving love forms the foundation for our relationship with God, others and ourselves. The cause of all spiritually-rooted disease is the inability to give and receive love. Love has the power to break rejection and fear.

Rejection tells us that we will never belong. Even though we desire to be a part of something, we never feel like we belong. We attempt to become involved in family, church, a group of friends or some organization, or we strive to fit in at work. Yet, we just can't accept the fact that we belong. This sense of not belonging is rejection. Shame and guilt result from rejection, making us feel uncomfortable, so we don't fit in. We're not good enough. "I've been working at the same job for sixteen years, but no one really likes me down there. They still won't let me sing at the picnic. Julie won't even talk to me. Well, I talk too much. I understand. Why would anyone want to be my friend?"

A person who is plagued by rejection is given to irrational and continual self-introspection. They walk around with their heads hanging down, are unable to look you in the eye, but seem to always be looking for approval and acceptance from others. They're constantly on guard, watching to see if someone notices them.

Rejection produces double-mindedness. "I know God said He loves me, but I don't feel His love, and He certainly never answers my prayers. I want to believe His promises, but why should I?" We constantly argue with God's eternal truth, bolstered by Satan's eternal lies. Rejection robs us of our true identity in Christ Jesus, preventing us from becoming the special person that God created us to be. It creates internal instability and restlessness. James 1:8 says, "A double-minded man is unstable in all his ways."

Rejection causes us to run and hide, or to search for our identity in all the wrong places. It prevents us from really facing down our problems. Ironically, rejection drives us to seek some level of intimate contact with others — job, church, groups, individuals — but continuously drives us away from establishing intimate contact.

What began as our own irrational fear of rejection evolves into real rejection. "I can't stand being around Bob. He's so negative about himself. I don't want to hear any more of it!"

In the church, rejection drives people to focus on their position. They want an identity, title and status. They don't necessarily want to serve; they want recognition. Their need for acceptance causes them to constantly check to see if they are being noticed.

A person who has a healthy, true identity rooted in Christ knows who he is and is content. He doesn't strive for position or status, and because of this, others often seek him out for leadership.

Rejection is an acknowledgement of agreement with Satan's lies. Believing Satan's lies is calling God a liar.

Scripture teaches that rejection is just as dangerous as unbelief and faithlessness. Rejection claims that God's acceptance of us rests on us first winning man's acceptance. It puts man in the place of God, because it gives irrational weight to man's acceptance.

GOD'S TRUTH

God created us in His image and gave us His Son to make us whole. This is the ultimate act of acceptance, but we still seek to win man's approval before going to God. We see our true identity in man's opinion of who we are, and whether or not we win human approval becomes vitally important to us. We let humans define our reality, choosing them instead of God.

God said to come unto Him and He will not cast us out. He said to come in our sins and fallen state, accepting His forgiveness. And He asks us to live a life focused on Him, not other people. To do otherwise is to call God a liar.

God the Father, God the Son and God the Holy Spirit — the Godhead — are greater than any created being. If God is for us, and He is, who can be against us? (Romans 8:31b).

When we make winning man's approval our god, we are in idolatry. Idolatry is addressed in the First Commandment. Idolatry carries a curse down a family line through the third and fourth generations. Exodus 20:3 says, "Thou shalt have no other gods before Me."

Rejection is a form of idolatry: self-idolatry and idolatry of other humans. Rejection values the opinions of other men more than it values God's truth.

David wrote in Psalms 139 that God created us and knew us intimately since before the foundation of the world. We're no accident or mistake. It makes no difference what the circumstances were by which we were conceived, we are known and accepted by God through Jesus Christ. God created us, He makes no mistakes and we have great value. To say otherwise is calling God a liar.

God knows the thoughts and intents of our heart (Hebrews 4:12). We can't hide from Him. Rather, we need to be cleansed by God and run toward Him, basking openly in His love.

Consider the Genesis story of Cain and Abel as it relates to the results of rejection and bitterness. Genesis 4:1-8 says, "And Adam knew Eve his wife; and she conceived, and bare Cain, and said, I have gotten a man from the LORD. And she again bare his brother Abel. And Abel was a keeper of sheep, but Cain was a tiller of the ground. And in process of time it came to pass, that Cain brought of the fruit of the ground an offering unto the LORD. And Abel, he also brought of the firstlings of his flock and of the fat thereof. And the LORD had respect unto Abel and to his offering: But unto Cain and to his offering He had not respect. And Cain was very wroth, and his countenance fell. And the LORD said unto Cain, Why art thou wroth? and why is thy countenance fallen? If thou doest well, shalt thou not be accepted? and if thou doest not well, sin lieth at the door. And unto thee shall be his desire, and thou shalt rule over him. And Cain talked with Abel his brother: and it came to pass, when they were in the field, that Cain rose up against Abel his brother, and slew him."

Why did God reject Cain's offering? God had decreed that only a blood offering could cover sins. Cain disobeyed God's requirement by bringing the fruits of his field, rendering his offering as unacceptable to God.

When Adam and Eve sinned in the Garden of Eden, they tried to hide from God in the woods. They realized that they were naked, and took fig leaves and covered themselves, thinking they were unclean. This is a picture of what we do when we sin, hiding from others to avoid the pain of a confession or confrontation.

The Lord came looking for Adam and Eve in the cool of the evening, as was His custom. This is a beautiful picture of God's desire to know all of us. We might try and hide, but He still seeks to have a relationship with us.

God killed an animal and made clothing for Adam and Eve from its skin. Though He expelled them from the Garden of Eden, He still dressed them in His love. God's slaughter of an animal provided the first blood sacrifice to meet the needs of a sinner. This was a foreshadowing of the Sacrificial Lamb that would die on Calvary's cross. Jesus Christ died to take away the rejection men had toward Him, others and themselves, a rejection rooted in Satan's lies.

Cain offered his crops, but they were inadequate to pay for his sins. Abel brought a firstling. A firstling was an animal that was without spot or blemish, the best that he could offer. Burning the fat sent a sweet-smelling savor to God. Abel's was the sacrifice God required.

The first result of rejection is bitterness. Bitterness carries unforgiveness, resentment, retaliation, anger, wrath, hatred, violence, and murder. We teach about bitterness first because it is so powerful and too often negatively affects so much of our life.

Cain's offering stemmed from duty and a requirement. Abel rooted his in a heart of worship and obedience. These two men were offered a choice. One obeyed God and the other obeyed Satan. Bitterness took root in Cain.

If Cain had dealt with bitterness, when that spirit of rejection came he wouldn't have listened to it. He would have said, "Jehovah, how come my offering is not acceptable?"

God would have shown Cain His love, and offered grace and mercy. God would have carefully explained why Cain's offering was not acceptable. Did God reject Cain? No! Genesis 4:7 says, "...and if thou doest not well, sin lieth at the door. And unto thee shall be his desire, and thou shalt rule over him."

God may have said, "Cain, you brought this sacrifice to Me because you had to. It wasn't your first fruit (your best). You gave it out of duty and religion, and I reject your offering, but I don't reject you." Did God replace Cain as the elder son? No. Did God reject Cain as a person? No. God only rejected his offering. But Cain took it personally. His countenance fell as bitterness, anger and wrath welled up within him.

Have you ever seen a rejected person smile? No. Have you ever seen a bitter person smile? No. Have you ever seen a jealous or envious person smile? Never.

With perfect twenty-twenty hindsight, we see clearly the ultimate result of bitterness: murder. Honestly evaluating what Cain did and why, helps us build discernment. Abel's murder was an external expression of internal pressures created by Satan. Be sure, God did not reject Cain as a man or as a leader; He just rejected his half-hearted and unholy offering.

Isaiah 53 is a prophecy about the coming Messiah. Verses 1-5 read, "Who hath believed our report? and to whom is the arm of the LORD revealed? For He shall grow up before Him as a tender plant, and as a root out of a dry ground: He hath no form nor comeliness; and when we shall see Him, there is no beauty that we should desire Him. He is despised and rejected of men; a man of sorrows, and acquainted with grief: and we hid as it were our faces from Him; He was despised, and we esteemed Him not. Surely He hath borne our griefs, and carried our sorrows: yet we did esteem Him stricken, smitten of God, and afflicted. But He was wounded for our transgressions, He was bruised for our iniquities: the chastisement of our peace was upon Him; and with His stripes we are healed."

Jesus understood sorrow and rejection. People despised Him so strongly they hid their faces from Him. He knows experientially this kind of abuse and pain; He will never reject us. Hebrews 13:5-6 says, "Let your conversation be without covetousness; and be content with such things as ye have: for He hath said, I will never leave thee, nor forsake thee. So that we may boldly say, The Lord is my helper, and I will not fear what man shall do unto me."

Zechariah 13:6 is a prophetic description of Jesus' death on the cross: "And one shall say unto Him, What are these wounds in Thine hands? Then He shall answer, Those with which I was wounded in the house of My friends."

God gave Jesus His power and authority. Jesus could have called down ten thousand angels to fight against Satan, but He didn't. Why did Jesus accept the abuse and rejection He received from the men He had created? He accepted it because, in perfect love, He chose us before the foundation of the world (Ephesians 1:4). He wants to have an intimate relationship with us. We can't totally understand the depth of His love, patience, acceptance, or forgiveness. We can choose to believe and worship Him.

Rejection wounds our spirit. Proverbs 18:8 says, "The words of a talebearer are as wounds, and they go down into the innermost parts of the belly."

A slanderer's words (an evil spirit of slander operating in another) hurt us in our innermost parts. The lie of rejection says we are not who God says we are. Words of rejection and slander wound our spirit and break our heart. We will feel it deep inside. Negative comments uttered years ago by our parents may have penetrated deep into our spirit, putting us under the curse of those words ever since. Proverbs 18:14 says, "The spirit of a man will sustain his infirmity; but a wounded spirit who can bear?" Proverbs 18:21 says, "Death and life are in the power of the tongue: and they that love it shall eat the fruit thereof."

Our words have power and they will be honored, either by God or the devil. We can curse or bless others. We can curse or bless ourselves. We can set evil spirits in motion by our words. "I wish I never had you. You're nothing but trouble." "I never wanted you in the first place. You were just an accident." "Your middle name is trouble. You'll never amount to anything." What thoughts entered your mind as you read these cruel lies?

Matthew 12:36-37 says, "But I say unto you, That every idle word that men shall speak, they shall give account thereof in the Day of Judgment. For by thy words thou shalt be justified, and by thy words thou shalt be condemned."

To defeat the curse of words we must fall out of agreement with them. Reject them and instead, believe God's Word. Accept God's will and His promises, and the power of an evil spirit to execute those words will be broken. If we spoke these kinds of evil words, we must take responsibility and repent, renounce and place them under the blood of Jesus Christ. He can destroy their power over us and over those whom we have harmed.

To deal with bitterness, jealousy and envy, or rejection, we must get at the root of the sin. We must exercise spiritual discernment to identify this root, and then deal with it decisively, preventing its regrowth.

A friend of mine had a tree blown down in a violent windstorm. The tree-trimmer came within an hour, cut the tree down, ground it into chips and drove away. He left the stump in the ground. Within days, suckers began to bloom on the stump and, without stump removal, threatened to create a new, more powerful tangle of trees. The root has to be dug up and destroyed.

THE ROOTS OF REJECTION

The roots of rejection are a tangled mess with four identifiable causes.

First, is the fear of rejection. Rejection by itself is tough enough, but when coupled with the fear of rejection it becomes even more powerful. The fear itself produces more rejection. Compare faith to fear. Faith is the substance of things hoped for (Hebrews 11:1). Fear is the substance of things not hoped for. Faith says the eventual outcome of events will be for the better. Fear says all things happen for our detriment (Job 3:25). The fear of rejection immobilizes us, preventing us from venturing out. We feel rejected even though we've done nothing at all except thought about being rejected. We withdraw into a shell.

There are three powerful demons that answer to fear and rejection working in tandem. They are fear of man, fear of failure, and fear of rejection. All three must be defeated!

When we're under spiritual attack, too often we run toward rejection and bitterness. But it's really the ideal time to run toward God.

God says to be anxious, i.e., nervous or distraught, about nothing. Believers are to be free of anxiety. The Bible promises perfect peace to those whose minds are stayed on God. Stayed refers to focus. The person whose focus is on God is blessed with a heart at peace. Isaiah 26:3 says, "Thou wilt keep him in perfect peace, whose mind is stayed on Thee: because he trusteth in Thee."

Second, is self-rejection. Self-rejection tells you that even you know you don't measure up. Perhaps we learned this as a child. "You will never amount to anything." We heard a lie, and believed it. The lie became self-rejection.

Self-rejection often results in an intense and sometimes irrational drive to succeed. There is a need to prove to our parents, the world and ourselves that we are valuable and useful. But rejection is never satisfied, and if being accepted becomes our focus, we are driven deeper into the pit of self-rejection. We will never be good enough to satisfy rejection.

If we grew up in a home without unconditional love and acceptance, and were treated as someone with very little value, we may well experience rejection and self-rejection even as adults.

If you haven't grasped the seriousness of the attacks of self-hatred or unloving spirits, you might want to review it now. Self-hatred and self-rejection are networked with unloving spirits.

The third aspect is rejecting others. We habitually reject others first, before they reject us. In this way, we protect ourselves from the hurt of future rejection. We fear becoming vulnerable and transparent with others, and we have a hard time trusting anyone. All of this sets off a chain reaction in our relationships that continues a vicious circle of rejection. The only winner is Satan.

Once we learn to be free from rejection, we can also become vulnerable without fear. II Corinthians 12:10 says, "Therefore I take pleasure in infirmities, in reproaches, in necessities, in persecutions, in distresses for Christ's sake: for when I am weak, then am I strong."

The fourth aspect is the desire for rejection. This is the most perverse result of rejection. It is the fruit of an unloving spirit of self-hatred. We actually set ourselves up for rejection by treating others poorly or with indifference. In reality, we are seeking rejection from them. Being rejected allows us to continue dodging the real spiritual issues that hinder our freedom. As a result, when rejection occurs, it reinforces our lack of self-worth, and lack of identity. This feeds our belief that we are unworthy. Rejection becomes a self-fulfilling prophecy.

The following diagram is called the "Walls of Rejection." We suggest that you pray through each of the four walls or roots of rejection, repenting for allowing them into

BREAKING DOWN THE WALLS OF REJECTION

- Confess
- Repent
- Renounce the power of _____ in my life.
- Speak blessings over my life
- Seal my ears from hearing rejection
- Seal my eyes from seeing rejection
- Seal my mouth from speaking rejection
- Break the power of the spirit of _____ in my life
- Command the spirit of _____ to leave in the name and authority of Jesus Christ, under Whose blood I am covered

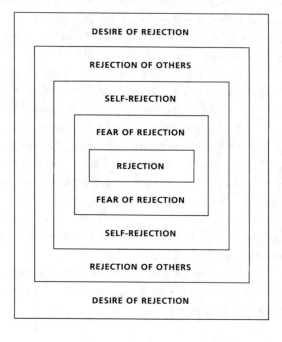

your life and repenting for this sin in your generation. We also suggest that you ask God to seal your ears from hearing rejection; your eyes from seeing rejection; your mind from perceiving rejection; and your mouth from speaking rejection.

Being rejected sets various defensive mechanisms in action. We withdraw from others like a turtle hiding in its shell. Rejection says, "I'm not going to let myself be vulnerable. I'm not going to let people reject me again. I'm never going to get close to anyone again." This comes from an attitude of fear. Adam and Eve hid after their sin. Withdrawal from people is a defense mechanism reacting to the fear of man.

Fear of failure drives a defense mechanism that prohibits us from taking chances in a relationship. By risk avoidance, we protect ourselves from rejection, but also miss much of life.

Anger and hatred give us a defense against rejection. They drive us to be aggressive, fighting bitterly against real or supposed enemies. Rejection couples with a root of bitterness and they reinforce and fuel each other.

Rejection naturally seeks for a meaningful identity outside of a whole, pure relationship with God. Rejection distorts us so no one, especially us, even knows our real self. Instead, our identity should be so strongly established in God that if someone smiles at us or invites us in, it is just a bonus.

Rejection looks for identity and comfort from other people, not God. Instead of patterning ourselves after Christ, we idolize other people. We are driven to have someone around us whom we can idolize, rather than making God the object of our worship. Yet, as we draw near to another human, we ultimately become rejected again, continuing the downward spiral.

Rejection searches for someone weaker than us with whom to hang out. Support groups are a popular place to find weak people all looking for someone weaker.

Rejection causes us to fabricate a personality. Since we don't know who we are, we make up someone and cling to that, until the fabrication is revealed and once again, we are rejected.

Fear, rejection, and rebellion are the volatile ingredients of insanity. Accepting who we are with Jesus Christ as our strong defender is the antidote to insanity. Galatians 4:7 says we are God's sons, daughters and heirs through Christ. A healthy self-image looks beyond the "now" to the future, when in Christ we are perfected. Doing so solves our identity problem (II Timothy 1).

POSSIBLE SOURCES OF REJECTION

Fatherless homes often produce children subject to rejection. Fatherless homes lack a clear identity, causing the children to miss out on the fullness of feeling loved and accepted. The father establishes the identity and emotional stability in the home. The head of the woman is the man, and the head of the man is Christ. I Corinthians 11:3

says, "But I would have you know, that the head of every man is Christ; and the head of the woman is the man; and the head of Christ is God."

Rejection can stem from the lives of our ancestors. Spiritual problems can be inherited. Abraham lied to Abimelech, telling the king that Sarah was his sister. Isaac made the same lie forty years later. Then Jacob lied to his father, Isaac. Ten of Jacob's sons lied to him. Sin can continue from generation to generation unless someone repents and puts a stop to it.

Rejection can occur at conception if one or both of the parents are not happy about the coming of the baby. If a child is unwanted, a door opens for a spirit of rejection to enter into the child while in the womb. This often happens when the child was an "unplanned accident," conceived in lust or between unwed parents: a bastard. The Scriptures teach that the bastard's curse continues for ten generations unless it is broken (Deuteronomy 23:2).

God gave all of us life and He knew each of us before laying the foundation of the world. His hands knit us together in our mother's womb. God has a plan and purpose for each of us. He knows the exact number of hairs on our head, and has engraved us on the palm of His hand. He loves us unconditionally and through His Son, Jesus Christ, He made provision for us to spend eternity with Him. By claiming God's truth, we break the bastard's curse for all generations. When God in Christ Jesus adopted us as His children, He abolished the curse of sin passed down from our ancestors!

Sometimes parents are disappointed with their baby's gender. The father complains, "I don't know what to do with you. If you were a boy, it'd be different." This can result in rejection and self-rejection. Fathers sometimes build up great resentment toward their infant child because of all the attention it receives from the mother. A spirit of rejection transfers from the father to the baby, and that child matures caught in the vicious cycle of rejection.

Blended families are ripe for the growth of influence of the spirit of rejection. The newly married parents need time to get to know each other. Each worries over their own blood offspring, and often resent the lack of attention provided by the other parent, both to them and their own children. These parents need to take great care to ensure that a generous amount of love flows between and through them to the stepchildren.

If a parent dies when a child is young, the child sometimes resents or even hates the dead parent. They feel abandoned and rejected. "Why did mommy have to die and leave me alone?" the little girl asks.

If there is strife and turmoil in the home during pregnancy or early childhood the child will have feelings of rejection, abandonment and fear.

Adopted children often struggle with a deep inner sense of rejection by their birth parents. Most adoptive parents deeply love and provide tremendous care for their children, but many still struggle with rejection.

Middle children often feel rejected because the older and younger siblings get more attention. Psychologists label this "the middle child syndrome."

If a father, mother, wife or husband has rejected you, please understand that at some time since their conception, they were more than likely also rejected.

In these scenarios of rejection in children, spirits of fear, rejection and abandonment come into the children even while they are in womb. No matter the scenario, there is an answer and a cure for rejection. In children we teach the parents to repent for however they rejected their child. Then ask the child for forgiveness; bless the child with a mother's and/or a father's blessing; and command the spirits of fear, rejection and abandonment to leave. God accepts all of us, and when we realize our true identity is in Him, rejection no longer has a chance with you.

If you were rejected by your parents in some way, choose to forgive them for their sin and release the bitterness.

WHO AM I IN GOD?

"The Word of God is quick and powerful, and sharper than any two edged sword..." (Hebrews 4:12). God's Word answers all questions, including how to deal with rejection. But in so doing, it can cut deeply into our presumptions, convicting us in the deepest recesses of our heart.

Isaiah 54 provides God's definitive Word on rejection. Isaiah 54:1 says, "Sing, O barren, thou that didst not bear; break forth into singing, and cry aloud, thou that didst not travail with child: for more are the children of the desolate than the children of the married wife, saith the LORD."

"Sing, O barren, thou that didst not bear." The inability to have a child — barrenness — is a major contributor to rejection. The barren woman feels rejected by God and by her husband. In many large families, she feels rejected by them as well, even by the community. Self-rejection, self-hatred and guilt well up in her spirit.

Paradoxically, rejection, fear of rejection, and self-hatred can produce barrenness. Many miscarriages result from an auto-immune dysfunction, where white corpuscles attack the umbilical cord. This produces swelling and edema resulting in a strangulation of the cord, preventing blood, oxygen and nutrients from getting to the placenta. The baby dies and the woman miscarries.

Anxiety and fear can cause frigidity and impotence. Obviously, without sexual contact, barrenness results.

Self-rejection and rejection can also produce barrenness because they affect the endocrine system. This system responds to emotions. The ovaries and testes are part of the endocrine system. They can malfunction from anxiety, stress and fear. Again, when this occurs, barrenness results.

Tied to being barren are the related female problems of PMS and menopause. We find these issues if a woman dislikes being a woman for any reason. Sometimes they resent how God made their bodies because they started to develop at a young age; do not like the monthly cycle; if there was molestation or rape, they reason, "if I were not a girl this would not have happened"; if dad wanted a boy, she might resent herself. These situations result in resenting being a female and thus producing physical problems.

"Sing, O barren, thou that didst not bear, Break forth into singing." When we receive deliverance from rejection we can become filled with joy. We can feel safe, secure, wanted, accepted and needed. Rather than brooding, we feel like singing and dancing. We have a freedom of spirit.

Rejection scars the human spirit and steals our joy. It keeps us from having a merry heart. "A merry heart doeth good like a medicine" (Proverbs 17:22), and when we don't have a merry heart, our whole body is affected. If God has accepted us just as we are, then we can truly understand that nothing else matters. Rejection itself is rejected, leaving us free to gain a merry heart.

Isaiah 54 continues, "Break forth into singing and cry aloud, thou that didst not travail with child, for more are the children of the desolate than the children of the married wife, saith the LORD." The devil cheats God of His children, because of the curse of sin. God says that more people on the earth have chosen against Him than for Him.

"Enlarge the place of thy tent," verse 3, "and let them stretch forth the curtains of thy habitations, spare not, lengthen thy cords, and strengthen thy stakes, for thou shall break forth on the right hand and on the left. And thy seed shall inherit the gentiles and make the desolate cities to be inhabited."

What does that mean? Rejection causes us to run and hide from others, staying isolated. Instead, we should walk out of our self-imposed prison, set free from condemnatory self-introspection. Let's break free of our feelings of self-hatred. To do this, we need to swing the doors open and enlarge our "place." We need to enlarge our "tent."

With rejection banished, we will interact freely with other people, without fear. We can be vulnerable without feeling threatened of exposure. We can entertain people in our homes. We can have fellowship with others.

Verse 4 says, "Fear not; for thou shalt not be ashamed: neither be thou confounded; for thou shalt not be put to shame: for thou shalt forget the shame of thy youth, and shalt not remember the reproach of thy widowhood any more."

This verse says, "fear not." "Fear not! For thou shalt not be ashamed." Shame accompanies rejection. The unloving spirit of shame robs us of our peace and destroys any chance we have to build relationships. As we feel shame, we avoid looking anybody in the eye, hang our head and feel great apprehension. Our self-talk says, "I'm guilty, I'm rejected, don't look at me." Why? Because rejection produces shame. How wonderful it is to be set free from shame!

"Neither be thou confounded." This means not to be confused. Rejection produces double-mindedness and it walks with confusion. We want to accept love and yet, we can't receive it. We want to feel, "I'm the righteousness of God, through Christ Jesus" (Philippians 3:9). But the devil says, "You old worm. You know you're no better than a filthy rat." We find ourselves agreeing with the devil. This is the attack of a spirit of confusion, seeking to make us double-minded. James 1:8 says, "A double-minded man is unstable in all his ways."

In contrast, God says you shall not be confounded, you shall not be confused, you shall not be double-minded, and you shall not be put to shame. Isaiah 26:3 supplies God's truth in this matter: "Thou wilt keep him in perfect peace, whose mind is stayed on Thee: because he trusteth in Thee."

Pay close attention to what the LORD is saying in verse 4. "For you shall forget the shame of your youth." Hallelujah! We denounce inherited shame and childhood rejection. God says we can forget the shame, rejection and guilt from our past. We are set free! Hallelujah!

But the devil accuses, "I know what you did when you were seventeen. Do you want to talk about that abortion? Do you want to talk about that little immoral relationship you had? Do you want to talk about what you did to Marvin?"

Claiming Christ's forgiveness, we can stare down that accusing spirit, saying, "Excuse me, evil spirit, but would you just mind going up to the throne and telling my heavenly Father what you're telling me in my head right now, and see what He has to say about it." No devil will do this. II Corinthians 10:5 provides the key, explaining what to do: "Casting down imaginations, and every high thing that exalteth itself against the knowledge of God, and bringing into captivity every thought to the obedience of Christ."

When we examine those fiery darts that Satan throws around in our minds, exposing them to the light of God's Word, we can discern truth. Truth sets us free. Jesus said in John 14:6, "I am the way, the truth, and the life...." John 8:32 says, "And ye shall know the truth, and the truth shall make you free."

To conquer rejection, we need to let the devil know that we know who we are. Galatians 4, says we are an heir. We're joint heirs with Jesus, sons and daughters of God. God accepted us. There is no more rejection by the One who really matters. We may be despised and rejected by men, but God accepts us. God's promises are eternally important to us, and Satan's temporal attacks fall harmlessly aside.

Rejection prevents us from understanding who we are in God and what Jesus did for us. It doesn't want us to believe that God created us from the foundation of the world.

God says, "Give a testimony to George, the man who works alongside you." Then comes a different voice, saying, "No, I better not do that. I might sound stupid. George will laugh at me. Besides, I really don't know what to say." That's rejection rooted in the fear of man and fear of failure.

Rejection reminds us of youthful sins and accuses us with shame, but God says repent, and then to forget the shame of our youth (Isaiah 54:4). Perhaps you were involved in various shameful and sinful activities before making peace with God. Yet, even though God forgave you, you hang on to youthful shame. So, what's the solution? "Father God, I'm sorry, will you forgive me?"

"Yes, my child, I forgive you," He says.

"You mean you're not going to judge me for these things in the Day of Judgment?"

"No, because you're dealing with them now."

"You mean you're not ashamed of me, Father God?"

"No, as a matter of fact, I'm very proud of you. I am proud that you took care of it now. And what's more, I declare you righteous and free from shame."

I John 1:9 says, "If we confess our sins, He is faithful and just to forgive us our sins, and to cleanse us from all unrighteousness." This powerful promise carries a condition. To receive God's forgiveness of sin requires us to confess those sins to Him. What follows is an intimate relationship with Him and freedom from shame and rejection. II Timothy 2:21 says, "If a man therefore purge himself from these [sins], he shall be a vessel unto honour, sanctified, and meet for the Master's use, and prepared unto every good work." God blesses our faithfulness.

God says, "I'm proud of you, daughter; I'm proud of you, son. Thank you for having the guts to deal with rejection and fear, and for coming before Me and saying, 'Father, in the days of my youth, I followed the devil and I did this or that.' Thank you for listening to my Word, thank you for admitting this to Me; your sins are forgiven. Go your way and sin no more."

God uses our confession as a tool to purge rejection from our lives. James 5:16 says, "Confess your faults one to another that you may be healed." We confess faults, rejections, and bitterness to receive healing.

Either we will move forward in faith, allowing God to drive rejection from our lives, or we will fall backward in fear, paralyzed by rejection.

Proper interpretation and application of Scripture requires a three-dimensional approach. First we examine God's statement to people at the time it was given. Next, the statement is examined in light of what God says to His people about the future. And there is the literal and spiritual application to our lives today.

Isaiah 54:4 says, "And thou shall not remember the reproach of thy widowhood anymore." The Scriptural context is about our relationship with God.

An application of this verse applies to ninety percent of our ministry caseload — women. This phenomenon is driven by the commonality of rejection women experience from their fathers and husbands. On this earth, men represent God the Father to their children, and as husbands they represent Jesus.

A woman whose relationship with her father has been shattered is often separated from her heavenly Father as well. Fear of her earthly father is transferred to an unholy type of fear of God.

Ephesians teaches husbands to love their wives as Christ loved the Church, calling the Church the Bride of Christ. If a husband rejects his wife or treats her cruelly, then the woman develops an unholy fear of Jesus.

A poor relationship with both the father and husband is an indicator of a poor relationship with God and His Son. She feels unloved and she falls from rejection. She is spiritually fatherless, and a spiritual widow.

Most of the women that we work with in ministry are married, but there is some sort of disconnect between them and their husbands. Or, their fathers may be physically alive, but they are uninvolved in their children's lives. Practically speaking, the wives are like widows, and her children are virtual orphans. The principle of how fathering and husbanding affect this war against rejection is essential to understand if you desire to win your freedom.

"Thou shalt not remember the reproach of thy widowhood anymore." The LORD is also talking about His wife. The Hebrew word for LORD as it is used here is *Jehovah*. In many Old Testament references Jehovah is described as our Savior, Redeemer and Creator — here as our Husband. Our Creator, Savior and Redeemer is Jesus Christ. His Bride is the Church.

Isaiah 54:5 says, "for thy Maker is thy husband." Thy Maker is God the Word. Who is God, the Word? The Hebrew word used for "maker" means, "master, captain, chief man, and lord" (Strongs 1167). It is a picture of authority. John 1:1 says that the Word — Jesus Christ — dwelt with and was God, the Father. God created all things through Jesus Christ, the Word (Colossians 1:16). God the Father created all things visible and invisible through Jesus Christ, the Word. Thy Maker is Jesus.

The other Hebrew words translated "husband" are Strong's 582 and 376. They have the meanings of "man, champion, mighty, steward, and worthy." God calls Jesus our husband, seeking an intimate relationship with each of us, and setting an example for men in their relationship with their own wives.

Jesus is our captain and spiritual leader. We are to submit to Him. He is our spiritual husband and He created us. Then He left His heavenly throne to come down to this planet because He loved His dying wife. He redeemed her and sent His Holy Spirit to shepherd her. Against all this, rejection stands no chance.

It was not just Jesus loving us. John 3:16 says the Father sent Him. "For God [the Father] so loved the world that He gave His only begotten Son." The Father loves us. Jesus loves us.

God the Father willed the creation, but God the Son — the Word — spoke it into existence. The Holy Spirit performed it. The fullness of the Godhead is responsible for and endeared to us. If we reconcile with God, through Jesus Christ, empowered by the

Holy Spirit, rejection stands no chance in our lives.

Understanding this helps us be healed of our earthly father's or husband's rejection. God is our real Father and Jesus our real Husband. In an eternal sense, no one else counts.

Verse 5 says, "For thy Maker is thy Husband, the Lord of hosts is His name and thy Redeemer, the Holy one of Israel, the God of the whole earth shall He be called." This verse describes our true husband, the Lord Jesus Christ.

Verse 6 says, "For the LORD hath called thee as a woman forsaken and grieved in spirit and a wife of youth, when you were refused, saith thy God."

Wow! Look closely at this. "For the LORD [that's Jesus] hath called thee as a woman, forsaken and grieved in spirit." What does it mean to be grieved in spirit? Rejected. And forsaken? Rejected. Who calls to us from our youth, even in our rejection? The Lord Jesus.

He says, "I love you. You are not rejected. I am here, come unto Me all of you who are laden with heavy burdens. I will give you rest." If God be for me, who can be against me? These powerful truths drive us toward God and obedience to Him. God wants a personal, intimate relationship with each one of us.

Verses 7-8 say, "For a small moment have I forsaken thee." But listen to this, "But with great mercies will I gather you. In a little wrath I hid my face from thee for a moment, but with everlasting kindness will I have mercy on thee, saith the LORD, [Jesus] thy Redeemer." Who is our Redeemer? Jesus.

Our husband left heaven to bring us to Himself, even though we are disobedient. In our disobedience, He offers us life. He gathers us because He hasn't rejected us; He loves us. Even though we serve the harlot, He waits for the moment that He can snatch us out of our sin. We just need to listen and respond to His voice.

Isaiah 54:8-11 says, "In a little wrath I hid my face from thee for a moment; but with everlasting kindness will I have mercy on thee, saith the Lord thy Redeemer. For this is as the waters of Noah unto me: for as I have sworn that the waters of Noah should no more go over the earth; so have I sworn that I would not be wroth with thee, nor rebuke thee. For the mountains shall depart, and the hills be removed; but My kindness shall not depart from thee, neither shall the covenant of My peace be removed, saith the Lord that hath mercy on thee. O thou afflicted, tossed with tempest, and not comforted, behold, I will lay thy stones with fair colors, and lay thy foundations with sapphires."

Read verse 11 again. "O thou afflicted tossed with tempest and not comforted." Be honest. Have you ever felt that way when you were deep into rejection? Rejection made you feel afflicted, tossed about with the storms of life, and lacking comfort. Rejection prevented you from being comforted. When your spouse says, "I love you," rejection says, "No, get away from me. I will not be comforted, I will not allow you to love me."

But Jesus says, "O thou afflicted, tossed with tempest and not comforted. Behold

I will lay thy stones with fair colors. And lay thy foundations with sapphires." This kind of relief goes far beyond anything you can gain from rejection. Jesus covers you with jewels. He will come with fine clothes, dress you up and place a crown on your head.

Verses 12-13 say, "And I will make thy windows of agates and thy gates of carbuncles and all thy borders of pleasant stones. And all thy children shall be taught of the LORD and great shall be the peace of thy children." There is no room for rejection here. Rejection's stranglehold on your family tree is severed today and for all eternity! You shall be established in righteousness!

Verse 14 says, "You shall be far from oppression for you shall not fear: and from terror." Panic and nightmares sometimes attack us in the middle of the night. Psalms 91 talks about Satan using terror by night to stalk us. But Jesus set us free!

Verses 14-15 continue, "You shall not fear, from terror for it shall not come nigh thee. Behold they shall surely gather together but not by me. Whosoever shall gather together against thee shall fall for thy sake." When terror starts coming against us, God is going to defend us. Why? He's our Husband.

Verse 16, "Behold I have created the smith that bloweth the coals in the fire and that bringeth forth an instrument for his work, and I have created the waster to destroy. No weapon that is formed against thee shall prosper and every tongue that shall rise against thee in judgment, LORD ye shall condemn it. This is the heritage of the servants of the Lord, and their righteousness is of Me, saith the LORD."

Isaiah 53 describes the ultimate rejection; the object here is our Redeemer, Savior and Husband. The world cruelly rejected Christ, but He defeated this rejection.

Isaiah 54 describes the redemption of the rest of us, including those who have been desolated by accusing spirits, rejection and unloving spirits. God says to listen to Him, believe and act on what He has said and done for us and He will defeat rejection in our lives. Let God be true and every man a liar.

Revelation 1:6 says, "And hath made us kings and priests unto God and his Father; to Him be glory and dominion for ever and ever. Amen."

Revelation 5:10 says, "And hast made us unto our God kings and priests: and we shall reign on the earth."

You are an uncondemned king and priest of Jesus Christ. Romans 8:1 says, "There is therefore now no condemnation [rejection] to them which are in Christ Jesus, who walk not after the flesh, but after the Spirit."

RECEIVING REJECTION IS IDOLATRY

We cannot prevent people from rejecting us but we can control how we respond. If we have responded by receiving the hurt and pain, we have fallen into idolatry. It is idolatry because we have allowed more importance to their words or actions than we have to God's. Anything that we allow to become between us and God, is idolatry or a form of occultism. Picture the moon coming between the sun and the earth, thus blocking the sun from view. This is called an occult moon. We do the same thing when we allow another person's actions or words to block us from His truth.

This is an important principle to deeply understand. It will set you free, as you workthrough it. Receiving the pain from rejection is therefore a sin.This means that we do not have to receive the pain. We must learn to remember who we are in the eyes of God, not man.

When we are whole and secure in who we are in God, we will be able to minister to others in their sin, instead of being hurt and offended.

RELEASE FROM REJECTION

Do you want release from rejection? Take these four steps:

First, accept God's love once and for all. James 1:6-8 says, "But let him ask in faith, nothing wavering. For he that wavereth is like a wave of the sea driven with the wind and tossed. For let not that man think that he shall receive any thing of the Lord. A double-minded man is unstable in all his ways." Don't vacillate. You are God's heir and Christ's king and priest. You are accepted, not rejected. God the Father is the giver of every good and perfect gift. If it is not good and perfect, it is not from God.

Second, we must get rid of all self-rejection. Review the chapter on the principality of self-bitterness and make sure that you have worked through every issue. God is for you; who can be against you? Since God has accepted you, you must accept yourself. Otherwise you make God a liar. Do you want to call God a liar?

Third, do not let other people's rejection of you get to you. We must always remember receiving the pain of rejection is idolatry. We cannot stop people from rejecting us but can control how we react. If we react by receiving the pain, we have sinned. If you take time to really understand what I am teaching, it will set you free. Realizing that it is a sin to receive the pain from rejection, means that we do not have to receive the rejection. It is the sin of idolatry because we are putting the actions or words of the person above God's.

People who feel rejected will still reject you. If they have bitterness, they will express bitterness to you. If they have jealousy and envy, they will express it to you. But you do not have to receive their words or actions into your heart.

Understanding this, and being prepared in your heart, being secure in God, and in your position in Him, defeats rejection. This security in Christ gives you all the power you need to resist Satan and banish rejection. Remember that God doesn't reject us even though some people might.

Develop a close fellowship with God the Father, Jesus the Word, and the Holy Spirit. II Timothy 1:7 says that God hasn't given you the spirit of fear, but of power, love and a sound mind. The antidote for fear is the power of the Godhead. The Holy

Spirit gives us power. The Father gives us love. The Word of God, Jesus, gives us a sound mind. Fellowship with the Godhead drives fear away. Start your day in fellowship with God. Walk in His spirit all day long.

False love depends on someone else's approval. If we receive their approval, they will allow us to build a relationship with them. They can steal away their approval at any time.

Real love is unconditional. It is built on an already established relationship, not anyone's approval. It's built on a true and eternal principle: your miraculous relationship with God through Christ Jesus. This kind of love makes us strong even in our failures.

Fourth, we must repent for the sin of rejection. Quit believing the devil and his lies. We suggest that you pray through and accept the truth of what God thinks of you. You are the apple of His eye, the bride of Christ, the righteousness of God by faith, a son or daughter of God, the heir of all creation, known and planned before the foundation of the world, unique, and special. God has a place for you in the universe, and your place will, and already has, changed the future of the world.

Deuteronomy 32:9-10 says, "For the LORD's portion is His people; Jacob is the lot of his inheritance. He found him in a desert land, and in the waste howling wilderness; He led him about, He instructed him, He kept him as the apple of His eye."

Psalms 17:7-8 says, "Shew thy marvelous lovingkindness, O thou that savest by thy right hand them which put their trust in thee from those that rise up against them. Keep me as the apple of the eye, hide me under the shadow of Thy wings."

Isaiah 49:14-16 says, "But Zion said, The LORD hath forsaken me, and my Lord hath forgotten me. Can a woman forget her sucking child, that she should not have compassion on the son of her womb? yea, they may forget, yet will I not forget thee. Behold, I have graven thee upon the palms of my hands; thy walls are continually before me."

Romans 3:21-22 says, "But now the righteousness of God without the law is manifested, being witnessed by the law and the prophets; Even the righteousness of God which is by faith of Jesus Christ unto all and upon all them that believe: for there is no difference."

II Corinthians 5:21 says, "For He hath made Him to be sin for us, who knew no sin; that we might be made the righteousness of God in Him."

Galatians 5:5 says, "For we through the Spirit wait for the hope of righteousness by faith."

II Timothy 4:8 says, "Henceforth there is laid up for me a crown of righteousness, which the Lord, the righteous judge, shall give me at that day: and not to me only, but unto all them also that love His appearing."

Ephesians 1:4-12 says, "According as He hath chosen us in Him before the foundation of the world, that we should be holy and without blame before Him in love: Having predestinated us unto the adoption of children by Jesus Christ to Himself, according to the good pleasure of His will, To the praise of the glory of His grace, wherein He hath made us accepted in the beloved. In whom we have redemption through His blood, the forgiveness of sins, according to the riches of His grace; Wherein He hath abounded toward us in all wisdom and prudence; Having made known unto us the mystery of His will, according to His good pleasure which He hath purposed in Himself: that in the dispensation of the fullness of times He might gather together in one all things in Christ, both which are in heaven, and which are on earth; even in Him: In Whom also we have obtained an inheritance, being predestinated according to the purpose of Him who worketh all things after the counsel of His own will: That we should be to the praise of His glory, who first trusted in Christ."

You are precious to God, accepted by Him. Enjoy Him and His creation from this day forward.

PRAYER AND PROCESS FOR OVERCOMING REJECTION

Make a list of all the ways that you have been rejected by others, perceived yourself as rejected, or been the one to reject others. Write a list of those people and events. We need to confess and repent before Almighty God of believing rejection, receiving rejection, and rejecting others. The stronghold that rejection has held in your life will be destroyed, and Satan's power over you will be legally cancelled. Here is an example of a prayer you can use to deal with rejection and eliminate it from your life:

> *Dear Heavenly Father, in the name of Jesus, I ask you*
> *to forgive me for:*
>
> *1. Any fear of rejection*
> *2. Ways that I have rejected others*
> *3. Ways that I have rejected myself*
> *4. Ways that I have desired rejection*

(It is important to pray through each specific way that you may have sinned.)

> *I purpose and choose to forgive myself and release myself*
> *from (the above specific sin). In the name of Jesus I*
> *cancel all of Satan's power and authority over me in this*
> *issue. Because God has forgiven me and I have forgiven*
> *myself, in the name of Jesus, I command the spirit of*
> *rejection to go.*
>
> *Holy Spirit please come and heal my heart, and tell me*
> *your truth about this situation.*

When the Holy Spirit speaks to you, write down His message in the space provided. When you have finished this prayer for each person or situation on your list, command the principality of rejection to go in the name of Jesus.

REJECTION (RECEIVED OR PERCEIVED FROM, HELD AGAINST OTHERS):

THE HOLY SPIRIT'S ANSWER (TRUTH):

_____   _____

_____   _____

_____   _____

_____   _____

_____   _____

_____   _____

_____   _____

_____   _____

_____   _____

_____   _____

_____   _____

_____   _____

_____   _____

_____   _____

_____   _____

_____   _____

_____   _____

_____   _____

_____   _____

_____   _____

CHAPTER TEN

Principality of Fear

DEFINITION

First, let's define fear. Satan is the master counterfeiter. He will always take what God has meant for good and distort it for his purposes.

The dictionary defines "fear" as "the emotion of being afraid, of feeling danger, or that evil is near, an uneasy or anxious thought." Synonyms are dread, or alarm. Dread is defined as "a great fear."

Fear can warn us of danger so that we can protect ourselves. If we are standing next to a cliff, it warns us to be careful. In times of danger fear also creates a "flight-fight" response in our bodies. This flight-fight response causes the adrenal glands to secrete large amounts of adrenaline, which causes several different physiological responses in our bodies. The primary one is an increase in strength to protect us. But many live in a constant state of flight-fight as they think about the things that have happened to them. The over-secretion of adrenaline and cortisol will destroy your immune system and the calcium in your bones.

Scripture teaches us that we are to fear God. This does not mean that we are to be afraid of Him.

The Hebrew word used for this kind of fear is *yir'ah* (Strong's 3374). It means to have reverence for God. He is the giver of every good and perfect gift. But all too many of us are afraid of Him. The Hebrew word for this kind of fear is *yare* (Strong's 3372). It means cause to be frightened, to make afraid or dread.

God the Father is love. In Matthew 22:37 Jesus said, "Thou shalt love the Lord thy God with all thy heart, and with all thy soul, and with all thy mind." We are to love God the Father, not be afraid of Him. God is the only one that loves each of us perfectly.

The Greek word *deilos*, translated fear in the New Testament, means "to dread; timid," i.e. (by implication) it means "faithless or fearful." Fear is equated with being faithless (Matthew 8:26, Mark 4:40, II Timothy 1:7, Revelation 21:8). Matthew 8:26 illustrates this meaning: "And He saith unto them, Why are ye fearful, O ye of little faith? Then He arose, and rebuked the winds and the sea; and there was a great calm." Mark 4:40 says, "And He said unto them, Why are ye so fearful? how is it that ye have no faith?"

Scripture records four occurrences of little or no faith: 1) concerning necessities of life (Matthew 6:30); 2) concerning danger (Matthew 8:26); 3) concerning working miracles (Matthew 14:31); 4) concerning food (Matthew 16:6-12).

In this chapter we will establish the fact that this kind of fear is a sin, and learn how to defeat it. We will see what fear has done and is doing to us, and how it functions. Being afraid, uneasy or anxious, and having great fear can cause extreme problems spiritually, physically and mentally.

Psalms 56:11 says, "In God have I put my trust: I will not be afraid what man can do unto me." We will see how these powerful words can deliver us from Satan's grasp and heal our diseases.

The Bible gives us many antidotes — remedies — to fear. The entire Bible is written to and about God's people. The Bible is written to the Old Testament church and the New Testament church. The Bible is not written about or to sinners, but to believers.

I John 4:18 says, "There is no fear in love; but perfect love casteth out fear: because fear hath torment. He that feareth is not made perfect in love." If we are in fear we are not made perfect in love. In other words, our fear prevents us from receiving His love. In fear we are calling Him a liar and telling Him that we do not trust Him. This kind of fear is unbelief.

Fear often uses torment to affect our minds and bodies, causing mental and physical disease. Medical textbooks list more than forty diseases that result from anxiety and stress.

Since Scripture links fear to faithlessness, then fear must be a form of sin. This is a new thought to most people. Searching the Scriptures helps us better understand what God says about fear.

Revelation 21:8 says, "But the fearful, and unbelieving, and the abominable, and murderers, and whoremongers, and sorcerers, and idolaters, and all liars, shall have their part in the lake which burneth with fire and brimstone: which is the second death."

Fear is linked with some very serious and damaging sins in this verse. The penalty, too, is very serious: spending eternity in the lake of fire, the second death. God takes sin seriously, and again, He lists fear as sin, right next to murder, sorcery, idolatry and lying.

God is testing our hearts. Mankind has been on probation for six thousand years as God examines us to discern whether He has another Lucifer on His hands. He tests us for the kind of rebellion revealed in the hearts of one-third of all of heaven's angels. Do we harbor any rebellion? Unbelief and faithlessness are forms of rebellion. As we live out our days, will we be God's ambassadors or leaders of another rebellion against Him, like Lucifer?

We need a reality check now, because now is the time that our hearts are being perfected for eternity. As people saved by faith and who are on daily probation, we work out our salvation with fear and trembling. God expects us to live triumphantly, in His power and for His purpose. Philippians 2:12 says, "Wherefore, my beloved, as ye have always obeyed, not as in my presence only, but now much more in my absence, work out your own salvation with fear and trembling."

Ephesians 2:8 says, "For by grace are ye saved through faith; and that not of yourselves: it is the gift of God." We are saved by faith, but faith is never alone. James 2:17 says, "Even so faith, if it hath not works, is dead, being alone." We are to work out our salvation by showing our faith by our works James 2:18 says, "Yea, a man may say, Thou hast faith, and I have works: shew me thy faith without thy works, and I will shew thee my faith by my works."

It is clear that we have a responsibility to live in a manner consistent with one who has been perfected, pressing on toward our high calling in Christ Jesus. Personal holiness, sanctification and righteousness give no room to fear. Fear stems from unrighteousness.

Our fear provides Satan's kingdom a foothold. Fear tells God that He's lost the battle and claims that Satan rules. It declares God powerless to do anything about it. Fear and faith are equal in this; they both demand to be fulfilled.

Hebrews 11:1 says, "Now faith is the substance of things hoped for, the evidence of things not seen." Fear consists of things not hoped for, the evidence seen, or at least vividly imagined. Fear focuses on temporal events, ignores the eternal, and plays a central role in our earthly existence.

It is a common — and false — Christian teaching that once we are saved, all of our problems disappear. This teaching results in great confusion. The evidence is that we all struggle with sin and disease. We cannot deny the evidence. In truth the war just begins when we become born again. But it is a war that we can win if we apply God's principles by becoming a doer of the Word.

The difference for a believer is that when we face problems, our relationship with the Godhead has given us the ability to successfully deal with them. Before Christ, we had no ability to conquer sin. Under the New Covenant we can defeat the works of the devil in our lives. Yet to defeat sin, we still must choose to do our part, and that is to obey God and resist the devil. God's part is to send the devil fleeing.

What does this mean? "...work out your own salvation with fear and trembling" (Philippians 2:12). I Peter 4:18 says, "And if the righteous scarcely be saved, where shall the ungodly and the sinner appear?"

The Bible adds that judgment begins at the house of God. I Peter 4:17 says, "For the time is come that judgment must begin at the house of God: and if it first begin at us, what shall the end be of them that obey not the gospel of God?"

Revelation 19:7-8 says, "Let us be glad and rejoice, and give honour to Him: for the marriage of the Lamb is come, and his wife hath made herself ready. And to her was granted that she should be arrayed in fine linen, clean and white." Are we ready for this?

Scripture says that we are dressed in fine linen. This fine linen is the righteousness of saints. It's a garment of righteousness, not a literal garment. Righteousness speaks to our right standing with God through Jesus Christ. God freely gave us, or imputes, Christ's righteousness at the time of our salvation. This legal position is not the same as our experience. We are also to be sanctified in our experience in our daily walk with God.

Isaiah 33:14 says, "The sinners in Zion are afraid; fear-fullness hath surprised the hypocrites. Who among us shall dwell with the devouring fire? Who among us shall dwell with everlasting burnings?"

The sinners in Zion are afraid. What does this describe? Zion represents the church in covenant with God. How can we have a covenant relationship with God and still be sinners? Does accepting Jesus as our Savior render us unable to sin? Of course not. God says no one is sinless. II Chronicles 6:36a says: "If they sin against thee, (for there is no man which sinneth not)."

II Chronicles 7:14 says, "If My people, which are called by My name, shall humble themselves, and pray, and seek My face, and turn from their wicked ways; then will I hear from heaven, and will forgive their sin, and will heal their land." This verse speaks to His people, God's people, believers.

No one is sinless. If we think we are sinless, we have been deceived. Romans 3:23 says, "For all have sinned, and come short of the glory of God."

When we stand before God and our works are tested by fire, whatever is not burned up will stand eternally. What areas of our lives would fail the scrutiny of the living God? Many areas.

HOW DOES FEAR ENTER OUR LIVES?

God's Word describes the characteristics of those who have good standing before Him. "He that walketh righteously and speaketh uprightly; he that despiseth the gain of oppressions, that shaketh his hands from holding of bribes, that stoppeth his ears from hearing of blood, and shutteth his eyes from seeing evil; He shall dwell on high: his place of defense shall be the munitions of rocks: bread shall be given him; his waters shall be sure. Thine eyes shall see the King in His beauty: they shall behold the land that is very far off" (Isaiah 33:15-17). The beauty and power of these promises bless God's people.

As believers, how does fear enter our lives? These verses suggest two ways. The person who walks righteously stops his ears from hearing violence, and shuts his eyes from seeing evil.

We have ministered to many adults and children who suffer from nightmares. In every case, Satan has haunted them with something they had watched or heard: a TV program, movie, a video game, Harry Potter or Pokémon. These created an entry point for the spirit of fear. II Timothy 1:7 says, "For God hath not given us the spirit of fear; but of power, and of love, and of a sound mind."

The spirit of fear is a tool of the devil that he sends to torment us. God has given His power, the Holy Spirit; His love, which is Himself; and a sound mind, which is

Jesus the Word. We give the spirits of fear access to us by the things we choose to watch or participate in.

We have also ministered to people with asthma, which is caused by fear, anxiety and stress. Fear causes the bronchial tubes and alveoli to become rigid, preventing the release of carbon dioxide. Trapped in the lungs, the carbon dioxide prevents the lungs from absorbing oxygen. Anxiety and fear may also cause inflammation. The inhaler that asthma sufferers use contains an anti-anxiety and muscle-relaxant drug. These drugs cause the cell walls to relax so a healthy exchange of carbon dioxide and oxygen can take place. Some inhalers also contain steroids to reduce the inflammation, and thus open the air passages. The drugs, acting as they do, bring real relief, but they also indicate a real problem rooted in fear, anxiety and stress. We have witnessed many children and adults win their freedom from fear and subsequently from asthma.

Fear affects allergies as well. I used to suffer from a disease called Multiple Chemical Sensitivity (MCS). Over the years, I harbored resentment and bitterness, weakening my immune system. I kept and "lived in" a record of wrongs against others and myself. This triggered the release of adrenaline and cortisol into my bloodstream, causing me to live in a constant state of flight-fight. God did not design the human body to function this way and eventually something has to give. The body wears itself out as these hormones destroy its immune system, constantly sending conflicting signals.

Allergies result from this breakdown in the immune system. Then we become fearful of the things to which we are allergic. We even begin to fear what we might become allergic to in the future. Every time I saw a doctor, my list of allergies grew right along with my fear level.

Once I learned to forgive others and myself, my immune system began the healing process. When I cast the spirit of fear out of myself, my allergies left me altogether. My allergic reactions were real, but fear and bitterness were their root cause. It is always an eye-opening but exciting process, for someone getting total relief from their allergies, to observe that one day something bothers them, and the next day it doesn't. The food did not change and neither did environmental factors. The only thing that changed was them!

Since I've been healed, I've shared my story with many others. They, too, have been healed of their allergies by conquering the sins of fear and bitterness. In fact, this is what formed the foundation of our ministry.

Our experience has taught us that as we get involved in people's lives, whatever they have opened their hearts to serves as a medium of transference from the kingdom of Satan into their soul.

How many times have we exposed our eyes to evil, saying, "well, I'm only watching (or reading, or listening); I'm not actually doing it; or, it is just entertainment, so it's okay"? Watching evil condones it. We become an accessory after the fact. We must chose to guard our eyes against evil. Most TV programming endangers your spiritual health, and that of your family.

Many video games are filled with violence, often resulting in antisocial behavior and rebellion. Pokémon, for instance, is straight from the pit of hell.

Pokémon means "pocket monster." It is a dangerous game for our children to play, as a version of Satanism for kids. Satanic worship invites people to gather more and more powerful demons inside themselves, giving them more powers and ability. The goal in Pokémon is to collect as many of the one hundred fifty different demons' cards as possible, because owning the card gives you the character's power. This is pure Satanism in its philosophy, principle and practice.

Harry Potter is seducing our children into witchcraft, wicca, black magic and the occult.

God says that we are to be called out and separated from other people — different from them, not leavened by them. "But ye are a chosen generation, a royal priesthood, an holy nation, a peculiar people; that ye should shew forth the praises of Him who hath called you out of darkness into His marvelous light" (I Peter 2:9). Yes, it's hard to live as called-out people given all the cultural distractions, but this is what Almighty God asks of us. God repeats this theme many times. I Thessalonians 2:12 says, "That ye would walk worthy of God, who hath called you unto His kingdom and glory."

Environmental illness is one of our most common fear and anxiety disorders. People become allergic to everything. We ministered to a lady who was allergic to literally all foods. She stood five-feet-five-inches, but weighed just seventy-nine pounds when we first met. Within two weeks of our first ministry session, she was eating more than fifty foods. She had gone from despair to joy as she learned to defeat fear. She no longer feared different foods, saying, "I was preparing to die because I could not eat enough to live. I thought I'd only get to enjoy food again in Heaven." Since casting down fear, she has regained normal weight and God has restored her health.

The person with this type of severe fear disorder usually meets one or more of the following four conditions: 1) they were verbally abused, 2) emotionally abused, 3) physically abused, or 4) sexually abused. This abuse often begins in childhood.

They also may have lived in a sterile environment, devoid of love. Perhaps their parents' love was conditioned upon meeting some set of difficult expectations. They rarely met the expectations of their parents. They were never quite good enough. These situations create a performance-orientated person. They feel that they must be good and perfect or they will not be accepted or okay. They live in the fear of being rejected.

I John 4:18 says, "There is no fear in love; but perfect love casteth out fear: because fear hath torment. He that feareth is not made perfect in love." Love gives no place to fear, but when we are not loved perfectly, fear finds an open door. I John 4:18b says, "Perfect love casts out fear." Then, "fear has torment." And, "he that feareth [because of the breakdown in love] is not made perfect in love."

When we're afraid because we've not been loved perfectly since our youngest days, we're not able to give or receive love without fear. That's what the Bible means by, "he that feareth is not made perfect in love."

Psalms 34:4-5 says, "I sought the LORD, and He heard me, and delivered me from all my fears. They looked unto Him, and were lightened: and their faces were not ashamed." When we have shame, we have fear. When we feel unworthy, we have fear. When we feel guilty, we have fear. When we feel condemned, we have fear. When we feel like second-rate citizens (self-condemnation), we have fear.

FEARS THAT TORMENT US

It is very important for us to recognize the various kinds of fear that trouble us. Number one on the list is fear of man. What is fear of man? It is fear of others, including our mother, father, grandmother, grandfather, brothers, sisters, pastors, parents, bosses, and schoolteachers: fear of anyone or everyone. If we can't look people in the eye, we fear men. Most of us experience a time in our lives when we fear men, but we ought not to continue doing so.

The Word of God provides the antidote that combats the fear of man. When we feel intimidated by someone, God will take that weakness and make us strong. Hebrews 11:34 says, "...Quenched the violence of fire, escaped the edge of the sword, out of weakness were made strong, waxed valiant in fight, turned to flight the armies of the aliens."

John 3:30 gives us the formula for victory over sin by a proper relationship with our Savior: "He must increase, but I must decrease."

Next comes fear of rejection. So many of us feel sorry for ourselves because others reject us. Hebrews 13:6 says, "So that we may boldly say, The Lord is my helper, and I won't fear what man shall do unto me."

Believers should be neither surprised nor troubled by rejection, at least when it's for the right reasons. In Isaiah 53:3, we find that Jesus was rejected of men: "He is despised and rejected of men; a man of sorrows, and acquainted with grief: and we hid as it were our faces from Him; He was despised, and we esteemed Him not." Still, it often hurts to be rejected, even when it's for righteous reasons. Turn to Christ and draw your strength from Him. He says to cast all your cares on Him, because He cares for you.

On the other hand, if we are rejected because we are worldly, walking in the flesh, we need a change of direction. We need to walk in the Light of Jesus Christ, and let Him defeat the spirit of rejection for us.

The Bible says the enemies of a man can often be found in his own house. "For the son dishonoureth the father, the daughter riseth up against her mother, the daughter in law against her mother in law; a man's enemies are the men of his own house" (Micah 7:6). Even prophets have no honor in their own home. "But Jesus said unto them, A prophet is not without honour, but in his own country, and among his own kin, and in his own house" (Mark 6:4).

The rejection battleground in this war for our minds and hearts is in the family. And it spreads to the church, which is no stronger than the families it represents. Cities and nations are made up of families and reflect their strength or weakness. Families are no stronger than their individual members. Weak families populated by weak parents and defeated children are the consequence of homes filled with the fear of rejection.

Our Lord is acquainted with our sorrows and our grief. He feels our infirmities. "For we have not an high priest which cannot be touched with the feeling of our infirmities; but was in all points tempted like as we are, yet without sin" (Hebrews 4:15).

God hears all our words and knows all our thoughts. He is right here with us now. God stands ready to help us withstand abuse and defeat rejection.

Zechariah 13 provides strong teaching we have often used to help people who have been somehow abused in their own family. It is a prophecy about Jesus' enthronement during the millennium. The people from all the nations of the earth — natural people that came out of tribulation — come and bow before Him once each year, acknowledging that He is King of kings and LORD of lords.

As they bow before Him, they see the scars in His hands, still there after His resurrection. They ask Him how He got them. Zechariah describes the scene: "And one shall say unto Him, What are these wounds in Thine hands? Then He shall answer, Those with which I was wounded in the house of My friends" (Zechariah 13:6).

Christ resisted and withstood Satan to the point of death. We have not done so. Sure we have it tough sometimes, but nothing like our Savior. We need to abandon self-pity. Jesus died, murdered because of His love for us. He will say, "These are the wounds I received in the house of My friends."

Consider the gravity and power of these facts. God the Word, Whom Mary and Joseph named Jesus, left His heavenly throne where He lived with God. He voluntarily came to Earth, which sin had damned to extinction. The only way He could leave this earth was to die, and He knew it before He came. John 15:13 relates Christ's own word: "Greater love hath no man than this, that a man lay down his life for his friends."

Christ's sacrifice of Himself on the Cross is the greatest love story ever told. As we begin to understand this, fear can no longer touch us because we're already dead, i.e. we're dead to ourselves, and eternally alive in Him. "For whosoever will save his life shall lose it: and whosoever will lose his life for My sake shall find it" (Matthew 16:25). We must die to ourselves, and then find real life in a new relationship with God the Father, Jesus the Son, and God the Holy Spirit.

Fear of losing something holds great power over us. But a relevant question is, how can we lose anything if we're already dead? As believers, our lives are no longer our own. Whether we live or die, we are the Lord's. To be absent from our body is to be present with Him. "We are confident, I say, and willing rather to be absent from the body, and to be present with the Lord" (II Corinthians. 5:8).

Psalms 118:8 says, "It is better to trust in the Lord than to put confidence in man." Yet we live in fear of others even though we are "dead men walking." As believers, we're dead to our old self but alive in Christ. As new creatures, fearful events shouldn't make a bit of difference to us as we live each day. Does fear come knocking on our door? It knocks on every man's door. Does it sometimes stagger us? It staggers all men. But the hurricane force winds of fear are just a slight breeze against which we press as we walk in His light. Fear becomes nothing more than a gentle breeze of satanic resistance.

With fear conquered, we are no longer bowled over by what fear represents. Instead, we're able to keep our eyes focused straight ahead and moving toward Christ. If you have ears to hear this teaching, then the Spirit of God will speak to your heart today. This is a powerful lesson straight out of the Word of God.

Fear is a principality of Satan. Ephesians 6:12 says, "For we wrestle not against flesh and blood, but against principalities, against powers, against the rulers of the darkness of this world, against spiritual wickedness in high places."

II Timothy 1:7 is clear: "For God hath not given us the spirit of fear; but of power, and of love, and of a sound mind." The antidote to fear is a vital relationship with the Godhead. Power is the Holy Spirit, love is God the Father, and a sound mind is Jesus, the Word. When we are established in the Holy Spirit, the love of the Father, and the Word of God, Satan's fiery darts of fear can never hit us!

On the other hand, if we don't have a close relationship with the Father, the power of the Holy Spirit, or the living Word, we are like a leaf battered by the winds of life, subject at any time to be torn away and blown by fear's fiercest blast. A believer should build on the solid foundation God gave us in Jesus Christ, empowered by His Holy Spirit, standing strong like a tree planted by the waters, whose roots go deep into the ground.

The spirit of fear is never from God. Am I teaching that fear is an evil spirit? Actually, I'm saying more than that. There are many evil spirits of fear, but there is also a principality called fear. He's one of Satan's ruling princes of darkness.

Job 3:24-26 explains Satan's legal right to attack Job. Job had fear. "For my sighing cometh before I eat, and my roarings are poured out like the waters. For the thing which I greatly feared is come upon me, and that which I was afraid of is come unto me. I was not in safety, neither had I rest, neither was I quiet; yet trouble came."

Job 4:12-16 provides a clear description of the spirit of fear. "Now a thing was secretly brought to me, and mine ear received a little thereof. In thoughts from the visions of the night, when deep sleep falleth on men, Fear came upon me, and trembling, which made all my bones to shake. Then a spirit passed before my face; the hair of my flesh stood up: It stood still, but I could not discern the form thereof: an image was before mine eyes, there was silence, and I heard a voice, saying . . . ." Here we find an evil spirit that God's Word calls a spirit of fear. Have you had a similar experience? Have you ever felt evil's presence so strongly that you were terrified? I have.

Another fear is the fear of failure. One Scripture will defeat this evil spirit. Proverbs 24:16 says, "For a just man falleth seven times, and riseth up again: but the wicked shall fall into mischief." Though a righteous person falls, i.e. fails, seven times, the Lord's strong hand will lift him up. That is powerful news.

If we ever attempt anything in life, we will experience some failure. A major league baseball player with a three hundred batting average fails seven out of ten times. Nearly every successful author saw dozens, if not hundreds, of rejection slips before a publisher finally took a chance with them. Failure is common to mankind. It is not a question of failing; it's a question of how to respond to failure. You might say, "Well, if I never try out for the team, I can never be cut." That attitude in itself is a failure fueled by the fear of failure. Not acting on a Holy Spirit-inspiration because of fear of failure is failure.

God has made provision for the failures of His saints. He pledges to pick us up and set us on our feet again. Just as He did, we need to make provision for failure in our life. The fact that He created forgiveness proves that He made provision for our failures.

If we don't make provision for failure, we'll be bound by a spirit of fear. Instead, we'll go into denial and never deal with or do anything. By our inaction, Satan wins a battle.

Every one of us avoids dealing with certain areas of our life. Every church avoids dealing with certain structural or discipline problems. This avoidance arises out of fear, but it is certain that during the course of life, these problems will surface. And it makes no difference whether or not we are born again, or the church is filled with true believers. It's amazing how often we hear, "I never had these kind of troubles until I got saved." When we got saved we entered into a spiritual war that we must learn how to win. We would have had trouble anyway, but God saved us and gave us power to deal with the problems. God's grace worked on our behalf and we didn't even know it.

Every one of us has areas of life that bring us shame and produce failure. These are the areas that need to be sanctified and renewed. We're not to be afraid of failure, we are to learn from the failures and let God heal our broken hearts.

Avoiding the areas of our lives that need to be sanctified pushes us into denial and torments us. We can pray, "God, take this thorn from my flesh, but I want no part of its removal." That's not realistic. I John 1:9 says that if we ask, God will forgive. God will never remove our fears if we fail to face them and deal with them.

For a Christian, problems serve as stepping stones to maturity through their sancti-fying effect. Don't be afraid of problems or of sin. The problems, or spiritual attacks, in life are really opportunities to defeat Satan. In these problems or attacks, Satan has revealed his hand, giving us clear direction on how to defeat him. God helps us fight fear and make the choices that win success.

God never causes us to fail. The cause of failure is sin, and that started with Adam. It's in our family tree, and in our life, and it will eventually surface. Why not let God perfect us as we face and defeat our fears?

How many of us can honestly say that we don't like admitting we made a mistake or failed? Do you know why? Because we have fear of man and of rejection, and we don't want anybody to know we're weak.

God knows that we are weak, and that our human frame is but dust. "For He knoweth our frame; He remembereth that we are dust" (Psalms 103:14). He made provision through Jesus Christ for our infirmities, which are human weaknesses. II Corinthians 13:9 says, "For we are glad, when we are weak, and ye are strong: and this also we wish, even your perfection." In Christ, fear can be dealt a deadly blow. It can be faced head on. But denial is an act of fear.

We must consider one more fear: fear of abandonment. Fear of abandonment gains access to us through several life events. Children conceived or born out of wedlock and of divorced parents fear abandonment. If there has been or is arguing and strife in the home, the children will be plagued with spirits of fear, rejection and abandonment. They often feel rejected and abandoned by one of their parents, or both. A parent's death often has the same result.

Women fear abandonment by their husbands. The Scriptures teach that the woman was created for the man. The woman was to be a helpmate who followed the Godly leadership of her husband. She was created to be a follower. The man was created to be the leader of the family.

When the man's protection, safety, and security by which she is covered is stripped away, the spirit of fear moves in immediately to oppress her. God did not give her the same spiritual dynamics to handle these types of situations as He gave to man. When the family's protector flees or fails, she becomes fearful and distrustful. Her distrust lingers for a long time.

God intended for every wife and child to dwell safely in the father and husband's presence. God appointed the husband to be the guard dog at the door. God enabled him to handle all manner of problems, and provide the family's safety net.

This is the picture of Christ in Isaiah 54, the husband who cares for and protects His bride. Men need to be the husbands and fathers God has asked them to be.

Titus 2 gives a picture of a vital church, ministering to its various age groups. It shows older, more mature women caring for the younger single women, admonishing and teaching them. The covering for these ministering women is their husband, and over him, the Lord. The church and the family are like an umbrella, spreading out and protecting those beneath it. If the church practiced what Scripture teaches, there would be no abandonment issues with which to deal.

James 1:27 says, "Pure religion and undefiled before God and the Father is this, To visit the fatherless and widows in their affliction, and to keep himself unspotted from the world."

When death or disease takes away the man's protection from the woman and her family, God has made provision for them through "pure religion" — ministering to them by other believers. In the Old Testament, the widow was taken as a wife by the man's surviving brother or other male relative. Is there any less reason that in New Testament times, spiritual brothers shouldn't care for the widows? Of course not.

When the accusing spirit of fear starts to speak to us, it replaces our thoughts and feelings with its own. We need discernment to know these are not our thoughts. We are not to fear; we are to be strong in Christ.

When God viewed His creation, He called Adam and Eve "very good." He didn't look down and say, "This is my beloved creation, Fear, who is very good." He didn't say, "These are my beloved children, filled with self-hatred and fear, and I am so happy for them."

If God wanted us to fear, Psalms 34 wouldn't say that He would deliver us from it. II Timothy 1:7 says, "For God hath not given us the spirit of fear; but of power, and of love, and of a sound mind." God did not give us a spirit of fear, so fear should have no home in us. God would never deliver us from something that He created in us.

WHAT IS FEAR?

So what is fear? Fear is our enemy. It's a vital part of Satan's kingdom and his desire to control us and to steal our faith. He desires to send a plague of unbelief and doubt, binding us down with disease so he can defeat God.

God intends for us to stand and face our enemies, never to flee from them. If we run from an enemy, it is a spirit of fear that takes us away. Facing fear is uncomfortable and painful, but not facing fear results in spiritual cancer. Fear grows and festers, becoming ever more painful until we experience spiritual death. Instead, facing fear is the ultimate therapy. Once fear is extinguished, we experience freedom, joy and life.

God's grace and mercy are sufficient to meet and defeat every enemy in our life. He already gave us the victory, but we must appropriate it! God's will is that the devil should have no legal right to our lives. We give Satan a legal right through our sin. God's desire is that we turn from the sin of fear, walk the narrow path of repentance and sanctification, and live a victorious life.

Keep Philippians 2:12 in mind. "Wherefore, my beloved, as ye have always obeyed, not as in my presence only, but now much more in my absence, work out your own salvation with fear and trembling."

II Corinthians 3:18 reminds us that as believers, we're being changed: "But we all, with open face beholding as in a glass the glory of the Lord, are changed into the same image from glory to glory, even as by the Spirit of the Lord."

We are to crucify our flesh. God Himself will be its executioner. Romans 6:6 says, "Knowing this, that our old man is crucified with Him, that the body of sin might be destroyed, that henceforth we should not serve sin." Jesus provided the way but in our free will we must chose to do it.

We're to deal with the earthly kingdom, which Satan rules, that we inherited through Adam. It's a real part of our life that we need to be able to identify and defeat. That brings us into the next stage.

FEAR AND FAITH ARE EQUAL: ONE WILL ALWAYS REPLACE THE OTHER

Fear is a form of occultism. It is a counterfeit, the opposite of what God teaches. Fear comes from a lack of faith. Listed below are specific fears that provide armor to the principality of fear. Please read through this list and identify any with which you may be struggling. This is not a comprehensive list; feel free to add to it.

As you work through this list it will stir up memories. You may need to deal with them. For example, you might remember watching a horror movie and a certain scene sticks in your mind. You should repent for allowing that evil to enter your mind and command it to leave. Or you may recall a bitterness or resentment against someone. If so, confess it, repent of it, and forgive them.

FEAR	HOLY SPIRIT'S RESPONSE
Anxiety and stress (fear)	
Controlling others	
Distress	
Distrust	
Dread: projection of evil into the future	
Drivenness	
Fear of a wasted life	
Fear of abandoning others	
Fear of abandonment	
Fear of animals	
Fear of another's bitterness	
Fear of another's words	

Fear of authority _____

Fear of bad news _____

Fear of being alone _____

Fear of being controlled _____

Fear of being free _____

Fear of being robbed _____

Fear of being shamed _____

Fear of betrayal _____

Fear of bigotry _____

Fear of blood _____

Fear of buildings _____

Fear of change _____

Fear of commitment _____

Fear of criticism _____

Fear of death _____

Fear of deliverance _____

Fear of dependency _____

Fear of disability _____

Fear of disapproval _____

Fear of disease _____

Fear of disfigurement _____

Fear of doctors/hospitals _____

Fear of driving _____

Fear of dying prematurely _____

Fear of everything/
free-floating anxiety _____

Fear of evil _____

Fear of facial expressions _____

Fear of failure _____

Fear of father _____

Fear of fear _____

Fear of fire _____

Fear of foods, clothes,
i.e. allergies _____

Fear of germs _____

Fear of God/afraid of Him _____

Fear of harassment _____

Fear of humiliation _____

Fear of inadequacy _____

Fear of insanity _____

Fear of intercourse or sex _____

Fear of judgment _____

Fear of lack of food,
clothes, etc. _____

Fear of loneliness _____

Fear of losing children _____

Fear of losing life _____

Fear of losing salvation _____

Fear of loss of confidence _____

Fear of loss of relationships _____

Fear of loss of sexual ability _____

Fear of man _____

Fear of menopause _____

Fear of mother _____

Fear of natural disasters _____

Fear of noises _____

Fear of not being free   _____

Fear of own sexuality   _____

Fear of pain   _____

Fear of poverty   _____

Fear of pregnancy   _____

Fear of public speaking   _____

Fear of punishment   _____

Fear of rejection   _____

Fear of reproach   _____

Fear of reproof   _____

Fear of responsibility   _____

Fear of spouse   _____

Fear of success   _____

Fear of suffering   _____

Fear of the dark   _____

Fear of the dying process   _____

Fear of the enemy   _____

Fear of the future   _____

Fear of the unknown   _____

Fear of verbal rejection   _____

Fear of vomiting   _____

Fear of war/conflict   _____

Fear of water   _____

Fear of weapons   _____

Horror   _____

Inferiority   _____

Night terror, dreams
and visions   _____

Panic attacks, various
phobias   _____

Perfectionism   _____

Self-consciousness   _____

Shyness   _____

Speculative fear   _____

Superstitions   _____

Suspicion   _____

Trembling   _____

Now that you have identified various fears, it's time to get rid of them. This is the type of prayer you can pray, asking God to defeat these fears:

Prayer For Overcoming Fear

Heavenly Father, in the name of Jesus, I confess, and repent for allowing the (specific fear) in my life, and I repent for all my generations. I ask You, Lord Jesus, to forgive me. I purpose and choose to forgive myself, from my heart, for allowing this (specific fear) in my life and I release myself from this fear. In the name of Jesus, and by the power of His blood, I cancel all of Satan's authority over me in this fear. In the name of Jesus, I command this fear to go.

Holy Spirit, I invite you into my heart to heal me of this fear. Please speak your words of truth to me about this situation.

While you are praying this, the Holy Spirit might speak to you. Write down what the Holy Spirit spoke to you or what He did in you. This is His testimony to you. When you have prayed through each individual fear, command the principality of fear to go in Jesus' name.

God gave you the power and authority of His Son, Jesus Christ, to defeat fear. His Holy Spirit joins with yours to drive Satan's influence out of your life. You can live in courageous victory!

CHAPTER ELEVEN

Principality of Occultism, Pharmakia & Sorcery

DEFINITION
"Occultism" and "occult" are words usually associated with psychics, witches, warlocks, druids, wicca, or even Satanism. A dictionary provides a more thorough and useful definition.

Webster's Collegiate Dictionary defines "occult" as "1. Of or pertaining to any system claiming use or knowledge of secret or supernatural powers or agencies. 2. Beyond ordinary knowledge or understanding. 3. Secret; disclosed or communicated only to the initiated. 4. Hidden from view. 5. The occult, the supernatural or super-natural agencies and affairs considered as a whole. 6. To block or shut off (an object) from view; hide. 7. To hide (a celestial body) by occultation. 8. To become hidden or shut off from view, cover up (conceal)."

In astronomy, occultation is the passage of one celestial body in front of another, thus hiding the other from view: an eclipse. Occultation is especially applied to a moon passing between an observer and a star or planet. When the moon comes between the sun and the earth it is called an "occult moon" because it block us from seeing the sun.

A Biblical definition of occultism includes any belief or practice that opposes the law of God. It also means any belief or practice that comes between God and us, just as the occult moon comes between the earth and the sun. Occultism thus includes anything that blocks you from, or comes between, you and God. In your mind picture the moon coming between the sun and the earth and then think about anything in your life that comes between you and God. This is the Biblical definition of occultism.

Central to occultism is man's desire to be his own god. In practical terms, this means using any lawless and godless processes to seize control over our lives and the universe. In every appearance and application, occultism is rebellion against God and His authority.

Rebellion stems from self-righteousness and Phariseeism. When Satan, and later Adam and Eve, rebelled against God they didn't think of themselves as sinners. Instead, they saw themselves as freedom-fighters, heroic champions standing against a tyrannical and arbitrary God. Does this sound familiar? They saw sin only as an attribute of God because He had supposedly concealed from them their own claim to divinity and had lied about the consequences of human freedom. Satan said, "Ye shall not surely die," thus implying that God had lied. Satan told Adam that God doesn't want any of us to be like Him. "For God doth know that in the day ye eat thereof, then your eyes shall be opened, and ye shall be as gods, knowing good and evil" (Genesis 3:4-5). After Adam's fall, men certainly came to know evil!

Since then, rebellion has characterized mankind. They see it as a principle of freedom, self-realization, and self-development. People choose to believe that freedom from obeying His laws somehow released them from answering to His laws. They thought rebellion brought them some sort of earthly utopia. But they fooled themselves. Rebellion has not freed us from the temporal or eternal consequences of disobedience.

I Samuel 15:23 says, "for rebellion is as the sin of witchcraft, and stubbornness is as iniquity and idolatry." The word translated "witchcraft" can also be translated as soothsaying or divination.

Samuel equates opposition and disobedience to God to soothsaying, witchcraft, divination and stubbornness. In actuality, all disobedience is idolatry, because it places the human self-will on a par with God — like a god. Opposition to God's Word and commandments is really a rejection of God, thus idolatry and occultism.

Occultism is one of Satan's principalities. Many lesser, but still powerful entities or demons that we expose support it by name. Ephesians 6:12 says, "For we wrestle not against flesh and blood, but against principalities, against powers, against the rulers of the darkness of this world, against spiritual wickedness in high places."

We have separated the principality of occultism into two major types of deceptions. First, we see false religions or belief systems, and then, modern medical practices. It is important to remember God's definition of occultism as you study through this chapter.

BELIEF SYSTEMS

Satan is a master deceiver, seeking to counterfeit the Godhead. First, he wants to counterfeit the Father's will for mankind. He tries to lure us into thinking and seeing life in a way that is different than God's way. Jesus labeled him a liar and the father of lies (John 8:44).

Secondly, Satan wants to counterfeit God's Word, so he entices us with another gospel. Remember that Satan knows Scripture quite well. He began corrupting it from the beginning. As he spoke to Eve in the Garden of Eden, he made subtle changes in the commandments God gave to Adam and Eve. He did this to influence Eve to adopt his way of thinking.

He tried tricking Christ by misquoting Scripture while tempting Him in the wilderness. Luke 4 records the story. But Jesus, the Living Word, straightened Satan out!

Satan wants to teach men a gospel different from God's gospel. Satan's gospel is described as "Having a form of godliness, but denying the power thereof: from such turn away" (II Timothy 3:5). This also describes divination and occultism. It's a way of thinking that twists the truth, often using Scripture to establish some credibility. New

Age teachings run rampant with this type of pseudo-Christian thinking.

Thirdly, Satan wants to counterfeit the Holy Spirit. During his rebellion against God, Satan said, "I will ascend above the heights of the clouds; I will be like the most High" (Isaiah 14:14). Satan is a master plagiarist and illusionist. Satan mystically attaches Jesus' name to false teaching to give it credibility. He throws around the term "Christian" any time it helps him sell a lie. The teachings of Christian Science, Jehovah's Witnesses, and the Church of Jesus Christ of Latter-Day Saints, Moon and others provide examples. These churches twist God's truth and deceive mankind.

Satan attaches the word "Christian" to stars, heroes and personalities and uses their ungodly acts to trick people into changing their minds about him. God says to test the spirits to see whether or not they are His.

Satan is clever and he knows that Biblical principles applied in the lives of nonbelievers still bring blessings. Practicing the charity of I Corinthians 13 brings a blessing. The cheerful heart that gives financial aid to a hurting family receives a blessing. The man who refuses to be surety for another is blessed by this application of Proverbs 11:15.

Matthew 5:45 says, "...your Father which is in heaven: for He maketh his sun to rise on the evil and on the good, and sendeth rain on the just and on the unjust." God's laws apply to the saved and unsaved. But as it concerns eternity, the unsaved are headed straight for Hell, while the saved join the Savior, Jesus Christ, for all eternity.

Satan's subtle lie is that if you have evidence of what appears to be a blessing of God in your life, it is safe to assume that you belong to God. You receive a promotion, even though you cheated on a test, and Satan says, "See, God blessed you anyway." You pray to God because you have a financial need, and then you find a billfold full of money, and an identification card. You keep the money, because Satan says, "See, God answers prayers in unusual ways." Satan contends that the proof is in the blessing. Christian faith and the blessings it bestows are not based on experiences, but on obedience to God.

God speaks the truth in Matthew 16:26. "For what is a man profited, if he shall gain the whole world, and lose his own soul? or what shall a man give in exchange for his soul?"

And again in Mark 8:36, "For what shall it profit a man, if he shall gain the whole world, and lose his own soul?"

Our eternal life is at stake. We must accept God's gift of His Son to receive salvation. There is no other way. John 3:16-17 tells us clearly, "For God so loved the world, that He gave His only begotten Son, that whosoever believeth in Him should not perish, but have everlasting life. For God sent not His Son into the world to condemn the world; but that the world through Him might be saved."

Remember that Satan is a master illusionist and deceiver. II Timothy 3:1-7 says, "This know also, that in the last days perilous times shall come. For men shall be lovers of their own selves, covetous, boasters, proud, blasphemers, disobedient to parents, unthankful, unholy, Without natural affection, trucebreakers, false accusers, incontinent, fierce, despisers of those that are good, Traitors, heady, highminded, lovers of pleasures more than lovers of God; Having a form of godliness, but denying the power thereof: from such turn away. For of this sort are they which creep into houses, and lead captive silly women laden with sins, led away with divers lusts, Ever learning, and never able to come to the knowledge of the truth."

Sorcery can also be called "spiritual bewitchment." Sorcery enters our lives through doctrines of devils. I Timothy 4:1 warns us of this: "Now the Spirit speaketh expressly, that in the latter times some shall depart from the faith, giving heed to seducing spirits, and doctrines of devils." What are doctrines of devils? This refers to the teachings of Satan — counterfeit doctrine — taught to us by other men. A perverse mindset drives these theological, philosophical and ideological teachings. They distort and twist God's truth, and are heretical. They bring about spiritual bewitchment.

Matthew 24:23-24 tells us about another spiritual bewitchment: "Then if any man shall say unto you, Lo, here is Christ, or there; believe it not. For there shall arise false Christs, and false prophets, and shall shew great signs and wonders; insomuch that, if it were possible, they shall deceive the very elect."

The name "Christ" is not the last name of Jesus. It means the "anointed one" or "anointing." In the last days (today) there will be many false prophets, and they will demonstrate many signs and wonders in their false anointing. They will deceive many of God's elect.

We must always remember that the Lord will never call a stone building His temple ever again. I Corinthians 3:16 says, "Know ye not that ye are the temple of God, and that the Spirit of God dwelleth in you?" The primary application of the "abomination of the desolation" described in the book of Daniel is in each of us. We are His temple. The anti-Christ may set up his throne in a temple in Jerusalem but that will be too obvious to fool many. The real deception that we must watch for is within the church and thus within each of us.

Another spiritual bewitchment is the false, heretical doctrine of reincarnation. It is Satan's attempt to use human reason and teaching to convince us that we can avoid the penalty of the judgment. Hebrews 9:27 says, "...it is appointed unto men once to die, but after this the judgment." Men die once!

Spiritual bewitchment exalts itself against the knowledge of God. Proverbs 2:5 says, "Then shalt thou understand the fear of the Lord, and find the knowledge of God." II Corinthians 10:5 tells us to guard against Satan's tactics by, "Casting down imaginations, and every high thing that exalteth itself against the knowledge of God, and bringing into captivity every thought to the obedience of Christ." If we do not know His Word and precepts we will be deceived.

Reincarnation, standing on its foundation of spiritual bewitchment says, "You don't need to worry about the judgment, because you get a chance to come back again and again and work out your sin progressively through rebirth. Someday you, too, can be a god." This teaching is sorcery and a doctrine of devils.

The false doctrine of karma supports the lie of reincarnation. Karma refers to a person's actions and deeds. When karma is coupled to reincarnation, a false belief system results that teaches that every deed, whether good or bad, has an inevitable consequence. Its adherents liken this to the Biblical principle of sowing and reaping. It twists the meaning of Genesis 1:11-12, 21, 24-25 and 29. Galatians 6:7-9 teaches that a little sin, or even a minor false doctrine, corrupts our entire life and affects how we conduct ourselves.

Believers in karma say it explains man's present condition and proposes a way out of suffering. People are told to do good deeds to pay off all their bad karma. This places them in good stead for their next life, and positions them to eventually attain nirvana — a mythological state of perfect blessedness achieved through extinction of the self (as taught in Buddhism). They believe eventually they will become pure spirit through this process of evolution of the soul.

The spiritual bewitchment of karma and reincarnation are common New Age teachings. It teaches that spirit guides, who are highly evolved former humans, no longer need to reincarnate because they have paid off all their karmic debt. These spirit guides are available to help human seekers find good karma and so, make progress on their own road to nirvana. The promise of spiritual evolution is also found in the doctrines of Jainism, Buddhism, Hinduism and occultism.

The truth is that the laws of karma and reincarnation are really Satan's doctrine of self-salvation. They teach that a person who offends another pays the price of that offense himself. There is no need for Jesus Christ's atonement on the cross to pay for sin. By perverting the Biblical doctrine of sowing and reaping, karma and reincarnation create a Satanic doctrine where men become their own savior through the practice of good works.

God says in Romans 3:23, "For all have sinned, and come short of the glory of God." He loves us so much that He provided a way for us to achieve an intimate, personal and perfect relationship with Him. God wrote us a love letter in John 3:16, saying, "For God so loved the world, that he gave His only begotten Son, that whosoever believeth in Him should not perish, but have everlasting life."

Only our Creator God can fulfill the promise of perfecting sinful, fallen men and women. The combined good karma of mankind couldn't purchase a seat outside heaven's gate, much less nirvana.

There are many other Satanic deceptions. Others have written extensively about them in detail and it is not my intent to do so here. However, at the end of this chapter I have listed hundreds of these deceptions. We will discuss them later.

MEDICAL PRACTICES

The word *pharmakia* comes from the Greek word *pharmakeus* (Strong's 5332). It means "medication (pharmacy), and by extension, magic, either literally or figuratively, sorcery or witchcraft." The most literal translation is "medication from a pharmacy."

According to *USA Today*, April 24, 1998, and *Newsweek*, April 27, 1998, adverse reactions to prescription drugs are the fourth leading cause of death in America. The medicines that doctors use to heal us are now the fourth leading cause of our deaths. More recent studies show that about forty-five percent of all deaths are caused by medical mistakes, and/or adverse reactions to prescription drugs.

Are medications actually dangerous? And if so, when do medications become dangerous?

Medications often cover over real problems. When medications prevent someone from dealing with sin, the use of the drug itself becomes a sin. If a drug prevents a person from being sanctified by the Holy Spirit, and it interferes with God's work in them, it falls into the realm of the occult, obscuring the real problem. These uses of medication make them dangerous.

Would I use antibiotics to kill a bacterial infection? Yes, I would. However, first, I would also search myself to see if I entertained anger, bitterness, anxiety, or some other sin that weakened my immune system.

Is it wrong to take ibuprofen, aspirin or acetaminophen for temporary relief of a tension headache? Probably not, but it is essential that you understand that tension is a spiritual problem and that you must take steps to deal with it.

Many doctors recommend taking an aspirin a day as a blood thinner. They suggest this could prevent heart attacks and strokes. We would teach you a more excellent way. Rid yourself of the anxieties, fears and bitterness that are really the root of the problem.

We do not stand against the use of certain medications for temporary relief. But we will not recommend them as a permanent solution any more than we would recommend adultery as a way to get a dopamine rush to satisfy a need to be loved.

Medications can be a form of sorcery. Pharmakia and sorcery offer a type of healing that is not true healing. Addictive or habitual in nature, drugs offer a form of bondage in the name of "helps." However Jesus said, "Peace I leave with you, My peace I give unto you: not as the world giveth, give I unto you. Let not your heart be troubled, neither let it be afraid" (John 14:27).

The Lord Jesus offered to give us His peace, a supernatural, healing peace. Jesus wants our hearts to be free from fear and totally at peace.

Pharmakia and sorcery can only offer a chemically-induced peace, and there is no deliverance from the real enemy. There is a more excellent way (I Corinthians 12:31). Christ offers us peace of mind during this earthly life.

Medications have unwanted physical and psychological side effects. Advertisements for many wonder-drugs carry long, detailed disclaimers about them. "CuresAll (fictitious name) may cause intrauterine bleeding, nausea, thinning of the hair, headaches, scalp itch and bad breath. Some people develop delusions or hallucinations. CuresAll can only be taken with doctor's prescription. But for the relief of tension-caused back cramps, nothing beats CuresAll." We've all seen and read such ads.

Just as many medications have serious spiritual side effects. The disclaimers should read, "Taking CuresAll prevents you from dealing with the tension that causes your back cramps and will hamper your relationship with Jesus Christ."

In our ministry, we see spiritual and psychological problems producing chemical imbalances in people. For example, lack of acceptance of others or ourselves, self-hatred, and self-rejection can cause fear and stress to affect the balance of the delicate endocrine system. Depression is caused by a shortage of the neurotransmitter serotonin.

The primary endocrine system consists of nine glands that produce more than one hundred hormones, neurotransmitters or interleukins. The number is constantly growing as medical science learns more about our very complicated physiology. In fact, medical science is now teaching that virtually every cell in our bodies is part of the diverse endocrine system.

Our thoughts and emotions effect the secretion of each of these glands and every cell in our bodies. An over- or under-secretion of any of these hormones or neurotransmitters has a definite effect on our health. Most medications are designed to restore a chemical imbalance of some kind. Imbalances of hormones, neurotransmitters or interleukins cause the vast majority of our diseases.

As those to whom we minister study and apply God's truths to their lives, we see them come back into chemical and neurological balance. They come out of depression. We see many diseases that are caused by neurological and chemical imbalance go away. Praise God! This type of healing never requires an expensive and dangerous drug maintenance regime. It costs nothing to maintain because it's a new way of life. It's a better life. It's a better way. It's a more excellent way.

We don't believe God is pleased when we spend up to fifty percent of our income maintaining our health, taking vitamin and mineral supplements or prescription drugs. Many people spend hundreds of dollars each month this way. God has far better ways to use our time than watching us sit in doctors' offices trying to figure out what is wrong with us, and then waiting in drugstores to get prescriptions filled.

We are to strive toward the goal of III John 1:2: "Beloved, I wish above all things that thou mayest prosper and be in health, even as thy soul prospereth." Scripture shows a direct connection between health in our body and health in our soul. The Greek word for "prosper" describes a successful journey. As we mature in Christ (sanctification), our health should also prosper. And God gives us the kind of peace that only He can give, that passeth all understanding, the peace that is an alternative to the chemical peace of pharmakia (Philippians 4:7).

Reliable statistics indicate that eighty percent of all diseases are psychosomatic, including both psychological and biological diseases. A spiritual root lies behind every psychosomatic disease, and that is why a proper application of God's truths brings healing. Psychosomatic diseases are real diseases that are caused by thoughts and emotions, and affect both the mind and body. Though rooted in a lie, they are very real.

Proverbs 23:7 says, "For as he thinketh in his heart, so is he . . . ." Our thoughts have the effect of creating changes in our chemical balance, and they are very powerful. When our thoughts fall out of agreement with God and into agreement with His enemy, this often results in devastating consequences for our bodies and minds. Our health suffers.

The truth of the power of applying God's literal Word to human life is the basis of our ministry. We seek to return the body, soul and spirit to the model of creation and to cast out those things that are not of God.

Every thought, every impression, every feeling or emotion causes a chemical release or a neurological impulse. God created us as balanced creatures; the medical profession called that balance "homeostasis."

Homeostasis is the natural and balanced internal state of our body that brings stability to our physiology. God designed our psychological functions to be in balance as well, free from unhealthy tension and stress.

Spiritually, we can achieve homeostasis as well, when, ". . . the peace of God, which passeth all understanding, [which] shall keep your hearts and minds through Christ Jesus" (Philippians 4:7).

The occult consists of any thought, action or feeling that comes between us and the peace of God. The saying, "No Jesus, No peace; Know Jesus, Know peace," is a powerful scriptural concept with very real positive implications for a healthy life.

Romans 8:14 says, "For as many as are led by the Spirit of God, they are the sons of God." God's Holy Spirit resides within each believer, leading us into living "In holiness and righteousness before Him, all the days of our life" (Luke 1:75).

God wants each of us to have control of our peace. That's why He gave us specific instructions in II Corinthians 10:5-6. "Casting down imaginations, and every high thing that exalteth itself against the knowledge of God, and bringing into captivity every thought to the obedience of Christ; And having in a readiness to revenge all disobedience, when your obedience is fulfilled."

James 4:7 says, "Submit yourselves therefore to God. Resist the devil, and he will flee from you." We start with submission to God (agreeing with Him in thought, word and deed) and then, our stubborn resistance of the devil forces him to flee! Then we find peace.

God also tells us in Ephesians 5:26 that we are to be sanctified by Him and cleansed by the "washing of water by the Word." Spending daily time studying God's Word, praying, applying His Word to our lives and having fellowship with other believers are the keys to living a cleansed, peace-filled life.

God sanctifies and cleanses us through the Person of His Holy Spirit, granting us His peace and His rest. His peace is not conditioned upon taking drugs to bring chemical balance: pharmakia. It is a true peace, not some false or occultic peace. Hebrews 4:9 says, "There remaineth therefore a rest to the people of God." God gave us the right to claim that rest, that peace, each day.

What happens when we cannot be at rest, or are constantly restless? Our bodies malfunction neurologically and chemically. By definition, depression is the result of a chemical imbalance — a lack of the neurotransmitter serotonin — in the human body.

When we have depression, what does the doctor prescribe? An anti-depressant drug designed to bring us back into chemical balance. Serotonin is a neurotransmitter that makes us feel good about ourselves. An anti-depressant attempts to make it last longer in the nerves' synapse. It cannot produce more serotonin. The real cause for the shortage is the anger, stress, and fears that are in our life. But, the doctor cannot address the spiritual dynamic that caused the chemical imbalance in the first place. Taking the drug causes us to avoid dealing with the real underlying spiritual problem.

The side effects of the drug can be devastating. Sexual dysfunction and psychosis are the most common side effects.

Migraine headaches are caused by enlarged blood vessels in the side the head. The most common drug given today for migraines is Imitrex. Imitrex contains an anti-depressant, an anti-histamine and a pain reliever. Serotonin is also a vascular regulator; it regulates the size of blood vessels. Histamine is a vascular expander; it expands blood vessels. The under-production of serotonin and the over-production of histamine are caused by thoughts of guilt and conflict. When we have helped people deal with the guilt, shame and conflict in their lives, the chemical imbalances are healed and the headache disappears. This process often takes only a few minutes.

There are many examples of medications that only cover up real problems. Western medicine is designed to treat symptoms. When the symptoms are the root's cause, as in injuries or other traumas, it works very well. But the symptom is usually not the root cause. We need to learn to depend on God and discover those areas of our lives that do not conform to God's teaching. When we confess and repent disobedience, then the peace of God that passes all understanding floods over us, and His joy becomes our joy.

Many surgeries could also be considered occultic as they are performed to treat a disorder that is really caused by our thoughts and emotions. Many surgeries are performed to correct anxiety and stress disorders in our hearts and digestive systems. There is again a more excellent way.

There are many other medical practices that we consider to be ungodly. Before, when I had been sick and desperate, I tried just about anything that anyone said would help me. I experienced several methods of alternative healing, and as I studied, I learned that many were, at their root, ungodly.

Most alternative medical practices involve some form of adjusting the "yin and yang" or the "energy systems" in our body, or some type of homeopathic remedy. Let me briefly discuss two of these.

Western medical science doesn't believe, nor can it find scientifically, that our bodies have an energy system as taught by Chinese medical practitioners. Regardless of this, the real question is whether or not this type of healing is something Christians should seek? Yin and yang are other names for good and evil. Why would we Christians want to adjust the flow of good and evil in our bodies? We want to remove all evil. Good and evil are not equal as New Age practices would have us believe. The answer is to rid ourselves of the evil with the power of God. Any form of adjusting, or balancing, the yin and yang is really a form of worshiping a god from an Eastern religion.

Many homeopathic remedies are so diluted that only an image of the original substance remains. I received and gave to others many NAET allergy treatments. This treatment requires holding a small glass vial containing a clear liquid that was labeled "wheat, mold, dust, pollen, etc." As I held these vials the practitioner tapped me on the acupuncture points along my spine. After doing this, the practitioner told me that I was no longer allergic to the substance in the glass vial.

Later on I learned how the vials were prepared. They filled a vial with water and held it in one hand. The other vial with the substance was held in the other hand. The practitioner transferred the image from one vial to the other through his or her body. Some use a computer to do this. But, the treatments helped. Why?

Fear is a major cause of allergies. This treatment ritual superficially dealt with fear. It was a placebo. As I learned the real cause of allergies and applied God's principles to them, I was completely healed of environmental illness and multi-chemical sensitivity.

Many of the diagnostic tools used in alternative medicine involve some form of divination. Applied Kinesiology and the Toftness device both rely on an ungodly power.

As Christians, it is vitally important that we carefully investigate things with which we become involved. Putting God first and shunning false gods requires diligence.

We have compiled a lengthy list of occultic beliefs and practices. Please remember that occultism includes anything that we allow to come between God and us. If you disagree with any item on our list, I strongly suggest that you carefully investigate its background and origins and use in your life, and then re-examine your grounds for disagreement. If you still disagree, let's agree to disagree and still be friends.

Please carefully study the list and mark any items with which you, or anyone in all your generations, may have been involved. Each one of these forms a part of the supporting cast, or infrastructure, of the principality of occultism.

A Partial List of The Occult

Abortion

Acupuncture/acupressure, including
Chinese medicine, Chinese herbs,
5 Element theory

Akashic record

Alexander technique, Feldenkrais method

Altered states of consciousness

American Indian ceremonies:
dream catchers, medicine wheel

Amulets, amulet healing

Angel worship

Apparitions

Applied and behavioral kinesiology/
muscle testing/NAET

Aromatherapy

Ascended masters, including
Elizabeth Clair prophet

Astral projection

Astrology/Horoscope/zodiac signs
/astrotherapy

Attitudinal healing/Jerald Jampolsky

Auras/aura reading/aura therapy

Automatic writing/journaling (channeling)

Auric/chakra healing

Ayurvedic medicine/Deepak Chopra

Bach's flower therapy

Bahaism (Bahai Church)

Biofeedback/autogenic training

Biorhythms

Buddhism: Zen, Vipassana, Tibetan
Buddhism, Buddhist meditation

Cabala/Jewish mysticism

Cartoons, demonic comic material,
movies, videos

The Celestine Prophecy

Chakras

Chanting/mantras

Charms, including ankh, talismans, Italian
Horns, horseshoes,rabbit's foot, scarabs

Chi

Christian Science, Mary Baker Eddy

Christian Science Monitor

Christian Science reading rooms

Clairvoyant diagnosis

Clairvoyance, mental telepathy, ESP

Color therapy

Crystal balls, Eight Ball

Crystals, crystal healing, birthstones
(supernatural power of), power rocks

Cultural/pagan ceremonies, superstitions,
elves, fairies, genies, leprechauns,
godless worship,
mother earth (Gaia) worship, tooth
fairy, harmonic convergence

Course of Miracles/Helen Schueman/
Kenneth Wapnick/Gerald Jambolsky

Cursing/general swearing

Déjà vu

Dianetics

Diets, including macrobiotics, Gerson
Therapy, colonics, food combining,
rotation diets

Divination: tarot, fortune telling, tea leaf
reading, handwriting analysis, palm
reading, I Ching, numerology, false
prophecy

Death/dying movement, Elizabeth Kubler-
Ross, *Tibetan Book of the Dead,
Into the Light*

Dowsing (water-witching)

Drug trips, recreational drugs

Dreamwork/Jungian

Dungeons & Dragons

Eastern philosophies
Eckankar
Esalen
ESP
EST/Werner Erhard

Familiar spirits/necromancy, family
   spirits, table tipping, seances
Feng shui
Fetishes
Fire psyche by candles
Firewalking
Feminism/goddess worship
False prophets: Jean Dixon, Nostradamus
Financial bondage to the occult
Fortune telling

Geomancy (a form of di vination)

Hinduism/gurus/Transcendental Medita-
   tion, Hare Krishna/Deepak Chopra
Hypnotism, self-hypnotism, subliminal
   tapes
Humanism/human potential mo vement,
   EST, actualization

I Ching
Incense/moxibustion
Iridology
Inner peace movement
Islam/Moslems/Black Moslems

Jehovah's Witness/*Watchtower*
Jung, Carl (archetypes, dark shadows)

Kabalah (Jewish mysticism)
KKK/racism
Kundalini energy, Kundalini yoga

Levitation

Magic: white/black/stage magic
Massage techniques such as Esalen,
   psychic, Jin Shin Do, Shiatsu,
Reflexology, etc. that are designed to
   adjust the yin and yang.
Mind idolatry/Mensa
Mediums: Edgar Cayce, Arthur Ford,
   J.D. Knight, Swedenborg,
   Jane Roberts
MENSA (self-idolatry)
Metaphysics
Mormonism
Movies: Alien, Ghost, Exorcist,
   The Omen, Psycho, etc.
Martial arts: aikido, tai chi, karate, judo,
   kung fu, taikwon do and others
Masonic lodge/Masonry including
   Eastern Star, Shriners, Demolay,
   Rainbow Girls

New Age physics, the tao of ph ysics
   (Fritjof Capra)
New Age therapies, New Age thinking
Nostradamus
"Now signs" of the New Age: unicorns,
   rainbows, New Age symbols, rock
   music or hippie memorabilia
Numerology

Occult medicine, Occult meditation
Occultic music/demonic rock music,
   Gregorian chants, Stephen Halpern
Occult books
Oracles
Ouiji board
Out-of-body experiences

Pagan religion/paganism in Christianity

Palmistry

Past life regression (hypnotic)

Parapsychology/paranormal

Pendulum diagnosis/Radesthesia

Pokémon/Harry Potter

Polarity therapy/Randolph Stone, diet, bodywork, polarity yoga

Poltergeists

Precognition

Primal therapy/bioenergetics, Radix

Psi, the psi-tronics super-sensor dowsing rod

Psychic detectives

Psychic reading/psychic portraits

Psychic surgery

Psychokinesis

Psychocybernetics

Psychometry

Psychotherapy, including teachings of Carl Jung, Sigmund Freud, Fritz Perls, Carl Rogers, Abraham Maslow

Psychosynthesis

Qi gong

Radionics/psychic healing

Reiki healing

Rosicrucians

Satanism/Satan Worship, Halloween/ Pentagrams

Scientology/Dianetics, L. Ron Hubbard

Sauna therapy

Secret brotherhoods/sisterhoods; fraternities, sororities, blood oaths

Sensory deprivation tanks

Silva Mind Control/mind dynamics

Shamanism/Carlos Castaneda

Sorcery/pharmakia

Spiritism/spirit guides

Statues or idols: Diana, angels, Mercury, Venus, Virgin Mary, Jesus, Buddha, including idolization of movie stars like Elvis, musicians, athletes, the Pope, gurus, JFK Jr., Stonehenge

Therapeutic touch

Trance diagnosis

The Way International

Toftness technique

Touch for health

Transendental Meditation

Unification Church/Rev. Moon, Moonies

Unitarian Church

Unitarian-Universalist Church

Urantia

Unity/daily word/affirmations

Science of Mind

Scientology

Reincarnation

Vampires, including Anne Rice books

Visualization/guided imagery, including Carl Simonton's teachings

Voodoo/Santaria/Voudon/Macumba

Waterwitching/geomancy

Warlocks, witches, Wicca

Wilheim Reigh/Neo-Reichian bodywork

Witchcraft, spells, Jezebel/Ahab spirits, control and manipulation;

Matriarchial witchcraft

Wart charming

Yoga: Kundalini/chakras/third eye/ Tantra/Kamasutra

Deuteronomy 5:9 and several other passages teach that the sins of the father are passed on to the third and fourth generation of those that hate God. Nehemiah 9:2, Leviticus 26:40-45 and Daniel 9 give examples of people confessing the sins of their ancestors. We believe that we need to confess and repent for our involvement, and for that of past family members, in any of these practices.

As before, take a sheet of paper and mark down all or any of these influences by which Satan has affected you. Ask the Holy Spirit to be your teacher. You may add others to this list. Then confess each one using a prayer such as this.

Prayer for Overcoming The Occult

Dear Heavenly Father, in the name of Jesus I, confess and repent, for my involvement in (specific activity). I ask you to forgive me, and all my generations, for our involvement in (specific activity). I forgive myself, and my family members, for our involvement.

In the name of Jesus, and by the power of His blood, I cancel all of Satan's power and authority over me and my generations resulting from this activity. In the name of Jesus I renounce and break any and all curses in my family line from any form of witchcraft or occult practices.

I invite the Holy Spirit to come into my heart, and to heal me, and to speak His words of truth to me.

(Pause and let God speak His Word to your heart.)

Satan will do his best to twist your mind and resist your efforts. You may want to ask other believers to support you during this time of healing. After you have confessed each individual involvement in an occultic practice, command the principality of occultism to go in Jesus' name.

CHAPTER TWELVE

The Kinsman Redeemer

THE BLOOD AVENGER

By now, each of us should understand that Satan regularly attacks God's people. He commits spiritual warfare against each of us, and we are the prizes he seeks. Don't misunderstand. Satan doesn't care about any of us, but he wants to win the victory over God. He will do anything to win. His tactics are ruthless and he plays by no rules.

Satan's kingdom counterfeits God's kingdom. We have seen that sin had been in the world before Adam when Lucifer rebelled against God. We saw sin enter the human race through Adam. We've witnessed the results of Adam's sin, watching Cain's unforgiveness progress to Abel's murder.

Our world is filled with wickedness as attested to by daily news reports. All around us, in our own lives and families, neighborhoods, cities and towns, we see human tragedy. Sometimes our own sin overwhelms us. But, in all this, we must remember that God has a plan.

In our ministry sessions, stories of sexual, emotional and physical abuse shock us. It amazes us that some people involve themselves in Satanic ritual abuse. We are continuously amazed at how many people (and myself) buy into Satan's lies. Still, God has a plan.

We could tell many stories of men and women that God created in His image, who have become pawns of evil, entrenched in deception and headed for destruction. Yet we have witnessed many who had a miraculous turn of events when God checkmated the devil. They won freedom.

God has a wonderful plan for redemption. Every person who receives the Lord Jesus Christ receives the ability to tap into God's wisdom and know His plan. The New Covenant gives us the ability to destroy the works of the devil.

In Ephesians, Paul used the word "dispensation" or "administration" several times. This is a significant word in our study of spiritual warfare. Ephesians 1:9-10 says, "Having made known unto us the mystery of His will, according to His good pleasure which He hath purposed in Himself: That in the dispensation of the fullness of times He might gather together in one all things in Christ, both which are in heaven, and which are on earth; even in Him."

The English transliteration of the Greek word for "dispensation" is *oikkonomia*. It refers to administering a house or property. It is a mode of dealing with household affairs, and the arrangement, or administration of the same. In other words, God has a plan.

He has a plan for each of us, no matter how deeply we may have served Satan. As long as we have breath, our story is not finished and the enemy has not triumphed. God's plan will defeat our enemy.

Ephesians 3:8-10 says, "Unto me, who am less than the least of all saints, is this grace given, that I should preach among the Gentiles the unsearchable riches of Christ; And to make all men see what is the fellowship of the mystery, which from the beginning of the world hath been hid in God, who created all things by Jesus Christ: To the intent that now unto the principalities and powers in heavenly places might be known by the church the manifold wisdom of God."

"The fellowship of the mystery" is a very interesting phrase. The Greek word is *koinonia*. It implies a partnership or joint participation and applies to all men. God has established a partnership with us that began in Genesis 1 with the naming of all the animals and man's dominion over the earth. This partnership is also to show the principalities and powers in heavenly places His "manifold wisdom," and He does this through the Church. The Church consists of every believer. This shows that we have a very important position in God's plan, a position that carries great responsibilities.

Paul wrote that even before man sinned, God's plan had been set in motion to bring all things in the heavens and on the earth back under His authority. God's administration of this plan, however, would remain a mystery until He was ready to expose it. At that time, God would make His statement through the Church, in the presence of the angels, good and bad, and Satan. God's revelation would show that Satan never did blindside Him. It would show that He was never out of control.

Before the foundation of the world, God knew that Adam and Eve would disobey Him, bringing sin to all mankind. So before He created the world, God had a plan of redemption. He had developed the administration of justice through our salvation. At the right time, Jesus would leave heaven, take on the body of a man, and become the Son of Man, sacrificing Himself on the cross to pay the penalty for our sin. Jesus would be our Kinsman Redeemer.

Why did God go to so much trouble? Why didn't He just create obedient people who had no ability to sin, rebel or worship other gods?

God gave mankind a free will because He desired a relationship with people that would love Him by their own choice, and whom He could love in return. No one can make someone love him or her; God chose not to force His love on anyone, nor force them to love Him.

When the serpent deceived Eve, God wasn't taken by surprise. This anointed cherub, Lucifer, who had defected and taken a third of the angels with him, did not blindside God. God had a plan all the time!

The devil is not omniscient, so he couldn't know about God's plan except as He revealed it. Genesis 3:14-15 says that Eve would have a seed, and although the serpent bruised the heel of her seed, the seed would crush the serpent's head. God let Satan know what would happen, but He didn't tell him when or how. In fact, God didn't openly reveal this truth until people began passing it along to others, and Moses wrote it down hundreds of years later.

Satan's first attempt to destroy God's plan ended with the flood. God saved Noah and seven others to start anew.

God called Abraham and made a covenant with him. Through Abraham, He raised up Israel, a separate people, as His own possession. From this nation would come the One who would bruise the serpent's head. Eve's line, her seed, passed through Noah, Abraham, David, and then to Christ. Through this Seed, all the nations of the earth would be blessed. Still, the details of the administration of the blessing were kept a mystery.

Then Mary, a virgin, gave birth to Jesus, the Christ (Luke 1:27, 34). Had Jesus been born through the line of an earthly father, He would have carried Adam's seed and, thusly, been born in sin. That is why Scripture specifies the seed of the woman. It is the sins of the father that are passed on to future generations, not the sins of the mother (Exodus 20:5).

God created man to carry the responsibility of spiritual leadership. Adam did not exercise his leadership responsibilities to set aside Eve's sin; he participated in the same sin. If Jesus had been born of an earthly father, He could never redeem Himself or anyone else. But Jesus was born in God's line, not of corruptible seed. God was Jesus' Father and He was born outside of the slave market of sin.

Because Jesus had no sin, He fell outside the dominion of "the prince of the power of the air, of the spirit that is now working in the sons of disobedience" (Ephesians. 2:2). Jesus was the only human being over whom Satan never had power, unless Satan could persuade Jesus to sin. Satan did not have a place or legal right to Jesus (Ephesians. 4:27). Satan tempted Jesus every way he could, but He refused to sin. Jesus came for the express purpose of seeking and saving sinners (Luke 19:10). He refused to exchange God's cross for Satan's crown. Satan failed.

Jewish leaders had Jesus nailed to the cross. They thought they had won a victory; so did Satan. But exactly according to God's plan, Jesus took all the sins of the world from eternity past to eternity future on Himself. God provided Jesus as His Passover Lamb, His scapegoat for the Day of Atonement.

Satan believed he had delivered a deathblow to God. He saw Jesus hanging on the cross, humiliated and bruised beyond recognition. Jesus breathed His last breath and died. For a time, Satan's demons danced and rejoiced. But God bruised Satan's heel just a short time later.

Jesus rose and left the tomb, alive and victorious. The tomb sat empty! Men could be reconciled with God's holiness by the blood of Jesus. By raising Jesus from the dead, God crushed the serpent's head! Satan's absolute grip on death was gone. Jesus had paid the wages of our sin — in full.

Through the shedding of Christ's blood and His resurrection, God gave us a method to break Satan's power. God unfolded His plan in the plain sight of all who desired to see it. Jesus provided the forgiveness of sins, abundant life now, and eternal life later, to all that believe in Him. He became our Kinsman Redeemer!

After appearing to hundreds of witnesses, Jesus ascended to the Father, where He sits at God's right hand. Before His ascension, He told His disciples He would send the Holy Spirit to indwell and seal them until the day of their full redemption. The Holy Spirit is one of the three members of the partnership of the mystery that God planned before the foundation of the world. We live a victorious life as a result of the Holy Spirit living in us, following His voice as our guide.

God chose each and every member of His creation before the foundations of the world (Ephesians 1:4). Men and women, boys and girls, who have trusted Jesus Christ for their salvation, became part of His bride, the Church. The Church is composed of Jews and Gentiles from every tribe, tongue and people. These are Christ's redeemed who, by virtue of His payment for sin, are now seated with Him in the heavenlies, far removed from the power of the enemy, no longer slaves to sin.

Jesus gave us His power to free us from Satan's dominion. During this lifetime, we will fight many battles with Satan, but Christ guaranteed that we would win the war. I Corinthians 15:24 says, "Then cometh the end, when He shall have delivered up the kingdom to God, even the Father; when He shall have put down all rule and all authority and power."

At first glance it appears this fellowship, or partnership, is one-sided, as if God took upon Himself all the responsibility. Yet James 4:7 says we are to "Submit yourselves therefore to God. Resist the devil, and he will flee from you." Our role in the partnership is to submit to God and obey Him. As an act of obedience, we are to purge ourselves of all iniquities (II Timothy 2: 20-21), and we are to resist the devil, to evict him from our lives. God will send him fleeing.

Before He formed the Church, God hid His plan for a partnership and how He would redeem mankind. Satan didn't know that God would make a way for us to be placed beyond all his evil power. Satan did not know that God was making a way for believers to become holy, as He is holy in this life through the indwelling of the Holy Spirit. Yet the Old Testament teaching about the kinsman redeemer, to those who know to look and have ears to hear, did somewhat reveal this plan.

THE LAW OF THE KINSMAN REDEEMER

A Kinsman Redeemer, in Hebrew a *ga'al*, was the person who had the legal right to redeem by buying back, either a blood relative or a family's inheritance that had been lost either through debt or death.

Let's read Leviticus 25:47-55 and study the law of the Kinsman-Redeemer, "And if a sojourner or stranger wax rich by thee, and thy brother that dwelleth by him wax poor, and sell himself unto the stranger or sojourner by thee, or to the stock of the stranger's family: After that he is sold he may be redeemed again; one of his brethren may redeem him: Either his uncle, or his uncle's son, may redeem him, or any that is nigh of kin unto him of his family may redeem him; or if he be able, he may redeem himself. And he shall reckon with him that bought him from the year that he was sold to him unto the year of jubilee: and the price of his sale shall be according unto the number of years, according to the time of an hired servant shall it be with him. If there be yet many years behind, according unto them he shall give again the price of his redemption out of the money that he was bought for. And if there remain but few years unto the year of jubilee, then he shall count with him, and according unto his years shall he give him again the price of his redemption. And as a yearly hired servant shall he be with him: and the other shall not rule with rigour over him in thy sight. And if he be not redeemed in these years, then he shall go out in the year of jubilee, both he, and his children with him. For unto me the children of Israel are servants; they are my servants whom I brought forth out of the land of Egypt: I am the LORD your God."

The law of the kinsman redeemer is summarized well by Dake in his study notes:

Seven Commands for the Redemption of a Hebrew Slave

1. If a sojourner or stranger becomes rich and buys a Hebrew slave, he may be redeemed again (Leviticus 25:47-48).
2. One of his brethren, an uncle, nephew, or any other near kinsman may redeem him (Leviticus 25:48-49).
3. If he is able to redeem himself, he may do so any time (Leviticus 25:49).
4. The price of redemption shall be determined by the number of years until jubilee (Leviticus 25:50-52).
5. He shall be to the Gentile as a yearly hired servant, not as a slave (Leviticus 25:53).
6. One shall not rule over him with rigor or oppress him in the sight of men.
7. If he is not redeemed he and his children shall go free in the year of jubilee (Leviticus 25:54-55).

Some men fell on hard times and sold themselves into slavery. They remained a slave unless one of these seven provisions for their release was fulfilled.

The law specified that the redeemer had to be a blood relative of the slave. How does this relate to our warfare? John 8:34-36 says, "Jesus answered them, Verily, verily, I say unto you, Whosoever committeth sin is the servant of sin. And the servant abideth not in the house for ever: but the Son abideth ever. If the Son therefore shall make you free, ye shall be free indeed."

This is the reason God sent His Son: to set us totally free. The more that we know about our Kinsman Redeemer and what He did for us, the greater is our ability to stand against Satan!

Take a moment to read the book of Ruth. It is a beautiful story of one who was redeemed by a kinsman.

Paul stresses our position in Christ in Ephesians. Victory in our spiritual war is assured as long as we hold our position. We shun fear and rest in Christ's power and authority, using His power of attorney to send Satan scurrying away.

Our position in Christ is so important it calls for a deeper understanding of the law of the kinsman redeemer. Kay Arthur calls it "the law of the go'el." There are six qualifications that the kinsman redeemer had to fulfill in order to redeem a relative.

First, the redeemer had to be a blood relative. If we were all born in sin, who could redeem us? Angels can't. The blood of bulls and goats can't. We can only be redeemed by another human being, and yet every one of them was also held captive in sin's slave market.

The devil saw this and thought victory would soon be his. But God had a plan! Hebrews 2:16-18 says, "For verily He took not on Him the nature of angels; but He took on Him the seed of Abraham. Wherefore in all things it behooved Him to be made like unto His brethren, that He might be a merciful and faithful high priest in things pertaining to God, to make reconciliation for the sins of the people. For in that He Himself hath suffered being tempted, He is able to succour them that are tempted."

This sums up Paul's argument that Christ is superior to the angels. Christ didn't take on an angelic form, but chose the natural seed of Abraham. It was necessary that in all ways, Christ would become just like men, so that He might be a merciful and faithful high priest interceding for us with God, paying for our sins by His own atonement and, having experienced temptation, ministering to us as we are tempted (Hebrews 4:14-15).

Establishing that Christ was as a legitimate Kinsman Redeemer, Paul showed the Jews that He came as a man out of Abraham's seed; that He had a common heritage with the Jews; that redemption could not have been possible otherwise; that He had to suffer to redeem sinners; that He is able to deliver all men who are tempted.

Paul was also teaching the Jews that it was never possible to be justified by keeping the law. The law was given for the purposes of sanctification, never justification. But the Jews turned God's law into a curse through their legalistic efforts for justification (Galatians 2-3).

God provided us a Kinsman Redeemer through the incarnation. Jesus came as a blood relative of all mankind by being born of the seed of God. Mary, a human mother, gave Him birth, putting flesh and blood on God's Spirit. This was the first step, but being a blood relative is not enough.

Second, the kinsman redeemer had to be able to pay the price of redemption. There are two New Testament words for "redeem." *Lutroo* means to release on receipt of ransom, and *exagorazo* means purchasing a slave in order to grant his freedom.

What price would justice demand to redeem man from sin's slave market? How exorbitant a demand would the Judge of the Universe demand to satisfy Satan's evil grip? How much would it cost to buy every human's freedom from sin?

Leviticus 17:11 says, "For the life of the flesh is in the blood: and I have given it to you upon the altar to make an atonement for your souls: for it is the blood that maketh an atonement for the soul."

Hebrews 10:4-10 says, "For it is not possible that the blood of bulls and of goats should take away sins. Wherefore when He cometh into the world, He saith, Sacrifice and offering thou wouldest not, but a body hast thou prepared Me: In burnt offerings and sacrifices for sin thou hast had no pleasure. Then said I, Lo, I come (in the volume of the book it is written of Me,) to do thy will, O God. Above when He said, Sacrifice and offering and burnt offerings and offering for sin thou wouldest not, neither hadst pleasure therein; which are offered by the law; Then said He, Lo, I come to do Thy will, O God. He taketh away the first, that He may establish the second. By the which will we are sanctified through the offering of the body of Jesus Christ once for all."

I Peter 1:18-19 says, "Forasmuch as ye know that ye were not redeemed with corruptible things, as silver and gold, from your vain conversation received by tradition from your fathers; But with the precious blood of Christ, as of a lamb without blemish and without spot."

Ephesians 1:7-8 says, "In Whom we have redemption through His blood, the forgiveness of sins, according to the riches of His grace; Wherein He hath abounded toward us in all wisdom and prudence."

How do we benefit from Christ acting as our Kinsman Redeemer? Colossians 1:13-14 says, "Who hath delivered us from the power of darkness, and hath translated us into the kingdom of His dear Son: In whom we have redemption through His blood, even the forgiveness of sins."

Having a blood relative with the wherewithal to act as a Kinsman Redeemer means little if he is unwilling to do so. The third responsibility of the kinsman redeemer is that he must have the desire to perform his act of redemption.

Luke 19:10 says, "For the Son of man is come to seek and to save that which was lost." God's gift cost Him His Son, and cost Jesus His life.

John 15:13 says, "Greater love hath no man than this, that a man lay down his life for his friends."

I John 3:1 says, "Behold, what manner of love the Father hath bestowed upon us, that we should be called the sons of God: therefore the world knoweth us not, because it knew Him not."

Jesus came for one purpose: to redeem us. But as with every kinsman redeemer, He knew that in the process, He jeopardized His own inheritance. Our Kinsman Redeemer, then, not only had to have the desire to redeem us, but He had to will it to be done. This willingness fulfills the fourth requirement.

The book of Ruth tells us that the first blood relative with a right of redemption was unwilling to fulfill his obligation. He refused to jeopardize his own inheritance. He gave his right of redemption to Boaz, and it's a good thing Boaz followed through. Mary, Jesus' mother, several generations later, descended from this union.

It's absolutely true that Jesus came with the express purpose of being the Lamb who would shed His blood for our redemption. Yet, Scripture reports that He asked the Father three times to find another way. Still, He submitted to God's will.

Matthew 26:36-44 says, "Then cometh Jesus with them unto a place called Gethsemane, and saith unto the disciples, Sit ye here, while I go and pray yonder. And He took with Him Peter and the two sons of Zebedee, and began to be sorrowful and very heavy. Then saith He unto them, My soul is exceeding sorrowful, even unto death: tarry ye here, and watch with Me. And He went a little farther, and fell on His face, and prayed, saying, O my Father, if it be possible, let this cup pass from Me: nevertheless not as I will, but as Thou wilt. And He cometh unto the disciples, and findeth them asleep, and saith unto Peter, What, could ye not watch with Me one hour? Watch and pray, that ye enter not into temptation: the spirit indeed is willing, but the flesh is weak. He went away again the second time, and prayed, saying, O my Father, if this cup may not pass away from Me, except I drink it, Thy will be done. And He came and found them asleep again: for their eyes were heavy. And He left them, and went away again, and prayed the third time, saying the same words."

Why did Jesus pray this way? Was He unwilling to go to the cross? Hebrews 5:7-9 says, "Who in the days of His flesh, when He had offered up prayers and supplications with strong crying and tears unto Him that was able to save Him from death, and was heard in that He feared; Though He were a Son, yet learned He obedience by the things which He suffered; And being made perfect, He became the author of eternal salvation unto all them that obey Him."

Did God ever ignore Jesus' prayers? No, He always answered them. If Jesus begged God to help Him avoid the cross, wouldn't He have done it? Since this did not happen, what was Jesus really asking?

He prayed to be saved from the curse of death that plagues all humans, not from His death on the cross — He did die on the cross. And God The Father heard His prayer and saved Him from death at the hands of the Satanic powers that tried to kill Him in the Garden of Gethsemane before He could get to the cross. To fulfill prophecy, He needed to die on the cross and complete the atonement for sins. If Satan had killed Christ at any time from infancy to the road leading up to Golgatha, he could have defeated God's plan of redemption. Christ had to get to the cross in order to triumph over Satan (Colossians 2:14-17, I Peter 2:24).

Satan had Herod try to kill Christ as a baby. He tried to trick Christ into throwing Himself off a tall mountain. He inspired men in Nazareth to stone Him. Had Christ resisted arrest in the Garden, or if His men had fought for His freedom, He might have been slain. The Roman soldiers might have killed him by flogging.

But Christ needed to die on a cross, and He did!

There are many Scriptures that expressly tell us that Jesus was willing in obedience to go to the cross. Jesus knew that only His blood could pay for men's sins. Philippians 2:6-8 says, "Who, being in the form of God, thought it not robbery to be equal with God: But made Himself of no reputation, and took upon Him the form of a servant, and was made in the likeness of men: And being found in fashion as a man, He humbled Himself, and became obedient unto death, even the death of the cross."

Only a very special Kinsman Redeemer would be willing to pay such a price, to completely humble Himself, to leave His heavenly throne just to redeem undeserving people who had no other hope. But Jesus had shown His love for us from the beginning when He created us in His own image.

Romans 8:17 says, "And if children, then heirs; heirs of God, and joint-heirs with Christ; if so be that we suffer with Him, that we may be also glorified together."

Often life seems very unfair. Tragedies come our way, stealing our joy, peace, health and material possessions. Many of these tragedies result from our own disobedience. We either willingly or ignorantly choose to disobey God, and suffer the consequences. We live in a fallen world, inheriting Adam's infirmities. In all this, we need to remember that we have a Kinsman Redeemer who ultimately triumphs over Satan and brings him to justice for all he has done.

This brings us to the fifth responsibility: the kinsman redeemer had to serve as the judicial executioner on behalf of the murdered relative.

Scripture requires a heavy price to be paid for murder of another human. God instituted capital punishment. He did this because we are made in the image of God, making life very sacred. When someone kills another person, he is attacking God's sacred creation and the penalty is death to the murderer.

Genesis 9:5-6 says, "And surely your blood of your lives will I require; at the hand of every beast will I require it, and at the hand of man; at the hand of every man's brother will I require the life of man. Whoso sheddeth man's blood, by man shall his blood be shed: for in the image of God made He man."

If a beast killed a man, the beast would be killed. If a man murdered another man, the murderer's life would be taken. However, the slain man's brother, his kinsman, executed the punishment.

Exodus 20:13 says, "Thou shalt not kill." The Hebrew word *ratsach*, means "to dash in pieces, to kill (a human being), especially to murder, to put to death, kill, (man) slay

(-er), murder (-er)." Exodus repeats the commandment found in Genesis 9:5-6.

Deuteronomy 19:10-13 says, "That innocent blood be not shed in thy land, which the LORD thy God giveth thee for an inheritance, and so blood be upon thee. But if any man hate his neighbour, and lie in wait for him, and rise up against him, and smite him mortally that he die, and fleeth into one of these cities: Then the elders of his city shall send and fetch him thence, and deliver him into the hand of the avenger of blood, that he may die. Thine eye shall not pity him, but thou shalt put away the guilt of innocent blood from Israel, that it may go well with thee."

The English transliteration of the Hebrew word for "avenger" is *ga'al*, the same word used for "kinsman redeemer."

Numbers 35:15-25 says, "These six cities shall be a refuge, both for the children of Israel, and for the stranger, and for the sojourner among them: that every one that killeth any person unawares may flee thither. And if he smite him with an instrument of iron, so that he die, he is a murderer: the murderer shall surely be put to death. And if he smite him with throwing a stone, wherewith he may die, and he die, he is a murderer: the murderer shall surely be put to death. Or if he smite him with an hand weapon of wood, wherewith he may die, and he die, he is a murderer: the murderer shall surely be put to death. The revenger of blood himself shall slay the murderer: when he meeteth him, he shall slay him. But if he thrust him of hatred, or hurl at him by laying of wait, that he die; Or in enmity smite him with his hand, that he die: he that smote him shall surely be put to death; for he is a murderer: the revenger of blood shall slay the murderer, when he meeteth him. But if he thrust him suddenly without enmity, or have cast upon him any thing without laying of wait, Or with any stone, wherewith a man may die, seeing him not, and cast it upon him, that he die, and was not his enemy, neither sought his harm: Then the congregation shall judge between the slayer and the revenger of blood according to these judgments: And the congregation shall deliver the slayer out of the hand of the revenger of blood, and the congregation shall restore him to the city of his refuge, whither he was fled: and he shall abide in it unto the death of the high priest, which was anointed with the holy oil."

Numbers 35:30-31, 33 says, "Whoso killeth any person, the murderer shall be put to death by the mouth of witnesses: but one witness shall not testify against any person to cause him to die. Moreover ye shall take no satisfaction for the life of a murderer, which is guilty of death: but he shall be surely put to death. So ye shall not pollute the land wherein ye are: for blood it defileth the land: and the land cannot be cleansed of the blood that is shed therein, but by the blood of him that shed it."

Murder pollutes the land, and it can only be cleansed by shedding the blood of the murderer. A ransom can never replace execution, because it leaves the land polluted.

The Hebrew word *ga'al* refers to the next of kin, as the avenger of blood for his murdered relative. These three words, "avenger of blood," are almost always linked together in Scripture. The idea is that it must be the next of kin that effects the payment and the lost life of the relative must be paid for by the equivalent life of the murderer. The kinsman is the avenger of blood.

How did Jesus fulfill this responsibility as our Blood Avenger? Satan led Adam and Eve into sin that resulted in death. When Satan successfully deceived Eve and she ate of the fruit, she gave it to Adam. Adam ate it, and thus, mankind died spiritually and physically. All future humans resided in Adam's loins, and his seed carried a sinful heritage.

Satan caused Adam's death. Jesus describes in John 8:44. "Ye are of your father the devil, and the lusts of your father ye will do. He was a murderer from the beginning, and abode not in the truth, because there is no truth in him. When he speaketh a lie, he speaketh of his own: for he is a liar, and the father of it."

Numbers 35:17-19 states that murderers should be put to death. The blood avenger himself will participate in the execution. This will occur when the two of them meet.

When Christ, our Kinsman Redeemer, returns to earth, He will meet the destroyer face to face, bind him for a thousand years, and then loose him for a short time. Then, acting as our blood avenger, Jesus will bind Satan and cast him and his angels into the lake of fire where they will be tormented for eternity (Matthew 25:41). Satan and his minions are guilty and won't ever be set free. God is just.

Scripture repeatedly tells us not to take vengeance on others, nor return evil for evil. Instead, we are to love our enemies, to do good to those that despitefully use us and turn the other cheek. All this is true, but we still need the protection of the Law.

I Timothy 1:9-11 says, "Knowing this, that the law is not made for a righteous man, but for the lawless and disobedient, for the ungodly and for sinners, for unholy and profane, for murderers of fathers and murderers of mothers, for manslayers, For whoremongers, for them that defile themselves with mankind, for menstealers, for liars, for perjured persons, and if there be any other thing that is contrary to sound doctrine; According to the glorious gospel of the blessed God, which was committed to my trust."

One of the primary purposes of law is to protect us. Laws should restrain man's ungodly behavior. Still, some people commit horrible deeds, often hurting innocent people, and never get caught by the police. Will they ever be brought to justice? Yes! Our Kinsman Redeemer is a righteous judge who will execute judgment on all (Jude 15, Romans 12:17-21).

The sixth responsibility of the kinsman redeemer is to redeem the land and remove all the squatters and invaders currently occupying it.

Leviticus 25:23-25 says, "The land shall not be sold for ever: for the land is mine; for ye are strangers and sojourners with me. And in all the land of your possession ye shall grant a redemption for the land. If thy brother be waxen poor, and hath sold away some of his possession, and if any of his kin come to redeem it, then shall he redeem that which his brother sold."

When Adam and Eve sinned, the serpent gained dominion over mankind and rulership of the earth. Adam and Eve forfeited to Satan the power and authority that rightfully belonged to them (Genesis 1:26-28). Satan became known as the ruler of this world.

John 14:30 says, "Hereafter I will not talk much with you: for the prince of this world cometh, and hath nothing in Me." John 12:31 says, "Now is the judgment of this world: now shall the prince of this world be cast out." II Corinthians 4:3-4 says, "But if our gospel be hid, it is hid to them that are lost: In whom the god of this world hath blinded the minds of them which believe not, lest the light of the glorious gospel of Christ, who is the image of God, should shine unto them."

Satan's worldly throne is a temporary position. Our Kinsman Redeemer has the power and authority to remove all squatters and invaders off of the land that had once belonged to His kinsman. Jesus Christ will evict Satan and his kingdom from the world, bind him and cast him into the lake of fire forever and ever. The day of vengeance and the battle or Armageddon will be the day of His second coming.

Remember the prophecy of Genesis 3:15? The serpent bruised the heel of the woman's seed, but the woman's seed would eventually crush Satan's head. Christ crushed Satan's head at the cross when He died, becoming our Kinsman Redeemer, providing a legal remedy for our sins. Then He rose again, becoming our Kinsman Redeemer Blood Avenger.

We have not yet seen all the results of the crushing of the serpent's head. But, when Christ delivered the deathblow at Calvary, He gave us a mighty weapon to use in our war with Satan. His successful frontal attack on Satan destroyed Satan's ability to maintain authority and power over us.

Throughout His earthly ministry, Jesus repeatedly said that His time had not yet come, until six days before the final Passover. Then He said this in John 12:23-33. "And Jesus answered them, saying, The hour is come, that the Son of man should be glorified. Verily, verily, I say unto you, Except a corn of wheat fall into the ground and die, it abideth alone: but if it die, it bringeth forth much fruit. He that loveth his life shall lose it; and he that hateth his life in this world shall keep it unto life eternal. If any man serve Me, let him follow Me; and where I am, there shall also My servant be: if any man serve Me, him will My Father honour. Now is My soul troubled; and what shall I say? Father, save Me from this hour: but for this cause came I unto this hour. Father, glorify Thy name. Then came there a voice from heaven, saying, I have both glorified it, and will glorify it again. The people therefore, that stood by, and heard it, said that it thundered: others said, An angel spake to Him. Jesus answered and said, This voice came not because of Me, but for your sakes. Now is the judgment of this world: now shall the prince of this world be cast out. And I, if I be lifted up from the earth, will draw all men unto Me. This He said, signifying what death He should die."

Verse 31 is written in the present tense, making it very clear that, "now is the judgment of this world, now shall the prince of this world be cast out." Now the time had arrived for the next part of God's plan to be revealed. It was time to crush the enemy's head. What our Blood Avenger began at Calvary, He will complete when He reclaims the earth, rids it of all squatters and casts Satan into the lake of fire.

Colossians 2:9-10 says, "For in Him dwelleth all the fullness of the Godhead bodily. And ye are complete in Him, which is the head of all principality and power."

Christ, who has authority over all principalities and powers, completed His work in us.

Colossians 2:11-15 says, "In whom also ye are circumcised with the circumcision made without hands, in putting off the body of the sins of the flesh by the circumcision of Christ: Buried with Him in baptism, wherein also ye are risen with Him through the faith of the operation of God, who hath raised Him from the dead. And you, being dead in your sins and the uncircumcision of your flesh, hath He quickened together with Him, having forgiven you all trespasses; Blotting out the handwriting of ordinances that was against us, which was contrary to us, and took it out of the way, nailing it to His cross; And having spoiled principalities and powers, He made a shew of them openly, triumphing over them in it."

Wow! What do we have to fear? When Christ saved us from sin, He put off the body of sin from us, and spoiled the principalities and powers, making an open "shew" of them, triumphing over them! Now all we have to do is appropriate what Jesus has accomplished. We do this by being obedient to forgive others, as God to forgive us, and resist the devil. We are to purge ourselves from all iniquity to become vessels of honor fit for his service (II Timothy 2:20-21).

Paul's writing reveals how God's Church unites believing Jews and Gentiles into one body. God also gave Paul the awesome privilege of understanding and explaining another mystery hidden since creation: the mystery of "Christ in you, the hope of glory" (Colossians 1:26-27). With Christ in us we have authority over the old nature, the flesh, the body of sin and Satan.

As he reveals this mystery, Paul assures us that when Christ died on the cross, the price was paid for all our sins. We must do our part of this partnership and apply His blood to our sins. Matthew 6:14-15 say, "For if ye forgive men their trespasses, your heavenly Father will also forgive you: But if ye forgive not men their trespasses, neither will your Father forgive your trespasses." Our part of this partnership is to forgive others whether they ask our forgiveness or not.

We also must ask God to forgive us our sins. I John 1:9 says, "If we confess our sins, he is faithful and just to forgive us our sins, and to cleanse us from all unright-eousness." This begins with an "if." If we confess He will cleanse us. What if we do not confess?

This is a critical truth because Satan gains power over us through sin. When we accept Jesus Christ as our personal savior, His death removes Satan's power of death. Our spirit can now be made alive to God again. We then have the power over sin. Through the indwelling of the Holy Spirit we conquer sin in our lives. We can defeat the old nature and crucify the flesh. God gives us an abundant life while here on planet Earth, and eternal life with Him.

At the instant we die we enter eternity with God. Romans 6:22-23 says, "But now being made free from sin, and become servants to God, ye have your fruit unto holiness, and the end everlasting life. For the wages of sin is death; but the gift of God is eternal life through Jesus Christ our Lord."

When the kinsman redeemer buys back property, he gains the right to possess the property. The prior owners must vacate. Colossians 2:15 says, "And having spoiled principalities and powers, He made a shew of them openly, triumphing over them in it."

What does this mean? Jesus defeated the enemy publicly. He knows it, Satan knows it, and everyone knows it! Sometimes we need to remind Satan of this fact.

Throughout the Gospels, the demons recognized Jesus as the "Son of God." Whenever they came face to face with Him, they cried out saying, as in Mark 5:7-8, "What have I to do with thee, Jesus, thou Son of the most high God? I adjure Thee by God, that Thou torment me not. For He said unto him, Come out of the man, thou unclean spirit." These demons were squatters holding captive those that Christ came to set free, so Jesus cast them out! Why? Matthew 12:28 says, "But if I cast out devils by the Spirit of God, then the kingdom of God is come unto you."

The Kingdom of God stepped into their presence, and those demons knew it immediately! Psalms 110:1 says, "The LORD said unto my Lord, Sit Thou at My right hand, until I make Thine enemies Thy footstool." Jesus is saying to the Father that He will make His enemies His footstool. I Corinthians 15:25-28: "For He must reign, till He hath put all enemies under His feet. The last enemy that shall be destroyed is death. For He hath put all things under His feet. But when He saith, all things are put under Him, it is manifest that He is excepted, which did put all things under Him. And when all things shall be subdued unto Him, then shall the Son also Himself be subject unto Him that put all things under Him, that God may be all in all." Being under someone's feet symbolized total contempt.

Satan and his demons recognize and fear God's power. When we appropriate His power, they recognize it immediately. It's ironic, but demons believe God's Word and tremble before Him, while we doubt His Word and tremble before demons. Obviously, something is wrong with this picture. John 14:12 says that we will do greater works than Christ. Are greater works happening in your life?

Have you ever wondered what it will be like after our Kinsman Redeemer rids the earth of the enemy and completes His work as our Blood Avenger? Revelation 5:1-14 and 6:1 tell the story.

Revelation 5:1-14: "And I saw in the right hand of Him that sat on the throne a book written within and on the backside, sealed with seven seals. And I saw a strong angel proclaiming with a loud voice, Who is worthy to open the book, and to loose the seals thereof? And no man in heaven, nor in earth, neither under the earth, was able to open the book, neither to look thereon. And I wept much, because no man was found worthy to open and to read the book, neither to look thereon. And one of the elders saith unto me, Weep not: behold, the Lion of the tribe of Judah, the Root of David, hath prevailed to open the book, and to loose the seven seals thereof. And I beheld, and, lo, in the midst of the throne and of the four beasts, and in the midst of the elders, stood a Lamb as it had been slain, having seven horns and seven eyes, which are the seven Spirits of God sent forth into all the earth. And He came and took the book out of the right hand of Him that sat upon the throne. And when He had taken the book, the four beasts and four and twenty elders fell down before the Lamb, having every one of them harps, and golden vials full of odours, which are the prayers of saints. And they sung a new song, saying, Thou art worthy to take the book, and to open the seals thereof: for Thou wast slain, and hast redeemed us to God by Thy blood out of every kindred, and tongue, and people, and nation; And hast made us unto our God kings and priests: and we shall reign on the earth. And I beheld, and I heard the voice of many angels round about the throne and the beasts and the elders: and the number of them was ten thousand times ten thousand, and thousands of thousands; Saying with a loud voice, Worthy is the Lamb that was slain to receive power, and riches, and wisdom, and strength, and honour, and glory, and blessing. And every creature which is in heaven, and on the earth, and under the earth, and such as are in the sea, and all that are in them, heard I saying, Blessing, and honour, and glory, and power, be unto Him that sitteth upon the throne, and unto the Lamb for ever and ever. And the four beasts said, Amen. And the four and twenty elders fell down and worshipped Him that liveth for ever and ever."

Revelation 6:1: "And I saw when the Lamb opened one of the seals, and I heard, as it were the noise of thunder, one of the four beasts saying, Come and see."

Compare this Revelation passage to Jeremiah 32:6-15. "And Jeremiah said, The word of the LORD came unto me, saying, Behold, Hanameel the son of Shallum thine uncle shall come unto thee, saying, Buy thee my field that is in Anathoth: for the right of redemption is thine to buy it. So Hanameel mine uncle's son came to me in the court of the prison according to the word of the LORD, and said unto me, Buy my field, I pray thee, that is in Anathoth, which is in the country of Benjamin: for the right of inheritance is thine, and the redemption is thine; buy it for thyself. Then I knew that this was the word of the LORD. And I bought the field of Hanameel my uncle's son, that was in Anathoth, and weighed him the money, even seventeen shekels of silver. And I subscribed the evidence, and sealed it, and took witnesses, and weighed him the money in the balances. So I took the evidence of the purchase, both that which was sealed according to the law and custom, and that which was open: And I gave the evidence of the purchase unto Baruch the son of Neriah, the son of Maaseiah, in the sight of Hanameel mine uncle's son, and in the presence of the witnesses that subscribed the book of the purchase, before all the Jews that sat in the court of the prison.

"And I charged Baruch before them, saying, Thus saith the LORD of hosts, the God of Israel; Take these evidences, this evidence of the purchase, both which is sealed, and this evidence which is open; and put them in an earthen vessel, that they may continue many days. For thus saith the LORD of hosts, the God of Israel; Houses and fields and vineyards shall be possessed again in this land."

Verses 37-44 reveal that God will, one day, restore His people to their land.

What is written on the sealed scrolls? Kay Arthur says it is the deed, the title, to the earth. Jeremiah calls it the "deed of purchase." Remember, "the earth is the LORD's and the fullness thereof" (Exodus 9:29, Deuteronomy 10:14, Psalms 24:1, I Corinthians 10:25-28). God may give title to the earth to whomever He pleases, just as He gave the Promised Land to the Israelites. God gave clear title to all of mankind in Genesis, but Adam lost it to Satan when he sinned. Jesus Christ has redeemed the title to the earth.

Jeremiah 32:27 says, "Behold, I am the LORD, the God of all flesh: is there any thing too hard for me?" No! The LORD signed the deed, put His seal on it and put it in an earthen jar to preserve it. The Lord will clean out the squatters and invaders, and punish those that had murdered His people.

The Lord Jesus Christ, our Kinsman Redeemer, will return as King of Kings and LORD of Lords. He will open and secure the deed to the earth. He is the only person who has the legal standing to do so because He was a man who never sinned, who willingly shed His blood to pay the price of Satan's claim on us. Revelation chapters 6-20 describes how Jesus will rid the earth of Satan and his demons.

John 20:21 says, "Then said Jesus to them again, Peace be unto you: as my Father hath sent Me, even so send I you."

Through Christ's resurrection, we have the power and authority to defeat and destroy the works of Satan. We are warriors in this spiritual warfare. Warriors know their enemy and they know, serve and obey their captain. Our Captain is the giver of life-abundant life in this world and eternal life with Him.

CHAPTER THIRTEEN

The Armor of God

God gave us spiritual armor to use in our warfare with Satan. Many books have been written and sermons preached about this armor, but it is a subject that is greatly misunderstood and, therefore, misapplied. God's armor is not some sort of magic that our minds apply to fend off the devil. It is not something that we apply or take off each day. We need a clear idea of the make-up, purpose and use of the armor of God.

Ephesians 6:10-18 says, "Finally, my brethren, be strong in the Lord, and in the power of His might. Put on the whole armor of God, that ye may be able to stand against the wiles of the devil. For we wrestle not against flesh and blood, but against principalities, against powers, against the rulers of the darkness of this world, against spiritual wickedness in high places. Wherefore take unto you the whole armor of God, that ye may be able to withstand in the evil day, and having done all, to stand. Stand therefore, having your loins girt about with truth, and having on the breastplate of right-eousness; And your feet shod with the preparation of the gospel of peace; Above all, taking the shield of faith, wherewith ye shall be able to quench all the fiery darts of the wicked. And take the helmet of salvation, and the sword of the Spirit, which is the word of God: Praying always with all prayer and supplication in the Spirit, and watching thereunto with all perseverance and supplication for all saints."

In Ephesians 6:10, Paul says to be "strong in the Lord and in the power of His might." "Be strong" is the Greek word *endunamoo*, meaning empowered. So to be strong is to be empowered by God and to appropriate His strength. Paul prays in Ephesians 1:15-23 and 3:14-21 that we would recognize that the power of the resurrection is ours. He commands us to act accordingly.

Ephesians 6:11 says to "Put on the whole armor of God, that ye may be able to stand against the wiles of the devil." Scripture lists two kinds of armor:

1. Defensive armor, for protection:
   - The helmet: protecting the head, comes in various forms embossed with many kinds of figures
   - The girdle, or belt: protecting the loins to brace the armor tight against the body, and support daggers, swords and other weapons
   - The breastplate in two parts: one covers the breast and the other covers the back, protecting the vital organs of the body; it extends down to the legs
   - The greaves, or sandals, cover the shins: a form of a sole was often used to protect the feet from rocks, thorns, etc.
   - The shield: to protect the entire body from blows and cuts

2. Offensive armor for conquest:
  • The sword is used to destroy the enemy and bring his surrender. Besides the sword, other weapons of offense included the spear, lance, battle-axe, club, bow and arrows, and sling.

The phrase, "that ye may be able to stand against the wiles of the devil," describes three blessings received from the armor of God:
1. The ability to stand against all enemies (Ephesians 6:11-14)
2. The ability to withstand all attacks (Ephesians 6:13)
3. The ability to quench Satan's fiery darts (Ephesians 6:16)

"Having done all to stand," or "to stand" is a military term meaning to hold one's position; having already conquered, stand ready again to do battle.

"Wiles" is the Greek word, *methodeia*, referring to the methods one would use to accomplish a task. In this context, it includes the different means, plans, and schemes used to deceive, entrap, enslave, and ruin men's souls.

The defensive armor is a soldier's personal armor, used for protection. The offensive armor is for conquest, bringing the enemy into surrender, or slaying the enemy. Paul uses these common military tools to make a spiritual application. Ephesians 4 and 5 encourage us to appropriate the things that are of God. It warns us of many ungodly practices as well. Paul tells us to take up, or put on, the armor of God giving us the power and authority to do those things that we should do, and not do the things that we should not do.

Putting on the armor doesn't just happen; it takes effort. It is not a ritual of some kind. As believers, God gives us access to His armor, but we are commanded to put it on — all of it. This is a result of doing, believing, embracing, responding, and studying to gain knowledge and truth.

Until Jesus comes, as long as we breathe we will be in continuous warfare. Satan will do anything to defeat God, including attacking us. In verse 12, Paul says that we "wrestle not with flesh and blood." The word for "wrestle" in Greek is *pale*. It indicates a hand-to-hand fight, a wrestling match. Wrestling is a type of fighting that includes trickery, cunning, strategy and often, using an opponent's own strengths against him. Satan has three objectives in this wrestling match.

First, he wants to destroy our unity with God, the body of Christ, and our families. If he persuades us that we are cut off from the Father, he knows we will question the source of our hope and our power. If God is not for us, we might as well give up.

In ministry we have seen people who have given up. People who believe their sin is so grievous that there is no way God will forgive them. They may even believe that they have blasphemed the Holy Spirit, and are now cut off from God forever. They buy Satan's lies and half-truths, instead of clinging to God's truth.

Satan uses our lack of assurance of God's power and love to separate us from God. He causes us to question the reality of our faith. It is imperative that we examine ourselves to make sure we are believers, but once that is settled, we need to believe and trust what God has said. Trust and obey and you shall be saved! Believe it. Rely on it.

Another common satanic tactic is making us wonder if God is withholding something good from us. By so doing, Satan causes us to think that God is somehow evil. It's what he did to Eve with the apple, and what he tried to do to Jesus in the wilderness when he challenged Him to turn stones into bread.

Satan's second objective is to entice us to sin, to gain a place in our life. I John 3:8 says, "He that committeth sin is of the devil; for the devil sinneth from the beginning. For this purpose the Son of God was manifested, that he might destroy the works of the devil." He wants us to sin so that we will be destroyed.

Satan's third objective is to put us under the influence of false teaching. He strives to keep us from the light of truth and lure us into greater darkness. The rise of cults, New Age mysticism, Eastern religions and even atheism indicate a multi-directional assault by false teachers. Satan's false teaching especially affects our children through the influence of godless teaching; he seeks to destroy our nation. Public schools are filled with violence, illegal drugs, open sexuality, and all fed by perverse textbooks.

The most serious deception is with in our own churches. A serious study of the seven churches in Revelation 2 and 3 would reveal that we are facing an even greater challenge today. Why are there as many divorces in the church as out? Why is the use of pornographic materials no different in the church or out? Why are alcohol or drug addictions no different in the church or out?

Where is the power of God in our lives? It is missing because we have been taught that obedience is good, but not absolutely necessary for salvation. We have been taught a form of Godliness that denies His power in the doctrines that teach the gifts of the Holy Spirit have passed away. We have been given a false security with the "once saved, always saved" theology. If there is not fruit, if there is not a change in attitude and behavior, there is no salvation. Salvation is not just a verbal assent; there must be a change of heart.

Have you ever been taught how to be a vessel of honor fit for his service? Have you ever been taught what it means to be an overcomer? Do you know how to achieve these? If not I strongly suggest that there is nothing more important to learn.

Either the devil keeps us blind to his existence and his activities, or tries to take us to the other extreme, of taking our eyes off of God and focusing them on him and his evil influences. He gains a perverse sense of joy when we credit him for all our problems and defeats. "The devil made me do it" is among Satan's favorite testimonies. Satan is very deceptive in how this manifest.

Satan assumes responsibility for all sorts of power so that we live in fear of him, rather than in reverential fear of God. In contrast, Jesus told us not to fear the one who is able to kill the body, but to fear Him who is able to cast both body and soul into hell (Matthew 10:28).

THE BELT OF TRUTH

In Ephesians 6:14, Paul names the Belt of Truth as a primary piece of the Armor of God. Why begin with the Belt? Why not the sword or the shield? Satan's first tactic is to cast doubt on God's Word. That is why our defense begins by having girded our loins with truth.

Truth must dominate our lives. In the first three chapters of Ephesians, Paul explains the relationship and position of a person saved by Grace. As believers, each of us becomes a member of the body of Christ. God gives us resurrection power, and seats us with Him in the heavenly places above all earthly rulers, power and authority. Our position is set forever in heaven. Though we gain this position in Christ, we still must live out our faith in our daily lives.

In the first three chapters, Paul makes six doctrinal statements that spell out our position in Christ:

1. God has selected us. God chose us. Ephesians 1:4 says, "According as He hath chosen us in Him before the foundation of the world, that we should be holy and without blame before Him in love." When Satan whispers or screams in your mind that you have been cut off from God, remind him that God chose you. God has chosen every man, woman and child that He created in His image.

2. God not only selected us, He saved us. Ephesians 1:7 says, "In Whom we have redemption through His blood, the forgiveness of sins, according to the riches of His grace." God spent His Son's blood to redeem us, giving us forgiveness of sins. Satan holds no power of death over us. James 4:7 instructs us to resist the devil and says he will flee. Because He saved you, Jesus gave you His power to use against Satan. But you must use it.

3. We are sealed. Ephesians 1:13 says, "In Whom ye also trusted, after that ye heard the word of truth, the gospel of your salvation: in whom also after that ye believed, ye were sealed with that Holy Spirit of promise." Satan wants to demoralize us, taking away our hope. He wants us to doubt the security of our relationship to God. God gave you His Holy Spirit to seal your faith and guarantee your redemption.

4. Positionally, we are seated at the right hand of God. Ephesians 2:6 says, "And hath raised us up together, and made us sit together in heavenly places in Christ Jesus." As you survey the battlefield, what better place to sit than immediately next to the Supreme Commander of the Earth. This is your position.

5. We are secure. We will be seated with Christ for all eternity. Why? Ephesians 2:19 says, "Now therefore ye are no more strangers and foreigners, but fellow citizens

with the saints, and of the household of God." Ephesians 3:6 says, "that the Gentiles should be fellow heirs, and of the same body, and partakers of His promise in Christ by the gospel." You are a citizen, heir, and of the same body as Christ.

6. Our position is one of strength. Ephesians 3:16 says, "that He would grant you, according to the riches of His glory, to be strengthened with might by His Spirit in the inner man." You need to be strong in the Lord and stand firm on the authority of these truths. You never have to run away, or be defeated! You put on the full armor of God to be able to resist the enemy, and taste God's victory. If you don't resist, Satan loves it.

Roman soldiers wore at least one of three different kinds of belts or girdles. One was like a leather apron worn to protect the lower abdomen; the second carried the sword; the third was a special belt, or sash, that designated the rank of an officer or high-ranking official.

The belt that carried the sword was absolutely necessary when going into battle. No soldier would purposely go to war without his weapon. Besides holding his sword's scabbard, this belt kept his tunic in place so he would not get tangled in it. And it secured the breastplate, which protected his chest. The belt kept everything else in place. The spiritual belt of truth performs a similar function in our lives. Truth lets us discern right from wrong, or recognize a violated standard.

All our lives, we have been subjected to Satan's lies, and he is the father of lies. We have believed and lived lies. We have told lies. But when we came to faith in Christ, God's Grace opened our spiritual eyes so we could see the Truth...and the Truth set us free. We no longer fell under the authority of Satan's lies. God's truth, as found in His Word, and our response to it sanctifies us and sets us apart for his service. His truth continues the sanctification process.

John 17:14-17 says, "I have given them thy Word; and the world hath hated them, because they are not of the world, even as I am not of the world. I pray not that Thou shouldest take them out of the world, but that Thou shouldest keep them from the evil. They are not of the world, even as I am not of the world. Sanctify them through Thy truth: Thy Word is truth." God the Father chose each of us. He sanctified or set each of us apart, and we are also required to sanctify ourselves. We are required to set ourselves apart to God.

I Peter 5:8-9 says, "Be sober, be vigilant; because your adversary the devil, as a roaring lion, walketh about, seeking whom he may devour: Whom resist stedfast in the faith, knowing that the same afflictions are accomplished in your brethren that are in the world." The truth of God's Word gives us the power and authority to defeat Satan.

II Peter 1:19-21 says, "We have also a more sure word of prophecy; whereunto ye do well that ye take heed, as unto a light that shineth in a dark place, until the day dawn, and the day star arise in your hearts: Knowing this first, that no prophecy of the Scripture is of any private interpretation. For the prophecy came not in old time by the will of man: but holy men of God spake as they were moved by the Holy Spirit."

Satan leads us into false beliefs so that we doubt God's Word. We actually help him in this, because many believers keep God in a tiny box, limiting what He can do in their lives by putting some areas off-limits. We must let God be God. Who are we to limit Him? We must decide whether or not we will believe the Bible and act on it, or continue to be tossed about by Satan.

II Timothy 3:16-17 says, "All Scripture is given by inspiration of God, and is profitable for doctrine, for reproof, for correction, for instruction in righteousness: That the man of God may be perfect, throughly furnished unto all good works."

Matthew 5:17-18 says, "Think not that I am come to destroy the law, or the prophets: I am not come to destroy, but to fulfill. For verily I say unto you, Till heaven and earth pass, one jot or one tittle shall in no wise pass from the law, till all be fulfilled." Jesus did not come to destroy or set aside the law. He came to give us a way to fulfill the law. We can fully keep the law, thus accomplishing the purpose of the law, which was sanctification. Salvation or justification has always been by faith. But true faith is never alone (James 2:17).

Luke 24:25-27 says, "Then He said unto them, O fools, and slow of heart to believe all that the prophets have spoken: Ought not Christ to have suffered these things, and to enter into His glory? And beginning at Moses and all the prophets, He expounded unto them in all the Scriptures the things concerning Himself."

When Jesus reached back into time, quoting from the law and prophets, did He believe them to be true? Did Jesus lie to those He taught? When the Gospel writers recorded their words about Jesus' life, did they make it all up? Can we count on Scripture to reveal truth?

The validity of God's Word is a central issue. If it is God-given, God-breathed, God-protected, and God-preserved, then we must study and obey it. If we pick and choose which parts of it we believe, then all of it fails. Satan likes to get us to doubt parts of Scripture, especially those parts that make us uncomfortable. Once he's got us doubting, he will devour us and we will at best become lukewarm Christians. God says he spews lukewarm Christians out of His mouth. We have a choice to make. Either we walk in our own understanding with Satan as our tour guide, or we can walk in God's truth with the Holy Spirit leading the way.

John 14:6 says, "Jesus saith unto him, I am the way, the truth, and the life: no man cometh unto the Father, but by Me."

John 17:17 says, "Sanctify them through Thy truth: Thy Word is truth."

John 8:32 says, "And ye shall know the truth, and the truth shall make you free."

If we refuse to accept God's truth, then we are not heirs to God's kingdom; instead, we inherit Satan's eternal damnation. There is no middle ground.

John 8:44 says, "Ye are of your father the devil, and the lusts of your father ye will do. He was a murderer from the beginning, and abode not in the truth, because there is no truth in him. When he speaketh a lie, he speaketh of his own: for he is a liar, and the father of it."

Make up your mind. Whom will you trust and follow? With whom will you walk? God gave you a free will to choose to manifest His Spirit, or manifest Satan's spirit.

II Corinthians 11:2-15 says, "For I am jealous over you with godly jealousy: for I have espoused you to one husband, that I may present you as a chaste virgin to Christ. But I fear, lest by any means, as the serpent beguiled Eve through his subtlety, so your minds should be corrupted from the simplicity that is in Christ. For if he that cometh preacheth another Jesus, whom we have not preached, or if ye receive another spirit, which ye have not received, or another gospel, which ye have not accepted, ye might well bear with him. For I suppose I wasn't a whit behind the very chiefest apostles. But though I be rude in speech, yet not in knowledge; but we have been thoroughly made manifest among you in all things. Have I committed an offence in abasing myself that ye might be exalted, because I have preached to you the gospel of God freely? I robbed other churches, taking wages of them, to do you service. And when I was present with you, and wanted, I was chargeable to no man: for that which was lacking to me the brethren which came from Macedonia supplied: and in all things I have kept myself from being burdensome unto you, and so will I keep myself. As the truth of Christ is in me, no man shall stop me of this boasting in the regions of Achaia. Wherefore? because I love you not? God knoweth. But what I do, that I will do, that I may cut off occasion from them which desire occasion; that wherein they glory, they may be found even as we. For such are false apostles, deceitful workers, transforming themselves into the apostles of Christ. And no marvel; for Satan himself is transformed into an angel of light. Therefore it is no great thing if his ministers also be transformed as the ministers of righteousness; whose end shall be according to their works."

Never forget that our warfare is not against flesh and blood, but against Satan and his kingdom. Never forget your real enemy.

I Timothy 4:1-3 says, "Now the Spirit speaketh expressly, that in the latter times some shall depart from the faith, giving heed to seducing spirits, and doctrines of devils; Speaking lies in hypocrisy; having their conscience seared with a hot iron; Forbidding to marry, and commanding to abstain from meats, which God hath created to be received with thanksgiving of them which believe and know the truth."

What happens to us when we refuse to put on the belt of truth and tighten it up for battle? From the beginning of the Christian faith it has always been a challenge for believers to become well established in the Word of God. In Ephesians 4, Paul exhorts believers to stay unified in the Spirit until all of us come to unity in faith and reach spiritual maturity. Zealous Christians who step into positions of leadership before they have a solid understanding of truth spread much error.

Ephesians 4:13-15 teaches that properly equipped believers won't be like children who are tossed around by waves and winds of false doctrine, or by men's trickery, craftiness or deceitful scheming. The one behind all these tactics is our enemy, Satan, who wants to lead us away from the simplicity and purity of God's Word and simple faith in the Lord Jesus Christ. This is why he disguises his servants and himself as angels of light.

When a believer is led astray, what should we do? Ephesians 4:15 says, "But speaking the truth in love, may grow up into him in all things, which is the head, even Christ."

When we see Christians in our fellowship or circle of influence that are doctrinally wrong, we must refute their error. We do this in a spirit of unity, peace and love. Peace and love are key motivations. We must approach an erring brother with patience, instructing him in truth, with humility. We must avoid spiritual pride and arrogance, being sure not to fall into the same doctrinal error, or one even worse. Galatians 6:1 teaches us to gently restore a fallen brother, thereby protecting ourselves from falling into the same sin.

I've taken quite a bit of time with the importance of wearing the belt of truth. I want you to have confidence that God's Word is truthful, and the source of all truth. God doesn't mind if you test His Word. Apply it and it will work. I pray that you have taken the reliability and truthfulness of Scripture to heart, as a primary step toward winning victory in the struggle against Satan.

How do we put on or take up the belt of truth? Do we say a magical prayer or visualize picking it up and putting it on?

Putting on the armor is not a passive action. The armor is not automatically put in place when we accept Jesus. It requires an act of doing, believing, embracing, responding to, and studying God's Word, and is accomplished over time. This is a basic issue we deal with in every ministry session. It is the most basic, foundational principle of spiritual warfare.

Ephesians 6:12 says, "we wrestle not against flesh and blood, but against principalities, against powers, against the rulers of the darkness of this world, against spiritual wickedness in high places." As it concerns each individual believer, the high places referred to here are between our ears.

II Corinthians 10:5 says to hold all of our thoughts captive to the subjection of Christ. What does this mean? It means that we are to examine each thought that enters our mind, and compare it to the plumb line (inerrant truth) of Scripture. We ask, "Does this thought come from God or Satan? Is it a good or evil thought; the truth or a lie?"

Hebrews 5:12-14 says to quit feeding on the milk of God's Word and start to feed on the meat. We are to become mature in our walk with God. Verse 14 describes discernment, saying that we should exercise our senses to know the difference between good and evil. Exercising our senses implies hard work. Christian maturity requires discernment and obedience to the truth. It requires us to know truth to be able to recognize error.

We put on the belt of truth by studying and applying God's Word to our lives.

James 4:7 says to "submit to God, resist the devil, and he will flee." There is a very specific order to this verse. It starts with submission. If we fail to submit and have sin in our lives, then the devil won't flee! How important is wearing the belt of truth? Nothing is more important if we desire to win at spiritual warfare and live a victorious, healthy Christian life.

THE BREASTPLATE OF RIGHTEOUSNESS

The Romans soldier's breastplate covered all his vital organs, both in front and behind. It was usually made of metal. In Ephesians 6:14, Paul drew a very important connection to our life in Christ from the breastplate's purpose.

Paul called this piece of spiritual armor, "The Breastplate of Righteousness." Putting on this breastplate is a process requiring the identification and removal of sin from our lives. It is an active process that requires a strong will to put God first.

One of the first issues we discuss with individuals in our ministry is total submission to God. If they are unwilling to seek God's kingdom and righteousness as their first priority, then we can't help them.

God promised to draw nigh to us if we will draw nigh to Him (James 4:8). Drawing nigh to God requires that we deal with the stuff in our life that is not of Him. That means we must identify and remove sin from our lives.

Almost everyone with whom we work has become very discouraged in their spiritual walk with God. They desire a close relationship, but can't seem to achieve it. They question whether or not God really cares about them or listens to their prayers. They feel separated, alone, condemned, unhappy, fearful and rejected. They're filled with anxiety, self-condemnation and self-pity.

Why do they feel like this? One thing separates them from God: sin.

Many of us knowingly tolerate certain types of sin, rationalizing that the sins we entertain are not as grievous as those we shun.

If you tolerate sin, deal with it now. Examine yourself to identify your sin. Name it, confess it, and ask God for His forgiveness. "If we confess our sins, he is faithful and just to forgive us our sins, and to cleanse us from all unrighteousness" (I John 1:9).

Many of us sin without realizing that our actions or attitudes constitute sin. We evaluate our sin based on the culture. Yet the culture constantly debates right and wrong. Today American culture calls good evil, and evil good. Cultural icons declare that there is no absolute truth, and since truth is relative, each person decides their own sense of morality. Eventually, a lack of moral consensus leads to chaos and instability. America needs a spiritual revival, but you need a standard. Look for your sense of right and wrong in the Scriptures, not the soap operas.

WHAT DOES SCRIPTURE TEACH ABOUT IMMORALITY?

Romans 1:22-27 says, "Professing themselves to be wise, they became fools, And changed the glory of the uncorruptible God into an image made like to corruptible man, and to birds, and fourfooted beasts, and creeping things. Wherefore God also gave them up to uncleanness through the lusts of their own hearts, to dishonour their own bodies between themselves: Who changed the truth of God into a lie, and worshipped and served the creature more than the Creator, who is blessed for ever. Amen. For this cause God gave them up unto vile affections: for even their women did change the natural use into that which is against nature: And likewise also the men, leaving the natural use of the woman, burned in their lust one toward another; men with men working that which is unseemly, and receiving in themselves that recompense of their error which was meet."

I Corinthians 6:9-11 says, "Know ye not that the unrighteous shall not inherit the kingdom of God? Be not deceived: neither fornicators, nor idolaters, nor adulterers, nor effeminate, nor abusers of themselves with mankind, Nor thieves, nor covetous, nor drunkards, nor revilers, nor extortioners, shall inherit the kingdom of God. And such were some of you: but ye are washed, but ye are sanctified, but ye are justified in the name of the Lord Jesus, and by the Spirit of our God."

I Corinthians 6:18 says, "Flee fornication. Every sin that a man doeth is without the body; but he that committeth fornication sinneth against his own body."

Ephesians 5:1-13 says, "Be ye therefore followers of God, as dear children; And walk in love, as Christ also hath loved us, and hath given Himself for us an offering and a sacrifice to God for a sweetsmelling savour. But fornication, and all uncleanness, or covetousness, let it not be once named among you, as becometh saints; Neither filthiness, nor foolish talking, nor jesting, which are not convenient: but rather giving of thanks. For this ye know, that no whoremonger, nor unclean person, nor covetous man, who is an idolater, hath any inheritance in the kingdom of Christ and of God. Let no man deceive you with vain words: for because of these things cometh the wrath of God upon the children of disobedience. Be not ye therefore partakers with them. For ye were sometimes darkness, but now are ye light in the Lord: walk as children of light: (For the fruit of the Spirit is in all goodness and righteousness and truth;) Proving what is acceptable unto the Lord. And have no fellowship with the unfruitful works of darkness, but rather reprove them. For it is a shame even to speak of those things which are done of them in secret. But all things that are reproved are made manifest by the light: for whatsoever doth make manifest is light."

I Corinthians 5:1-5 says, "It is reported commonly that there is fornication among you, and such fornication as is not so much as named among the Gentiles, that one should have his father's wife. And ye are puffed up, and have not rather mourned, that he that hath done this deed might be taken away from among you. For I verily, as absent in body, but present in spirit, have judged already, as though I were present, concerning him that hath so done this deed, In the name of our Lord Jesus Christ, when ye are gathered together, and my spirit, with the power of our Lord Jesus Christ, To deliver such an one unto Satan for the destruction of the flesh, that the spirit may be saved in the day of the Lord Jesus."

What does Paul mean when he says, "for the destruction of the flesh, that the spirit may be saved in the day of the Lord Jesus"? The purpose of delivering a sinner to Satan was to destroy the flesh. Christians were to withhold their fellowship and spiritual guidance from him, and to quit praying for him. Thus Satan had freedom to afflict his body. After suffering for a time under Satan's oppression, Paul believed such a person would come to repentance, receiving forgiveness and salvation. This Scripture teaches us about the power of prayer.

Destruction means to ruin, or a plague (I Corinthians 5:5, I Thessalonians. 5:3, II Thessalonians. 1:9, I Timothy 6:9). This kind of destruction did not kill the man; it brought him to repentance (II Corinthians 2:7). That the spirit may be saved means that physical affliction could not save a man's spirit unless it brought him to repentance. It wasn't the physical torment that saved the soul, but the repentance it stimulated. It is a consequence of disobedience and sin that allows Satan to have access to our lives (Deuteronomy 28).

Leviticus 20:10-22 describes God's attitude toward immorality. Verse 22 says, "Ye shall therefore keep all my statutes, and all my judgments, and do them: that the land, whither I bring you to dwell therein, spue you not out."

If God's commands took preference in our culture, AIDS wouldn't exist. Neither would abortion, murder, violence, hatred, suicide, rape, emotional and physical abuse, addictions, etc. The list of human maladies related to moral offenses is lengthy. If we obeyed God's commands, these things wouldn't be a major concern in our culture.

What we once condemned we now condone. People committed sinful acts in prior generations, but shame and cultural condemnation kept these sins from plaguing the society. The acts committed by past generations haven't changed in ours, but our cultural standards have ratcheted downward so they are no longer condemned. In fact, many of them are promoted. Homosexuality produces tremendous physical, psychological, emotional and spiritual suffering, yet our culture now calls it gay rights. Abortion kills the baby's body and leaves a huge moral vacuum in the heart of the mother, yet our culture calls it a woman's choice. Unbridled sexual images create sexual tension, and when compounded by confusion of gender roles, raise the incidences of rape and sexual abuse. Divorce divides families sometimes into three or four extended units, and Christians are just as vulnerable as non-Christians. We pay a terrible price for the abandonment of God's moral standards.

When we don't know the truth, or shun the truth, Satan's lies fill the void. Failing to put on the belt of truth gives Satan a huge edge in spiritual warfare. Without truth, we can't identify sin. Without first putting on the belt of truth, we cannot put on the breastplate of righteousness.

To be righteous, we must be forgiven. A forgiven person is blameless. I John 1:9 says, "If we confess our sins, He is faithful and just to forgive us our sins, and to cleanse us from all unrighteousness."

I Thessalonians 5:23 says, "And the very God of peace sanctify you wholly; and I pray God your whole spirit and soul and body be preserved blameless unto the coming of our Lord Jesus Christ."

II Peter 3:14 says, "Wherefore, beloved, seeing that ye look for such things, be diligent that ye may be found of Him in peace, without spot, and blameless."

Satan commonly attempts to conceal and pervert God's truth so that he can lead us into sin. He leads us to question whether or not we have really been forgiven of our sins. Satan nags us about our sins, constantly reminding us of how terrible we are, rendering us worthless to God and ourselves. He wants us to believe we are beyond God's forgiveness. Believing these lies removes our breastplate of righteousness leaving us susceptible to Satan's fiery darts.

To counter Satan, we must never forget God's promises. If we confess, He will forgive and cleanse us. As a forgiven person, we are blameless and declared righteous by God. His is the highest authority. Romans 8:1-2 says, "There is therefore now no condemnation to them which are in Christ Jesus, who walk not after the flesh, but after the Spirit. For the law of the Spirit of life in Christ Jesus hath made me free from the law of sin and death."

A REVIEW OF FORGIVENESS

In our ministry we ask people to prepare an affidavit as a tool to fight off Satan's attacks. In Matthew 6, Jesus taught us to forgive others and said that unless we forgive, God won't forgive us. In Matthew 18:34-35, Jesus said that if we don't forgive from our hearts we would be turned over to the tormentors. If we carry resentments, bitterness, and unforgiveness toward others or ourselves, the tormentors come in droves.

Through self-evaluation and inspection, we see how Satan's tormenters have attacked our peace and damaged our sound minds. Instead of peace, we have turmoil. Instead of health, we have ulcers caused by anxiety.

Our endocrine system responds to thoughts and emotions. The primary endocrine system has nine different glands that secrete more than one hundred different hormones, neurotransmitters or interleukins. If these glands secrete too much or too little of these hormones, it dramatically affects our mental and physical health. Now might be a good time to review the chapter on forgiveness.

James 5:16 instructs us to confess our faults to one another to receive healing. In our ministry we practice this principle. We work alongside people, helping them prepare their lists, praying with them as they seek forgiveness, and watch them shed the filthy rags of their sins. In doing this we help them put on the breastplate of righteousness.

At the end of the ministry time we each sign, date, and witness the affidavits. When Satan renews his attack, we reveal our breastplate of righteousness and order him to flee. He has no choice but to do so. He has no authority in our lives because we have been obedient to God and are now in right standing (blameless) before Him.

We don't need to live in bondage. God made a way for us to be free! John 8:36 says, "If the Son therefore shall make you free, ye shall be free indeed."

Romans 8:31-39 says, "What shall we then say to these things? If God be for us, who can be against us? He that spared not His own Son, but delivered Him up for us all, how shall He not with Him also freely give us all things? Who shall lay any thing to the charge of God's elect? It is God that justifieth. Who is he that condemneth? It is Christ that died, yea rather, that is risen again, Who is even at the right hand of God, Who also maketh intercession for us. Who shall separate us from the love of Christ? Shall tribulation, or distress, or persecution, or famine, or nakedness, or peril, or sword? As it is written, For Thy sake we are killed all the day long; we are accounted as sheep for the slaughter. Nay, in all these things we are more than conquerors through Him that loved us. For I am persuaded, that neither death, nor life, nor angels, nor principalities, nor powers, nor things present, nor things to come, Nor height, nor depth, nor any other creature, shall be able to separate us from the love of God, which is in Christ Jesus our Lord."

Amen! Knowing this truth gives us strength, but we still must take it into our heart so that we walk in it. God expects us to live righteously. Doing so requires that we confess our sins so that the devil has no opportunity to attack and put us back into bondage.

Ephesians 4:17-18 says, "not to walk as the gentiles walked." The Greek word for gentile means "pagan" or "heathen." Gentiles, the unsaved, take their walking instructions from Satan, not God. Whose kingdom are you taking instruction from?

Ephesians 4:22 says to put off the old man. The old man is Satan's spirit and nature. Romans 6:6 also refers to the old man. He is, "the prince of the power of the air, the spirit that now worketh in the children of disobedience" (Ephesians 2:2, Ephesians 4:22-24, Colossians 3:9, John 8:44, I John 3:8, 5:18).

Ephesians 4:23 says we need to be renewed. Being renewed means that the whole course of life flows in a different direction (II Corinthians 5:17-18). We renew our mind by renouncing its vanity (Ephesians 4:17), its darkness and blindness (Ephesians 4:18) and learning of Christ (Ephesians 4:20-21).

Ephesians 4:24 says to put on the new man. The new man is the Spirit and nature of God (Ephesians 4:23-24, II Peter 1:4, Romans 8:9, 14-16). Verse 25 says to lay aside the old man and put on the new man. Here we see a characterization of the two kingdoms. In an earlier chapter we listed behaviors identified with each kingdom. We have choices to make. We can manifest the fruit of the Holy Spirit, or the fruit and nature of Satan and his demons. What will your choice be? We put aside the old man each time we repent or forgive; each time we choose to do His will. This is called sanctification.

Ephesians 4:27 says, "Neither give place to the devil." This verse provides a very important insight and principle needing more attention. Sin gives Satan a place or opportunity to occupy our minds and affect our spirits. These are strong words with serious implications. The Greek word for "place" is *topos*, meaning "place, opportunity, position, home, license or room."

Warren Wiersbe wrote in *The Strategy of Satan*:

> If the believer cultivates in his life any known sin, he is giving Satan an opportunity to get a foothold, a beachhead in his life. Satan will then use this opportunity to invade and take other areas. Any sin that we harbor in our lives, that we know is there and yet we refuse to acknowledge and confess, will give Satan a beachhead for further attacks. It has been my experience that this includes material objects that are definitely related to Satanism and the occult. No Christian has any right to possess such objects because they give Satan the foothold he is looking for. When the Ephesian Christians burned their magic books (Acts 19:18-20), they were taking a giant step forward in defeating Satan.
>
> Finally, we must never look upon any sin or questionable object as a "little thing." Nothing is "little" if Satan can use it to attack you! I recall counseling a Christian student who had an obsession for food. She was ruining her health and her studies, and her anxiety was only making the problem worse. I asked her if she had anything in her possession that was related to the occult. She confessed that she did, and I urged her to get rid of it, confess her sin to the Lord, and claim the victory of Christ over whatever demons were using that object as a beachhead. She did all of this, and the Lord gave her wonderful victory. Illustrations of this kind of victory can be multiplied by pastors who have confronted occult powers.

Tolerating any sin in our lives opens the door to Satan, separating us from God. In our ministry, we ask people to read through an extensive checklist of occult practices. They check off those with which they have any contact. We expose any connection they have to things that are not Godly both in their lives, and in their generations. (See the chapter on occultism.)

Exodus 20:5 says the sins of the father are passed on to the third and fourth generations. In Nehemiah 9:1-3 and Leviticus 26:40-45, the people of Israel confessed the sins of their fathers. I believe it is just as important to do this today. I don't want Satan to gain any foothold, beachhead, place, opportunity, stronghold or entry point into my life.

We work through the occultic checklist, renouncing and repenting of any participation by ourselves or in previous generations. Two things happen: first, we identify sin that we had not understood to be sin; secondly, we are set free from sin through forgiveness. Praise God!

HOW DO WE PUT ON THE BREASTPLATE OF RIGHTEOUSNESS?

1. Make sure that we are God's child in accordance with Scripture.

2. Ask God to reveal any place where we have tolerated or opened ourselves to sin. Jeremiah 17:9 says that our heart is deceitful, who can trust it. God will let us know.

3. Apply I John 1:9. Confess our sin, specifically naming it, and agree with God that it is sin. Quit doing it. Ask God for His strength and discernment not to repeat the sin.

4. Thank God for His forgiveness, and what He continues to do in our lives.

5. If we have stolen, or if we have wronged others, we need to set these situations right. Sometimes we don't remember these situations. Ask God to reveal to whom we need make restitution. If the person has died, or if we have no way to make contact with them, go to God and ask for forgiveness. Ask for His supernatural peace.

6. When Satan comes to accuse, take the sword — God's word — and tell him out loud to be gone. Show him your affidavits, reminding him and yourself that you are forgiven and that you have forgiven others. Satan must obey your command to leave you alone. Speak out loud to Satan as he cannot hear your thoughts. Only God can hear our thoughts.

If we harbor sin in our lives, choosing not to forgive others or ourselves, then we lose our peace and fellowship with our heavenly Father. We cannot experience the joy of walking with God. This brings us to the next piece of armor Paul wrote about in Ephesians.

We put on the Breastplate of Righteousness through forgiveness: first by receiving God's forgiveness for our sin; and second, by forgiving those that have hurt us. Forgiveness quenches the firey darts of the devil. Forgiveness removes the pain from memories and experiences. Forgiveness is how God intended each of us to protect ourselves.

THE GOSPEL OF PEACE

Ephesians 6:15 says, "And your feet shod with the preparation of the gospel of peace." Peace and a sense of wellbeing are two of the greatest blessings of this life. If we live in peace with others and ourselves we can withstand almost anything life throws at us. But if that peace is disturbed, we are tormented. The parable of the rich man in Matthew 18:21-35 illustrates this very well.

Paul uses the soldier's shoes to teach us about the Gospel of Peace. The best equipped and most highly trained soldier will lose the battle if he is unable to stand on his feet.

Roman soldiers wore sandals that were bound by thongs over the instep and around the ankle, and the soles were thickly studded with nails. A common military practice of their day was to put sharpened sticks in the ground, concealing them — their version of land mines. A soldier who stepped on one of these ran the risk of receiving a severe, debilitating puncture. Unable to walk, he was effectively removed from battle.

The Greek word for "shod" means "to bind under" or "to strap on." How do we strap on our spiritual shoes to protect us from spiritual land mines? How do we put on "the preparation of the gospel of peace"?

Isaiah 52:7 says, "How beautiful upon the mountains are the feet of him that bringeth good tidings, that publisheth peace; that bringeth good tidings of good, that publisheth salvation; that saith unto Zion, Thy God reigneth!"

Romans 10:15 says, "And how shall they preach, except they be sent? as it is written, How beautiful are the feet of them that preach the gospel of peace, and bring glad tidings of good things!"

These two passages refer to spreading the gospel. But the context of Ephesians is spiritual warfare. The Greek word for "preparation" means, "to be prepared in readiness." It suggests making peace with God before the battle begins, being ready to meet Him. It also means having a solid foundation, a readiness of mind, flowing from the Gospel of Jesus Christ, a message of peace. Paul used the word "peace" in other verses in Ephesians as well.

Ephesians 2:14-17 says, "For He is our peace, who hath made both one, and hath broken down the middle wall of partition between us; Having abolished in His flesh the enmity, even the law of commandments contained in ordinances; for to make in Himself of twain one new man, so making peace; And that He might reconcile both unto God in one body by the cross, having slain the enmity thereby: And came and preached peace to you which were afar off, and to them that were nigh."

Ephesians 4:3 says, "Endeavouring to keep the unity of the Spirit in the bond of peace."

Ephesians 6:23 says, "Peace be to the brethren, and love with faith, from God the Father and the Lord Jesus Christ."

Paul teaches that our relationship with God should be one of peace. We should also live in peace with other Christians and with ourselves. Peace is required to be able to stand and fight. Living in peace with God and others assures me of withstanding the spiritual land mines that threaten to take me out of the battle.

Satan is a murderer and a destroyer. Anger, unforgiveness, bitterness and depression are four of the most common methods he uses to destroy us. All of these are listed in Ephesians 4:25-32 as things given no "place" in the life of children of God. Let's review these verses.

Ephesians 4:25 says, "Wherefore putting away lying, speak every man truth with his neighbour: for we are members one of another."

The lie must be put away. This also puts Satan away, he who is the father of lies (John 8:44, II Thessalonians 2:11). Heathen teachers have long declared that a lie is better than the truth when it is profitable and less hurtful. This is not Scriptural.

Ephesians 4:26 says, "Be ye angry, and sin not: let not the sun go down upon your wrath." This refers to being provoked to sin by Satan, but we are told not to yield to such provoking, or give any place to the devil (Ephesians 4:26-27). The only way to "be angry and sin not," is to be angry at Satan and evil. Even this anger needs to be put away before nighttime.

The words "anger" and "angry" are used 278 times in the Bible, but only twelve times in the New Testament. The emotion of anger is God-created and perfectly sinless in itself. Its misuse is what God condemns. We are never to be angry with others or ourselves. Righteous anger or hatred is only directed at Satan or evil.

God displayed anger many times, but His anger was a result of or directed at sin (Numbers 11:1, 10, 33, Numbers 12:9, Numbers 14:11, Psalms 7:11). If we express anger, our cause must be just (Matthew 5:22, Romans 1:18, James 1:19). The Gospel gives place to anger (Mark 3:5) but not to sin.

When anger rules us, we fall into trouble. According to Galatians 5:19-20, an angry outburst is one of the "works of the flesh," and when the flesh controls you rather than the Spirit, it is sin.

Harboring anger is sinful. Anger, justified or not, must be given to God. Harboring anger gives the devil a place in our lives. Anger wears away at relationships, and destroys our physical health. After giving it to God we are to stop being angry; we are to choose to stop sinning. A moment of anger should bring an opportunity for reconciliation.

Verse 27 says, "Neither give place to the devil." If we allow sin to have a place in our life, then Satan has also has a place.

God says in verse 28, "Let him that stole steal no more: but rather let him labour, working with his hands the thing which is good, that he may have to give to him that needeth." We are to work to satisfy our needs.

Verse 29 says, "Let no corrupt communication proceed out of your mouth, but that which is good to the use of edifying, that it may minister grace unto the hearers." This refers to useless, putrid and obscene communications (Matthew 7:17-18, Matthew 12:33, Matthew 13:48, Luke 6:43). God intended our words to edify others, to build up one another by our speech.

Verse 30 says, "And grieve not the holy Spirit of God, whereby ye are sealed unto the day of redemption." We will not grieve the Holy Spirit if we refuse to practice these forbidden things taught in Ephesians 4:17-18.

Verse 31 says, "Let all bitterness, and wrath, and anger, and clamour, and evil speaking, be put away from you, with all malice."

Hebrews 12:15 warns us not to let a root of bitterness spring up in our spirit. If we go to bed with unresolved anger or resentment, a root of bitterness will be evident the next morning. This is why Ephesians 4:26 tells us not to let the sun go down on our wrath.

Do you have any unresolved anger in your heart? Unresolved anger results from unforgiveness and leads to resentment, bitterness and depression. This is a very high price to pay for sin. Jeremiah 17:9 says that our heart is deceitfully wicked, and not to trust it. Ask God to show you if you any unresolved anger is still lurking in your spirit. Add it to your forgiveness list, confess it and renounce it. Resolve the issues that spawned it.

To gain peace you must give your anger to God. Ask and receive His forgiveness; ask Him to heal you of that memory or hurt. Then you can break Satan's power over you regarding this memory. Speak out loud telling Satan that in the name of Jesus his power over you is broken. Ask the Holy Spirit to come and heal the memory and the hurt. When you stand and resist the devil in this manner, he will flee. God promises it! Healing begins when we are willing to forgive!

Verse 32 says, "And be ye kind one to another, tenderhearted, forgiving one another, even as God for Christ's sake hath forgiven you."

Colossians 3:12-15 says, "Put on therefore, as the elect of God, holy and beloved, bowels of mercies, kindness, humbleness of mind, meekness, longsuffering; Forbearing one another, and forgiving one another, if any man have a quarrel against any: even as Christ forgave you, so also do ye. And above all these things put on charity, which is the bond of perfectness. And let the peace of God rule in your hearts, to the which also ye are called in one body; and be ye thankful."

II Corinthians 2:5-11 says, "But if any have caused grief, he hath not grieved me, but in part: that I may not overcharge you all. Sufficient to such a man is this punishment, which was inflicted of many. So that contrariwise ye ought rather to forgive him, and comfort him, lest perhaps such a one should be swallowed up with overmuch sorrow. Wherefore I beseech you that ye would confirm your love toward him. For to this end also did I write, that I might know the proof of you, whether ye be obedient in all things. To whom ye forgive any thing, I forgive also: for if I forgave any thing, to whom I forgave it, for your sakes forgave I it in the person of Christ; Lest Satan should get an advantage of us: for we are not ignorant of his devices."

This why we have been studying spiritual warfare, so that we would not be ignorant! We are God's children and He has set us free by His forgiveness. If we don't forgive others and ourselves, we move back under Satan's power.

Matthew 18:21-35 tells the story of a man whose master forgave him a very large debt, but he refused to forgive another of a very small debt. When the master heard of his unwillingness to forgive, he turned him over to the tormentors until his debt was paid in full. In verse 35, Jesus says the same thing will happen to us if we don't forgive others.

In the Lord's Prayer we are instructed to ask God the Father to forgive us in the same manner that we forgive others. Do you really want to pray this prayer? Each day and in every situation in life we are setting the standard for our own forgiveness.

We'd like to think that God will forgive all our sins if we just ask in faith. But these two teachings from Matthew indicate we have a role to play: forgiving others. These are tough lessons, but they from are God's Word. And they're vitally important, given that lack of forgiveness results in bitterness and resentment, two torments that steal our peace and health.

Life's hurts can seem very unfair. Some people are severely abused through no fault of their own. Satan works to keep these things fresh in our minds, causing us to live under their bondage. As people in bondage, our peace is shattered. Is that your desire?

Hebrews 12:1-4 says, "Wherefore seeing we also are compassed about with so great a cloud of witnesses, let us lay aside every weight, and the sin which doth so easily beset us, and let us run with patience the race that is set before us, Looking unto Jesus the author and finisher of our faith; who for the joy that was set before Him endured the cross, despising the shame, and is set down at the right hand of the throne of God. For consider Him that endured such contradiction of sinners against Himself, lest ye be wearied and faint in your minds. Ye have not yet resisted unto blood, striving against sin."

Have you resisted Satan "unto blood"? Jesus bled during His prayer at Gethsemane, from the whips of Roman soldiers, and at Golgotha. He fought Satan with the blood of His own body. The blood carries life to every cell of the body, and carries away the body's impurities. Voluntarily giving up His blood became the ultimate sacrifice for our sins.

You will have no peace until you are willing to submit everything, including your life, to God. Seek first the kingdom of God and His righteousness and then you will receive His peace, a peace that passes all understanding. You receive the Gospel of Peace by being obedient to God's Word.

THE SHIELD OF FAITH

Kay Arthur illustrates her study of the Shield of Faith with a story of an African bird and how it protects its young. She writes that the screeching of a bird perched high in a tree startled a hunter in the jungles of Africa. As the hunter watched the bird, he noticed a snake working its way up the tree. He saw that the bird had a nest and that there were baby birds in it. The mother bird made a tremendous racket but then, as suddenly as it began, it quit. As the snake got close to the nest, the mother bird flew off as if it were abandoning the nest. However, she came back quickly with a leaf in her beak.

She placed the leaf squarely over the nest, covering all the little babies. When the snake got to the nest, it turned back and slowly wound its way back down the tree. The hunter stood puzzled. He did not understand how a leaf would make the snake turn and leave its meal.

Later he shared what he had seen with local people. The leaf the mother bird placed over the nest was poisonous to the snake.

This is a picture of what God does for us as we engage in spiritual warfare. He didn't leave us defenseless. He didn't leave us without a shield and a helmet to ward off Satan's fiery darts. He gave us the Shield of Faith and the helmet of our Salvation.

Ephesians 6:16-17 says, "Above all, taking the shield of faith, wherewith ye shall be able to quench all the fiery darts of the wicked. And take the helmet of salvation, and the sword of the Spirit, which is the Word of God."

In verse 14, Paul said to put on the belt and the breastplate. Now he says to take up the shield and the helmet. It makes sense that a soldier would put on the main articles of his armor before taking up his helmet and shield. A breastplate alone wasn't enough protection. The shield is movable and able to catch or deflect the enemy's arrows, knives and spears.

The fiery darts in Roman times included any thrown missile: a javelin, spear, arrow, or stone. Fiery darts could include the combustible arrowheads that set fire to fortifications, ships, houses and shields made of wood and leather. Roman shields were made of iron, and were usually shaped like a door. They were large enough to protect the soldier, and some were covered with layers of leather soaked in water just before the battle to extinguish fire from flaming arrows.

The shield provides another great word picture. The Bible often compares the Word to water. Ephesians 5:26 says, "That he might sanctify and cleanse it with the washing of water by the Word." Just as a Roman shield that had been soaked in water put out flaming arrows, so the shield of faith quenches all of the enemy's fiery darts. Faith comes from hearing, believing and applying the Word, and without faith we cannot please God.

Knowing the truth is not good enough. We must apply it, taking up the shield of faith to deflect Satan's attack. Practically, this means using specific truths from God's Word to counteract various lies and accusations of the devil.

There is not a single lie or accusation of Satan that we cannot extinguish with the Word of God. If Satan's fiery darts burn us, it's because we haven't spent enough time in the Scriptures building up our faith. Just as the leather on Roman shields would dry out in the heat of battle, so will our shields of faith if we are not completely immersed in the Bible each day.

Satan's fiery darts consist of evil thoughts, lusts, passions and various temptations (I Corinthians 10:13-14, II Corinthians 10:4-6, James 1:13-15, Romans 6:12, I John 2:15-17).

How does Satan attack you? Have you examined your thoughts? Do you know their origin? Are they good or evil? Are they from God or Satan?

What do you think of yourself? What do you think of others? Write down every thought you have about yourself, your spouse and others you know. Write down how you feel about God. How do you feel about your earthly mother and father, even if they have died? Once you have done this, compare your thoughts to the truth of Scripture. Do your thoughts line up with the Word, or are some, or many, of them out of line?

Scripture commands us to examine our thoughts. II Corinthians 10:5 says, "Casting down imaginations, and every high thing that exalteth itself against the knowledge of God, and bringing into captivity every thought to the obedience of Christ."

Our thoughts are either curses or blessings. Philippians 4:8 says, "Finally, brethren, whatsoever things are true, whatsoever things are honest, whatsoever things are just, whatsoever things are pure, whatsoever things are lovely, whatsoever things are of good report; if there be any virtue, and if there be any praise, think on these things." How do the thoughts that you just wrote down compare to this verse? Do the thoughts you identified build up or tear down those on your list?

Hebrews 5:12-14 says that we need to quit feeding on the milk of the Word, and move on to the meat. Meat is a metaphor for spiritual maturity. Verse 14 says, "But strong meat belongeth to them that are of full age, even those who by reason of use have their senses exercised to discern both good and evil." Being of full age means to be mature, and maturity is defined as the ability to discern between good and evil.

Scripture commands us not to be ignorant of Satan's devices (II Corinthians 2:11). Not knowing the difference between good and evil reveals ignorance. This is why the command in II Corinthians 10:5 is so important. If we are to be successful in defeating Satan, we must examine our thoughts. We need to ask whether or not we are allowing Satan's lies into our hearts, or God's truth. If our thoughts are good and of God, then we need to readily accept them into our hearts with great joy. If they are evil thoughts, we are to reject them and rebuke Satan.

James 4:7 says submit to God and resist the devil and he will flee. Sending the devil fleeing starts with our total submission to God. This is an ongoing process. If submitting to God is our habit, then we will be able to resist the devil. To resist implies that there is something that we must actually do. God grants us the power to resist, but we must choose to do so. The mystery of the fellowship of the Church is that it is a partnership with God (Ephesians 3:9).

As we grow in our relationship with God our shield will also grow. As a young immature Christian our shield is small, unable to withstand all of the attacks of the devil. But as we mature and learn God's word by use and experience our faith grows.

THE HELMET OF SALVATION

The belt is truth, the breastplate is righteousness, the shoes are peace, the shield is faith, and the helmet is the assurance of salvation. It is the confidence that comes from knowing our salvation is sure.

The helmet symbolizes our position in Jesus Christ, showing that we are a member of His family and joint heirs with Him. Putting on the helmet demonstrates that we know and embrace our position in Christ. We have been selected, saved and sealed by and in Christ; we are seated with Christ at the right hand of God; we are secure in Him; in Him we have a position of strength.

We are assured of salvation, if our faith is not alone (James 2:17). Are there works of Righteousness in your life? Are you being changed (sanctified) in your experience? in your daily life? If so, rest assured that you are His.

By putting on the Helmet of Salvation, we show the enemy that he cannot crush us, touch us, nor do anything to us. Yet sometimes we still feel defeated. Why? It requires us to search our hearts and minds to see if we have given the devil an opening, then defeat him, sending him fleeing. Our salvation assures the ultimate victory through Christ.

The Helmet of Salvation demonstrates three aspects of salvation: I have been saved, I am being saved, and I will be saved.

The first is justification. This is our legal position in Christ. We were saved from the penalty of sin at the moment we accepted Christ's sacrifice on the cross. This aspect of salvation is past tense. Because we accepted His free gift, we are justified.

The second is sanctification. This is in the present tense. We are being saved daily from the power of sin. Sanctification is an ongoing process as we learn to walk with God and put aside sin and Satan's ways. It is a process of sharpening our ability to discern between good and evil, and then choosing the good (Hebrews 5:14). It is in this process that we become "vessels fit for His service" (II Timothy 2:20-21). We can be overcomers or non-overcomers. If we choose to be overcomers great rewards are promised (Revelation 2-3).

Sanctification comes as a result of submitting to His authority, and allowing the Holy Spirit to direct us. We can choose to walk by the spirit in God's Kingdom, or walk in the flesh in Satan's kingdom. We can choose to quench the Holy Spirit by not allowing Him to work through us to carry out His will. We can grieve the Holy Spirit by continuing to sin. Or we can walk as sanctified believers, in the power and light of the Holy Spirit.

Sanctification is the process of being trained to be His kings and priests for all eternity. We must learn to conquer the iniquity in us. In doing this we learn how to be His servants in all eternity.

The third is glorification. This is in the future. At the end of our earthly life, we will walk with our Heavenly Father and we'll be given a new body. The level of relationship and the level of authority that we have in heaven is determined by our obedience in this life.

I believe our new body will be just like Jesus' body was after the resurrection. He was recognizable, He still had the scars from His crucifixion, and yet He walked, talked and ate. He appeared in rooms without going through a door, and traveled instantly from one place to another.

Our spirit and soul are eternal, and will live with Him forever. This is fascinating. Even walking on earth, we are really in eternity. Only our body dies, and it is replaced with a new and better model.

Hebrews 13:5-6 says, "Let your conversation be without covetousness; and be content with such things as ye have: for He hath said, I will never leave thee, nor forsake thee. So that we may boldly say, The Lord is my helper, and I will not fear what man shall do unto me."

Whatever the spiritual battle in which we are involved, we can stand secure with our helmet on, confident in our identity in Christ. We are on the winning side. We have nothing to fear but fear itself. II Timothy 1:7 says, "For God hath not given us the spirit of fear; but of power, and of love, and of a sound mind."

Scripture labels it "the spirit of fear." Notice, Scripture doesn't say *a* spirit of fear, but *the* spirit of fear. The spirit of fear refers to Ephesians 6:12, where we're told, we wrestle not with flesh and blood but with powers and principalities. Our triune God has given us His power through His Holy Spirit, and His love through God the Father, and a sound mind through Jesus Christ, the Word."

Often as we teach about victory in Christ someone always brings up Job or Paul's thorn in the flesh. They suggest they are examples of Satan's victory in that God allowed, or tested them with disease or other calamities in their lives. Then they are used as an excuse for the problems in their own life. This is not so.

Galatians 6:7 says, "Be not deceived; God is not mocked: for whatsoever a man soweth, that shall he also reap." There are many other verses in both the Old and New Testaments that teach that we will always reap what we sow.

Job blamed God seventy-four times in the first thirty-one chapters for what happened to him. To blame means to belittle or curse. Job cursed the day he was born seventeen times. He wished he were dead or had never been born. He sinned greatly in each of these situations.

Additionally Job lived in fear. He had extreme fear that his children would sin in their partying and curse God. He also had his own fears. Job 3:25 says, "For the thing which I greatly feared is come upon me, and that which I was afraid of is come unto me." As we have studied in the chapter on fear, it is unbelief. Fear is the opposite of faith. In his fears, Job was cursing God.

Moreover, in chapter forty-two, Job repented for speaking about things that he had no knowledge of, and he forgave or prayed for his first three friends. He also completed the required animal sacrifice as covering for sins. Then God restored double what Satan had taken from him. If Job were not reaping what he had sown, why would he have to repent?

Elihu's response, in chapters 32-37, contains the answers to our problems in this life. I suggest that you study Elihu's wisdom from God with diligence. (I have written a detailed study of Job in my book, *The Continuing Works of Christ*.)

If you cannot agree with how I present Job, at least remember that he did not stay sick and defeated for long.

Let's take a closer look at Paul's thorn in the flesh.

II Corinthians 12:7 says, "And lest I should be exalted above measure through the abundance of the revelations, there was given to me a thorn in the flesh, the messenger of Satan to buffet me, lest I should be exalted above measure."

What was Paul's thorn in the flesh? The verse says plainly that it was a "messenger of Satan." The Greek word is translated "angel" 179 times and "messenger" seven times. It's never translated "disease" or "physical infirmity." Such an interpretation would be wrong. An angel of Satan, one of the spirit beings that followed him when God threw him out of heaven, buffeted Paul, tempting him with self-exaltation.

In II Corinthians 11:23-27 Paul lists some of the ordeals caused by this evil angel that kept him humble. There is not a disease in the entire list.

Paul's thorn must be understood in the same sense as Numbers 33:55, Ezekiel 28:24, and Hosea 2:6 where the same Greek word for thorn is found in the Septuagint. In these passages, the giants were called thorns in the sides of the Israelites. The giants resulted from the union of fallen angels with human women (Genesis 6:4, Jude 6, II Peter 2:4). They weren't diseases and plagues, bad eyes or a heart condition. They did cause suffering and war.

Those that teach that Paul's thorn was an eye disease use Galatians 6:11 to justify their case.

Galatians 6:11 says, "Ye see how large a letter I have written unto you with mine own hand." They reason that since he wrote a large letter, Paul must have had an eye problem. Some have gone so far as to describe it with running sores. The truth is simply that he wrote a long letter. The writing style of the day was also to use letters large in size. To make this an eye disease is a total fabrication of Scripture.

Paul asked three times for the thorn to be removed and God refused. He refused because the thorn was an evil spirit that was tempting Paul. It is not yet time for Satan and his demons to be removed from the world. That will happen in God's timing which is the Day of Vengences, the Second Coming of Christ. In truth each and every believer has the same thorn. We are all tempted and buffeted by Satan, and this will continue until Jesus put Satan away for ever.

These examples show that God could never violate His holy nature by allowing or testing with evil. If we disobey God, Satan has a right to sift us as he did Job, Paul, and Peter. The curses of Deuteronomy 28, and elsewhere in Scripture, are delivered by Satan, not by God. Our enemy is Satan.

God made many promises to each of us. I Corinthians 10:13 says, "There hath no temptation taken you but such as is common to man: but God is faithful, who will not suffer you to be tempted above that ye are able; but will with the temptation also make a way to escape, that ye may be able to bear it."

He has promised us a way of escape from the devil's wiles. This is a message of hope, love and peace. Still, we cannot be ignorant of his devices. We must know the entire truth, seek forgiveness and obey God's Word. Then we will receive peace. Satan's thorns will still be thrown at us, but we will deflect and defeat them.

Satan's primary objective is to entice us to sin, thereby separating us from God and rendering us useless in spiritual warfare. He targets our minds, with sin beginning in our thought life. That's why Paul insisted that we take every thought captive and avoid being snared by the devil.

Satan even targets our dreams. Have you ever had evil dreams, or dreams with sexual overtones? They surely didn't come from God. How do you deal with these? First, submit to God. Ask if there is a reason for the dreams? Is there a sexual fantasy running amok in your thoughts? If so, ask for God's forgiveness, and ask Him to remove harmful dreams, binding and breaking Satan's power. Satan will flee.

In our ministry we commonly find people who hear voices in their minds. Many fear talking about the voices thinking they might be labeled insane. I have found that all of us at least occasionally hear voices in our minds. They are evidence of the spiritual warfare in which we engage. Satan attacks us with evil thoughts in order to drown out the voice of God's indwelling Holy Spirit. Here is where we must diligently practice discernment. What is the origin of these voices?

James 1:8 says, "A double-minded man is unstable in all his ways." This speaks of someone who sometimes chooses God and His ways, and other times chooses Satan and his ways.

James 4:8 says, "Draw nigh to God, and He will draw nigh to you. Cleanse your hands, ye sinners; and purify your hearts, ye double-minded."

If we submit to God and resist the devil, he will flee from us. Then the ungodly voices and dreams will stop.

Satan wants us to blame others or ourselves for these voices. He wants us to believe there is something wrong with us. But we need to blame him and his demons. In some way, we gave Satan an opening and he moved into our thought life. Just as we gave him an opening, so we can close him out.

As the time for Jesus to cast Satan into the lake of fire draws closer, spiritual warfare will escalate. Revelation tells us that Satan won't just peaceably surrender. He will unleash his worst. Likewise, he won't leave us alone without a battle, and his primary battleground is our mind. He will constantly attack our thoughts.

Remember II Corinthians 10:3-5: "For though we walk in the flesh, we do not war after the flesh: (For the weapons of our warfare are not carnal, but mighty through God to the pulling down of strongholds;) Casting down imaginations, and every high thing that exalteth itself against the knowledge of God, and bringing into captivity every thought to the obedience of Christ."

Taking every thought captive is a continual challenge, and forms an important aspect of spiritual warfare. Bringing thoughts into captivity means to bring them under control. Then we can submit ourselves more completely to God.

The devil shoots a fiery dart, a thought, to our mind: a lie, thought of rejection, wrong doctrine, self-condemnation, a suggestion to do evil, etc. At the moment we become aware of the thought, we must evaluate it and hold it up to God's Word. Does it meet the Philippians 4:8 test? Does it meet the Hebrews 5:12 test? If it doesn't meet these qualifications, we must reject it as instructed by James 4:7-8.

Sin occurs when a wrong thought turns into an action. This creates an appetite that becomes a weakness, then a habit. The habit brings oppression from the enemy. James 1:14-15 provides a warning about the steps that lead to sin.

Our families form another major battlefield for Satan. He is determined to destroy them. Families form the foundation of our nation and society. If they are destroyed, our children and all future generations will be destroyed. Exodus 20:5 warns us that the father's iniquity is passed on to the third and fourth generations.

Satan targets the family because the relationship between husbands and wives, and parents and children, is an earthly example of the interaction of our heavenly Father with His family. If he can destroy your relationship with your earthly father, he has created a rift between you and your Heavenly Father. The habits and attitudes learned from our parents are passed on to our children. This perpetuates Satan's attack on the human race.

I teach a class called "The Power of Dad." We study in detail how the sins of the father are passed on from generation to generation, and what constitutes those sins. We learn how to restore broken relationships and break the generational chain of sin. We discuss how to re-teach our children if we have taught them error. But in all this, the key element is the father's attitude and desire to bring change to himself.

Even grown children don't have the ability to confront their dad. It lies with dads to examine their relationship with their children. What habits, fears, attitudes, beliefs or diseases have they learned or received from dad? If they have learned things that dad now regrets, then he must go to them and apologize, teaching them in God's way.

Our children reap the harvest of the sin sown by their parents. Satan works overtime to keep parents from loving their children, and to alienate children from their parents.

We need to take special care in our relationship with our spouse. Do we edify our mate, or tear him or her down? Do we neglect or take him or her for granted? Do we treat our spouse as a king or queen, or as our servant? We must guard our families. Ephesians 5:15-6:4 gives instructions. Study what God's Word says about nurturing and loving our families.

THE SWORD OF THE SPIRIT

Ephesians 6:17 says, "And take the helmet of salvation, and the sword of the Spirit, which is the word of God"

The sword of the Spirit is the Word of God. But the Belt of Truth and the Shield of Faith are also the Word. How are they different?

First, the sword is both a defensive and offensive weapon. You don't "put on" the sword and helmet, you "take" them.

The second difference is uncovered by a word study. The Greek word in Ephesians 6:17 for "word" is *rhema*. It refers to the spoken Word. When we put on the Belt of Truth or the Shield of Faith we put on the "logos," the entirety of Scripture. Using the sword of the Spirit requires quoting individual verses or passages as the Spirit brings them to mind when they are needed.

If we hide God's Word in our hearts, as we are attacked the Holy Spirit brings to mind a specific verse or passage of Scripture that we can use to defeat the devil.

The Greek word for "sword" is *machaira*. It means a knife or dirk, a short sword used by Roman soldiers in hand-to-hand combat. Its use required skill and practice. God's armor places the sword of truth in the scabbard hung from the belt of truth: individual verses held in the whole of His Word. The belt held the breastplate of righteousness in place. God has a plan that we can tap to win this spiritual warfare.

In Luke 4:1-13, Jesus used specific Scriptures to defeat Satan. It is critical that we are skilled in knowing and using the Word of God. We must know how to test our thoughts and actions, comparing them to the plumb line of God's truth. We need to know which word to pull out to defeat Satan in each situation.

As we mature in Christ our sword or knowledge of His Word grows. We begin with a small dagger and hopefully grow to a large two-handed sword that will defeat every wile of the devil. We must study to show ourselves an approved workman rightly dividing the Word.

It is also important to recognize and use the gifts of the Holy Spirit listed in I Corinthians 12. Among those gifts are words of knowledge and prophecy. God desires to speak to each of us today. His spoken or *rhema* word has not passed away. But we must remember to test all things back to His written word.

CHAPTER FOURTEEN

Our Power and Authority in Christ

Many different opinions are expressed about the nature of spiritual warfare. I believe we won't have complete agreement about this until we are with Christ. There are some aspects of this study with which you may not agree. I pray that the unity of the Spirit, in the bond of peace, will be maintained between us (Ephesians 4:3). None of us sees the whole picture clearly. Rather, we see through a glass darkly. One day we shall all see truth with absolute clarity.

This chapter may stretch some of your long-held beliefs. Please read and study this in the light of Ephesians 4:3. Have your sword of truth ready, and be sure you use it as God leads you.

First, let's examine Christ's power and authority.

Colossians 1:13 says, "Who hath delivered us from the power of darkness, and hath translated us into the kingdom of His dear Son...."

Colossians 2:15 says, "And having spoiled principalities and powers, He made a shew of them openly, triumphing over them in it."

John 12:31 says, "Now is the judgment of this world: now shall the prince of this world be cast out."

Hebrews 2:14 says, "Forasmuch then as the children are partakers of flesh and blood, He also himself likewise took part of the same; that through death He might destroy him that had the power of death, that is, the devil...."

I John 3:8 says, "He that committeth sin is of the devil; for the devil sinneth from the beginning. For this purpose the Son of God was manifested, that He might destroy the works of the devil."

Jesus came to earth to destroy the kingdom and works of the devil. He had the power to triumph over all principalities and powers. Demons recognized His authority, and they created a scene when Jesus confronted them. Luke 4:34 and Matthew 12:22-32 present such an account: "Then was brought unto Him one possessed with a devil, blind, and dumb: and He healed him, insomuch that the blind and dumb both spake and saw. And all the people were amazed, and said, Is not this the son of David? But when the Pharisees heard it, they said, This fellow doth not cast out devils, but by Beelzebub the prince of the devils. And Jesus knew their thoughts, and said unto them, Every kingdom divided against itself is brought to desolation; and every city or house divided against itself shall not stand: And if Satan cast out Satan, he is divided against himself; how shall then his kingdom stand? And if I by Beelzebub cast out devils, by whom do your children cast them out? Therefore they shall be your judges. But if I cast out devils by the Spirit of God, then the kingdom of God is come unto you. Or else how can one enter into a strong man's house, and spoil his goods, except he first bind the strong man? And then he will spoil his house. He that is not with Me is against Me; and he that gathereth not with Me scattereth abroad."

Matthew 12:43-45 says, "When the unclean spirit is gone out of a man, he walketh through dry places, seeking rest, and findeth none. Then he saith, I will return into my house from whence I came out; and when he is come, he findeth it empty, swept, and garnished. Then goeth he, and taketh with himself seven other spirits more wicked than himself, and they enter in and dwell there: and the last state of that man is worse than the first. Even so shall it be also unto this wicked generation."

The Gospels record at least sixteen incidents of Jesus encountering and casting out demons. During His earthly ministry, He went throughout all Galilee preaching and casting out demons.

Matthew 4:23-25 says, "And Jesus went about all Galilee, teaching in their synagogues, and preaching the gospel of the kingdom, and healing all manner of sickness and all manner of disease among the people. And His fame went throughout all Syria: and they brought unto Him all sick people that were taken with divers diseases and torments, and those which were possessed with devils, and those which were lunatick, and those that had the palsy; and He healed them. And there followed Him great multitudes of people from Galilee, and from Decapolis, and from Jerusalem, and from Judaea, and from beyond Jordan."

This Scripture implies that many more people were healed and there were more than sixteen occasions when demons were cast out. Why did Jesus do this?

He came to confront the enemy and set the captives free. He also set an example for us to follow in the continuing war against Satan. The kingdom of God came in the person of Jesus Christ, and with Him came the power and authority of heaven. Jesus cast out demons by the Spirit of God. He bound the strong man and plundered his house, setting those in bondage free and healing their diseases. Following His death and resurrection, we too were set free, and He gave us His Holy Spirit so that we could have power and authority over Satan.

The Sword of the Spirit and prayer are our two offensive weapons in this war with Satan. In warfare, if we want to win, we'll need power and authority greater than that of our enemy. God is on our side, and He gave us His authority and power.

Acts 1:8 says, "But ye shall receive power, after that the Holy Spirit is come upon you: and ye shall be witnesses unto Me both in Jerusalem, and in all Judaea, and in Samaria, and unto the uttermost part of the earth."

I John 4:4 says, "Ye are of God, little children, and have overcome them: because greater is He that is in you, than he that is in the world."

During His ministry, Jesus demonstrated absolute authority and power over the devil and his demons. He tapped God's authority and power, not His own.

Matthew 4:10 says, "Then saith Jesus unto him, Get thee hence, Satan: for it is written, Thou shalt worship the Lord thy God, and Him only shalt thou serve."

Luke 4:31-37 says, "And came down to Capernaum, a city of Galilee, and taught them on the sabbath days. And they were astonished at His doctrine: for His word was with power. And in the synagogue there was a man, which had a spirit of an unclean devil, and cried out with a loud voice, Saying, Let us alone; what have we to do with Thee, Thou Jesus of Nazareth? art Thou come to destroy us? I know Thee, who Thou art; the Holy One of God. And Jesus rebuked him, saying, Hold thy peace, and come out of him. And when the devil had thrown him in the midst, he came out of him, and hurt him not. And they were all amazed, and spake among themselves, saying, What a word is this! for with authority and power He commandeth the unclean spirits, and they come out. And the fame of Him went out into every place of the country round about."

Mark 9:17-29 says, "And one of the multitude answered and said, Master, I have brought unto thee my son, which hath a dumb spirit; And wheresoever he taketh him, he teareth him: and he foameth, and gnasheth with his teeth, and pineth away: and I spake to thy disciples that they should cast him out; and they could not. He answereth him, and saith, O faithless generation, how long shall I be with you? how long shall I suffer you? bring him unto Me. And they brought him unto Him: and when he saw Him, straightway the spirit tare him; and he fell on the ground, and wallowed foaming. And He asked his father, How long is it ago since this came unto him? And he said, Of a child. And ofttimes it hath cast him into the fire, and into the waters, to destroy him: but if thou canst do any thing, have compassion on us, and help us. Jesus said unto him, If thou canst believe, all things are possible to him that believeth. And straightway the father of the child cried out, and said with tears, Lord, I believe; help Thou mine unbelief. When Jesus saw that the people came running together, He rebuked the foul spirit, saying unto him, Thou dumb and deaf spirit, I charge thee, come out of him, and enter no more into him. And the spirit cried, and rent him sore, and came out of him: and he was as one dead; insomuch that many said, He is dead. But Jesus took him by the hand, and lifted him up; and he arose. And when He was come into the house, His disciples asked Him privately, Why could not we cast him out? And He said unto them, This kind can come forth by nothing, but by prayer and fasting."

Luke 13:10-17 says, "And He was teaching in one of the synagogues on the sabbath. And, behold, there was a woman which had a spirit of infirmity eighteen years, and was bowed together, and could in no wise lift up herself. And when Jesus saw her, He called her to Him, and said unto her, Woman, thou art loosed from thine infirmity. And He laid His hands on her: and immediately she was made straight, and glorified God. And the ruler of the synagogue answered with indignation, because that Jesus had healed on the sabbath day, and said unto the people, There are six days in which men ought to work: in them therefore come and be healed, and not on the sabbath day. The Lord then answered him, and said, Thou hypocrite, doth not each one of you on the sabbath loose his ox or his ass from the stall, and lead him away to watering? And ought not this woman, being a daughter of Abraham, whom Satan hath bound, lo, these eighteen years, be loosed from this bond on the sabbath day? And when He had said these things, all His adversaries were ashamed: and all the people rejoiced for all the glorious things that were done by Him."

Luke 22:31-32 says, "And the Lord said, Simon, Simon, behold, Satan hath desired to have you, that he may sift you as wheat: But I have prayed for thee, that thy faith fail not: and when thou art converted, strengthen thy brethren."

John 19:10-11 says, "Then saith Pilate unto Him, Speakest thou not unto me? knowest Thou not that I have power to crucify Thee, and have power to release Thee? Jesus answered, Thou couldest have no power at all against Me, except it were given thee from above: therefore he that delivered Me unto thee hath the greater sin."

These verses prove the absolute authority that Jesus has over the devil. He exercised God's authority and power. Through Jesus Christ, God gave this same power and authority to every believer.

True enough, God's power is not seen as mightily in some believers as in others. This is because either some don't believe they have it, or they don't know how to appropriate it. It is by use of the offensive weapons of the Word and prayer that you appropriate this power and authority.

Luke 9:1-2 says, "Then He called His twelve disciples together, and gave them power and authority over all devils, and to cure diseases. And He sent them to preach the kingdom of God, and to heal the sick."

Here Jesus sends out the twelve disciples granting them His power and authority. In Luke 10:1-20, He sent out seventy. They healed the sick and cast out demons. When He commissioned them, before they went out, there is no record of them receiving power over demons. When they came back, they were excited because even the demons obeyed them. I suspect they simply did what they had seen Jesus do when He dealt with demons.

Matthew 16:18-19 says, "And I say also unto thee, That thou art Peter, and upon this rock I will build My church; and the gates of hell shall not prevail against it. And I will give unto thee the keys of the kingdom of heaven: and whatsoever thou shalt bind on earth shall be bound in heaven: and whatsoever thou shalt loose on earth shall be loosed in heaven."

The Church consists of all who believe. The following verses describe many of the promises God made to believers.

Matthew 17:20 says, "And Jesus said unto them, Because of your unbelief: for verily I say unto you, If ye have faith as a grain of mustard seed, ye shall say unto this mountain, Remove hence to yonder place; and it shall remove; and nothing shall be impossible unto you."

Matthew 21:22 says, "And all things, whatsoever ye shall ask in prayer, believing, ye shall receive."

Mark 9:23 says, "Jesus said unto him, If thou canst believe, all things are possible to him that believeth."

Mark 11:22-24 says, "And Jesus answering saith unto them, Have faith in God. For verily I say unto you, That whosoever shall say unto this mountain, Be thou removed, and be thou cast into the sea; and shall not doubt in his heart, but shall believe that those things which he saith shall come to pass; he shall have whatsoever he saith. Therefore I say unto you, What things soever ye desire, when ye pray, believe that ye receive them, and ye shall have them."

Mark 16:15-20 says, "And He said unto them, Go ye into all the world, and preach the gospel to every creature. He that believeth and is baptized shall be saved; but he that believeth not shall be damned. And these signs shall follow them that believe; In My name shall they cast out devils; they shall speak with new tongues; They shall take up serpents; and if they drink any deadly thing, it shall not hurt them; they shall lay hands on the sick, and they shall recover. So then after the Lord had spoken unto them, He was received up into heaven, and sat on the right hand of God. And they went forth, and preached every where, the Lord working with them, and confirming the word with signs following. Amen."

John 14:12 says, "Verily, verily, I say unto you, He that believeth on Me, the works that I do shall he do also; and greater works than these shall he do; because I go unto My Father."

"He that believeth" means each and every believer, as it does in John 3:15-18, 36, John 5:24, John 6:35, 47, John 7:37-39, John 11:25, John 12:44-46, Mark 9:23, Mark 16:15-20, Acts 10:43, Romans 1:16, Romans 3:26, I John 5:1-10.

The Greek word for "works" means works, deeds, or acts. It is translated "works" 152 times, and "deeds" 22 times. It is clear that He is referring to miracles, healings, signs, wonders, and mighty acts of power (Matthew 11:20-23, Matthew 13:54-58, Matthew 14:2, John 5:20, 36, John 9:3, John 10:25, 32, John 14:10-12).

Jesus' works consisted of healing all manner of sickness and disease, casting out devils, raising the dead, cleansing lepers and doing innumerable acts of deliverance from all the works of Satan (Matthew 4:23-24, Matthew 9:35, Acts 10:38). Jesus controlled the elements, multiplied food, walked on water, restored a severed ear, and turned water into wine, completing everything He undertook to do in the material and spiritual realms.

"Shall he do also" is a promise that each believer will be endowed with power (Luke 10:19, Luke 24:49, Acts 1:4-8) and receive a limitless measure of the Spirit

(John 7:37-39), so he can do all of Christ's works, even greater works than He did. To present this as only applying to spiritual works, when Jesus did numerous physical and spiritual works, is a poor excuse for unbelief. To make it refer only to saving souls is to ignore facts, because Jesus also did this. To limit this power only to the works of the apostles robs believers of the benefits of the promise.

The greater works do not refer to reaching more people by means of radio, television and the printed page. These are natural means available to all men, saved or unsaved. No man receives greater power than Christ, for He received the Spirit without measure (John 3:34, Isaiah 11:2, Isaiah 61:1-2). Therefore, the greater works could not refer to doing greater things than Christ could have done had He had the occasion to do them.

The teaching is that each believer can tap power equal to Christ's to do the same works He did, and greater works if the circumstances require it.

"Because I go unto my Father" refers to the fact that Jesus sits at the right hand of the Father making intercessory prayer for us (Luke 22:32).

Dake lists twenty-one reasons that believers should experience greater works in our lives:

1. Satan is cast out (John 12:31).
2. Satan's defeat on the cross (Colossians 2:14-17, I Peter 2:24).
3. Completed redemption (John 19:30, Colossians 2:14-17, I Peter 1:10-12).
4. Spirit baptism which could not be given until Jesus was glorified (John 7:37-39, Acts 1:4-8, 2:33).
5. Christ's intercession for believers (Romans 8:34, Hebrews 7:25).
6. His restored glory (John 17:5).
7. High priesthood of Christ (Hebrews 4:14-16, 6:20, 7:11-28, 9:11-15).
8. Headship of all powers (Ephesians 1:20-23, I Peter 3:22, Colossians 2:10).
9. All authority was given to Christ to give to believers (Matthew 28:18-20, John 14:12-15, Acts 1:8).
10. Completed victory over death, hell and the grave (Hebrews 2:14-15, Revelation 1:18, Colossians 2:14-15).
11. His headship of the church (Ephesians 1:20-23, Colossians 1:16-18, 24).
12. Making of the New Covenant benefits based upon better promises (Matthew 26:28, II Corinthians 3:6-15, Hebrews 8:6) and confirmed by greater powers (Hebrews 2:1-4, Mark 16:15-20, Luke 24:49, II Corinthians 3:6-15, 2 Peter 1:1-10).
13. Fullness of grace is now possible in Christ (John 1:17, Colossians 2:10).
14. Full salvation glory that was to follow the sufferings (I Peter 1:10-12; Hebrews 2:1-4, II Corinthians 3).
15. Entrance into the holiest by every believer now possible (Hebrews 10:19-38, Ephesians 2:14-18).

16. Time for God to bless both Jews and Gentiles alike (Ephesians 2:14-18, 3:1-11, Romans 10:9-14).

17. Time to send men with full authority and power as God sent Christ (John 17:18, 20:21)

18. Time for each believer to receive all the gifts and fruit of the Spirit, which they could only receive in part in Old Testament times (John 7:37-39, 14:12-15; Matthew 17:20, 21:22, Mark 9:23).

19. Time of no limitations in Christ, in the Spirit, and in the full benefits of the gospel promises (Matthew 17:20, 21:22, Mark 9:23, 11:22-24, John 15:7, 16, II Peter 1:1-12).

20. Time for the universality of the plan of God to bless all nations (Matthew 28:18-20, Mark 16:15-20, Luke 24:47-49, Acts 1:4-8, Genesis 12:1-3). Believers carry out the full plan of the gospel demonstrating worldwide works of power to even a greater degree and kind than that of Christ, depending upon the needs.

21. Because Jesus returned to His Father and no longer would be here to continue His works or do greater ones, He gave His power to His disciples to carry on where He stopped. They will do greater things than He would have done if He had continued (John 14:12). He gave them authority to see to it that His work was carried on through them.

The book of Acts is our example. For years well-meaning teachers taught me that the book of Acts was for that time only, that the things that transpired then were necessary to substantiate the written Word, but were not an example for us to follow today. Where does God say that? Where does He say that we no longer have authority over Satan? Where does He say that the gifts of the Holy Spirit were for another time only?

Just before Jesus ascended into heaven He said, "And Jesus came and spake unto them, saying, All power is given unto Me in heaven and in earth. Go ye therefore, and teach all nations, baptizing them in the name of the Father, and of the Son, and of the Holy Spirit: Teaching them to observe all things whatsoever I have commanded you: and, lo, I am with you always, even unto the end of the world. Amen" (Matthew 28:18-20).

The One, Jesus Christ, who has all power and authority, has commissioned each of us. He told us He would be with us to the end of the world, not just to the end of the book of Acts. Put on the full armor of God and go in power and authority and destroy the works of the devil!

Revelation 12:11 says, "And they overcame him by the blood of the Lamb, and by the word of their testimony; and they loved not their lives unto the death."

Through this teaching and the power of Christ, I have been privileged to witness many of God's miracles. I have seen demons cast out. They have talked to me; just recently one told me that he "hated" me. Hallelujah! I know I'm on the narrow path of Christ when a demon hates me!

I have witnessed people being set free from many different physical and mental diseases. I've seen people go from despair to joy, from torment to the peace that passes all understanding.

I personally have been healed of Environmental Illness, about one hundred different allergies. My sister saw tumors in her body disappear.

The list of God's healing grows every week. Praise God! He is alive and active today! He is the same yesterday, today and forever. The only change has been in you and me. The book of Acts ends at chapter 28, but my favorite chapter is 29; the continuing works of our Lord and Savior Jesus Christ. In my book, *The Continuing Works of Christ*, I share more than sixty testimonies of people that God has healed.

You have been drafted into violent spiritual warfare, but you are ready for it if you have submitted to our Captain, Jesus Christ. You have been taught how to "stand." When the enemy attacks, you put on the belt of truth. When Satan tries to lead you into sin, or tells you that are not truly forgiven, put on the breastplate of righteousness. When he attacks, hold up the shield of faith to catch his darts. When he would bring disharmony between you and others, put on the shoes of peace. When Satan causes you to doubt your salvation or your worth in Christ, take up the helmet of salvation. Complete the victory by wielding the sword of the spirit. Your marching orders come from your Commander in Chief as you spend time on your knees in prayer.

Wellspring Ministry Resources

How to Minister to Others Seminar

Dr. Mathias provides training for those who desire to minister to others. It is our premise that all believers are ministers of the Gospel. We do not need to be "professionals" to be His ministers. This seminar is designed as a practical, hands-on approach. A workbook is provided to participants. Seminar available on Audio Cassettes with Workbook. $40.00 + shipping.

PERSONAL MINISTRY SESSIONS

Trained staff provides personal and telephone ministry sessions.
Call (907) 563-9033 to schedule appointments.
E-mail: akwellspr@aol.com
Website: akwellspring.com

Please check our website often, as we continually update our ministry and information.

Order Form

To order these books, please use this convenient order form, or call (907) 563-9033 or order from our online store: www.akwellspring.com.

ITEM	QUANTITY	PRICE/EACH	TOTAL
In His Own Image	_____	24.95	_____
Biblical Foundations of Freedom	_____	24.95	_____
Biblical Foundations of Freedom Study Guide	_____	10.00	_____
The Continuing Works of Christ	_____	24.95	_____
Biblical Foundations of Freedom Audio Tapes	_____	30.00	_____
Biblical Foundations of Freedom Video (VHS)	_____	119.95	_____
How to Minister to Others Audio Tapes	_____	30.00	_____
How to Minister to Others Workbook	_____	10.00	_____
		SUBTOTAL	_____
		POSTAGE & HANDLING	_____
		TOTAL	_____

Please print name clearly as it appears on your credit card:

_____
NAME

_____
ADDRESS

_____
CITY   STATE   ZIP

❏ VISA ❏ MC _____
            CARD #   EXP DATE

_____
SIGNATURE   PHONE

POSTAGE & HANDLING CHARGES ON ORDERS:

1-2 Books/Tapes	5.00
3-4 Books/Tapes	10.00
5-6 Books/Tapes	15.00
7-10 Books/Tapes	20.00

Above charges are for domestic orders only. Please call or email for shipping & handling on international orders.

THIS ORDER MAY BE MAILED TO:

Wellspring Ministries of Alaska
PO Box 190084
Anchorage, AK 99519-0084

or faxed to (907) 243-6623